Sociology for GCSE

SECOND EDITION

Christopher Townroe
George Yates

Longman

LONGMAN GROUP UK LIMITED
Longman House,
Burnt Mill, Harlow, Essex CM20 2JE, England
and Associated Companies throughout the world

First published 1987
Second edition 1990
Third Impression 1993

Set in 10/12 pt Times New Roman, Linotron 202

British Library Cataloguing in Publication Data

Townroe, C.
  Sociology for GCSE.
  1. Sociology
  I. Title   II. Yates, G.
  301   HM66

    ISBN 0–582–05118–5

Produced by Longman Singapore Publishers Pte Ltd
Printed in Singapore

Prepare for publication by
Jenny Lee Publishing Services

The publisher's policy is to use paper manufactured
from sustainable forests.

For Jenny, Annabel and Jackson

Contents

Acknowledgements

In writing this book, we have received advice and help from many people. In particular, we would like to thank the following: Clive Palmer, who kindly read through the whole manuscript and made many useful suggestions; Howard Cunnington, who scrutinised the chapter on religion; Richard Protasiewicz, Elwyn Durant and David Reville, who helped with a number of the photographs; and Jacqui King, who prepared many of the charts that appear in this book.

We would also like to thank many of the students of the School of Saint David and Saint Katharine, Hornsey, for their critical comments. And special thanks are due to Trevor Oughton, for his illustrations.

We are grateful to the following for permission to reproduce copyright material: Causeway Press Ltd for an adapted extract from *The Sociology of Youth* by Simon Frith (1984); the Author, Ajay Close for an adapted extract from her article 'Saying Farewell with Vivaldi' in *The Sunday Times* 26.2.89; The Economist Newspaper Ltd for extracts from *The Economist* 4.6.83, 12.10.85. Guardian Newspapers Ltd for an extract from an article by J. Joliffe in the *Guardian* 12.6.80; Hampstead & Highgate Express Printing & Pubg. Co. for an extract from the article 'Students wanted to kill us' in the *Hampstead & Highgate Express* 2.12.88; the Editor, Hornsey & Muswell Hill Journal for article 'Pupils in police charge alarm' in *The Hornsey & Muswell Hill Journal* 1.12.88; the Author, Daniel John for an extract from the article 'White collar crime-wave' by Mark Miller & Daniel John in the *Guardian* 4.2.89; Open University Press for an adapted extract from ch.1 'Women in the Family: Companions or Caretakers?' by Diana Leonard & Mary Anne Speakman in *Women in Britain Today* edited by Veronica Beechey & Elizabeth Whitelegg 1986; Times Newspapers Ltd for extracts from the articles 'The School ... Pupils attend' by P. Wilby in *The Sunday Times* 26.2.78, "Both the ... Steel Centres" by P. Beresford in *The Sunday Times* 29.9.85, 'Big Spending Woopies turn on Grey Power' by Jeremy Laurence & Chris Blackhurst in *The Sunday Times* 5.3.89. © Times Newspapers Ltd 1978, 1985 & 1989; and to the following examination boards for permission to reproduce past examination questions: London and East Anglian Group for GCSE (University of London School Examinations Council); Midland Examining Group (University of Cambridge Local Examinations Syndicate, Oxford and Cambridge Schools Examination Board); Northern Examining Association (Associated Lancashire Schools Examining Board, Joint Matriculation Board, North Regional Examinations Board, North West Regional Examinations Board, Yorkshire and Humberside Regional Examinations Board); Southern Examining Group; Welsh Joint Education Committee.

We would like to point out that any answers or hints on answers are the sole responsibility of the authors and have not been provided or approved by the groups mentioned above.

We are grateful to the following for permission to reproduce the following photographs and other copyright material: BBC Hulton Picture Library, pages 52, 71, 92 and 131; Bilderdienst Suddeutscher Verlag, page 34; Birmingham Museum & Art Gallery, page 84; Bridgeman Art Library, page 28; British Library, pages 57 and 206; Camera Press, pages 4 (photo Alan Grisbrook), 15 *left* (photo Jerry Watson), *right* (photo Alan Grisbrook), 49 (photo Snowdon), 110 *above* (photo MTI), *below* (photo David Holden), 199, 242 *above*, 258 (photo David Gaywood); J Allan Cash, pages 125, 151 and 197; Commissioner of Metropolitan Police, page 11; Co-op/Cath Tate, page 282; *Daily Mail*, page 188; Derbyshire County Council, page 169; *Employment News*, page 112 *centre*; Format, pages 44 and 58 (photos Margaret Murray), 112 *right*; Sally and Richard Greenhill, page 66; Guardian Newspapers Ltd., pages 7 (photo Jill Joliffe), 104, 189 and 217 *above*; Controller of Her Majesty's Stationery Office, Crown copyright reserved, pages 171, 174, 180 *below*; John Hillelson Agency, page 5 (photo Jim MacHugh/ Sygma); Hutchison Library, page 113; International Freelance Library, pages 2 (photo Jez Coulson), 25 (photo Angela Phillips), 79 (photo Mark Rusher), 114 (photo John Harris), 118 *centre* and 170 (photos Laurie Sparham), 181 *above* (photo Begonia Tamarit), 218 (photo Derek Speirs), 223 (photo Jez Coulson), 229 (photo John Sturrock); International Fund for Animal Welfare, page 201 *below*; MFI, page 117 left; W Murray, *Boys & Girls book 3b* Ladybird Keywords, page 17; NALGO, page 201 *above*; Network, pages 82, 99 (photo Barry Lewis), 123 *left* (photo Roger Hutchings), 123 *right* and 142 (photos Mike Abrahams), 163 (photo Roger Hutchings); Ann Oakley, *From Here to Maternity – Becoming a Mother* Penguin, page 254; Perrings, page 117 *right*; Photo Source, page 192 *below*; Pictorial Press, page 185; Press Association, page 192 *above*; Public Record Office/OPCS, Crown copyright reproduced by permission of the Controller of Her Majesty's Stationery Office, pages 57, 70; Report, pages 32 (photo Patrick Eagar), 63 *below* and 108 (photos Derek Speirs), 118 *above* and 119 *above* (photos John Sturrock), 119 *below* (photo Chris Davies), 140 *above* (photo Romano Cagnoni), 217 *below* (photo Peter Harrap), 219 (photo Derek Speirs), 225 (photo Stefano Cagnoni), 229 (photo John Sturrock), 240 (photo Andrew Wiard); Frank Spooner, pages 106 (photo Marie-Laure de Decker/Gamma), 154 (photo Abbas/ Gamma); the *Sun*, page 186 *left*; Syndication International, pages 20, 38, 186 *right* & *centre*, 242 *below*; Telefocus, page 112 *left*; © Times Newspapers Ltd., page 190; Topham, pages 89 (photo FE/Wiener Library), 156 (photo AP Wirephoto), 158 (photo Cook); Scope Features, page 194; Tropix, page 46; Volvo, page 233.

Cover: London, Chicksand St. & Bricklane, 1980. 'Promised Land', by Ray Walker, commissioned by Tower Hamlets Art Project. Photo by David Hoffman.

Guide to using this book

We have aimed to write a straightforward introduction to sociology which meets the requirements of the new GCSE syllabi and which refers mainly to recent studies published in the 1980s.

The order of the chapters

There is a certain logic to the order of our chapters: they follow the process of an individual's socialisation, or growing up in society, and then broaden out to consider the connected issues of social control and social change. Many of these chapters follow on from each other, but it is quite possible to read them in any order. Many teachers and students will find it useful to start by reading Chapters 17, 18 and 19.

The subject index

If a term such as 'census' or 'Class IIIN' is used without a full explanation then it should be possible to look it up in the subject index and find other references to the term which can be consulted. The census, for example, is discussed in Chapter 6 and the Registrar-General's classification of socio-economic groups is explained in Chapter 9.

The author index

Where we refer to a study at some length, the author of the study can be looked up in the bibliography for full details of the study. The bibliography also serves as an author index.

Activities

We have included a number of examination-style data response exercises and we have also offered activities in most sections which develop the ideas in the text. These activities are not just intended for individual written work in class; many of them lend themselves to fairly open-ended discussions. Some are appropriate for group work and others, such as 'mini-surveys', have to be undertaken outside the classroom. The last two chapters include some ideas for project work and a number of specimen GCSE examination questions.

Further reading

Our main recommendations for further reading are the latest edition of the annual HMSO publication *Social Trends* (which will enable you to update many of the figures given in this book) and the weekly magazine *New Statesman Society*.

CHAPTER 1 Introducing sociology

Socialisation – are we brainwashed to conform?

1 Sociology and social groups

The word **sociology** was first used in English in 1843 and it means the study of human societies. This book is an introduction to the ways in which sociologists can help us to understand modern British society.

Society is made up of social groups, ranging from our family or 'our local darts team' to large social institutions such as the Roman Catholic Church in Britain. The following case study shows how we belong to a range of social groups. Note that in each group we have a position which carries with it certain obligations and expectations, this is often called a person's **role**. For example, parents are expected to look after their children.

Case study: Mrs Catherine Wyatt, 28 years old

Types of social groups	The groups to which Mrs Wyatt belongs	Her positions or roles in the group
Family	The Wyatts	Daughter, mother, wife, sister, etc.
Occupational group	Data Processing Department	Computer programmer
Trade union	National Association of Local Government Officers	Health and Safety Representative
Recreational club	'The Dog and Duck' Darts Team	Treasurer
Church	The Church of England	Member of choir at St Peter's Church
Educational group	Thursday evening class on furniture restoration	Student
Parents' group	Hillview Estate Baby-sitting Circle	Organiser

Activities

1   Construct similar charts for (a) yourself and
    (b) an adult you know well.

2   Find out what is studied in the following
    social sciences: psychology and economics.

Sociologists are interested in how groups in society are changing: for example, the ways in which the numbers of church members or juvenile delinquents have altered. They also look at the relationship between different aspects of social life: for example how religion influences voting, how work influences leisure, how social class influences success at school.

Psychologists and biologists also study human behaviour but sociologists differ from them because sociology is primarily concerned with how humans behave in the context of social groups.

Some children, such as travellers, grow up in minority social groups.

2   Viewpoints on human behaviour

Sociologists are interested in the *social* aspects of human behaviour; that is, the ways humans behave in relation to others, in relation to social groups. When biologists look at human behaviour they are concerned with how the body works and psychologists focus on the workings of the mind. Let us illustrate this by asking three different specialists for some interesting facts on two common human activities: eating and sleeping.

Viewpoints on eating

Mrs A. Crania, a biologist, on eating: 'Did you know that the transit times vary between an average adult and a vegetarian? The time taken from eating to elimination by the body is on average forty-three hours but for a vegetarian it is thirty-seven hours. And even when no food is eaten about 7 to 8 grams of faeces are excreted daily.'

Mrs P. Brain, a psychologist, on eating: 'Have you heard of anorexia nervosa, the "slimmers' disease" where patients virtually stop eating altogether? Well, very often they are teenage girls of above average ability; hard-working high achievers under pressure to succeed from their parents. They have a negative self-image, thinking themselves to be fat and ugly when they are really just average in appearance. They are often frightened of growing up and in a way they can go back to girlhood by starving themselves because this stops their monthly periods.'

Mrs B. Snoop, a sociologist, on eating: 'Did you know that the South Wales miner does not regard convenience foods or fish and chips as a "real meal"? Traditionally, a real meal means meat, potatoes and two or three fresh cooked vegetables and the miner will insist that his wife produces this for him on most evenings of the week.'

The biologist has concentrated on the workings of the digestive system, the psychologist has discussed neurotic obsessions arising from unconscious fears in the mind, and the sociologist has looked at the customs or culture of a particular social group.

Viewpoints on sleeping

Mrs A. Crania, the biologist, on sleeping: 'A person loses from 28 to 42 grams in weight per hour of sleep or 300 grams per night; less urine is produced per hour of sleep and body temperature falls during normal sleeping time whether we are awake or not.'

Mrs P. Brain, the psychologist, on sleeping: 'The average new-born baby sleeps sixteen to seventeen hours a day but most adults have seven and a half hours sleep which breaks down into 100 minute-long cycles. During each cycle we go through four distinct stages, each with different brain wave patterns. During the fourth stage we enter a period with rapid eye movements and if woken then we will almost always report a dream.

Sleep deprivation is a form of torture and can cause hallucinations. When a New York disc jockey, Peter Tripp, stayed awake for 201 hours for charity he was assessed by doctors. At one stage he ran away from them because he believed that they were undertakers who had come to bury him. After the "wakathon" he became fairly seriously depressed for some time.'

Mrs B. Snoop, the sociologist, on sleeping: 'Did you know that most rock musicians are "night-owls"? They often choose to spend night-time rather than day-time working in recording studios. And when relaxing, like professional snooker players and professional criminals, they often set off for night clubs when most of us are returning home after our evening out. They then get home as late as 6 a.m. when the first trains and buses are running to get most people to work. Many rock musicians opt for a pattern of sleeping each day until one or two in the afternoon.'

Many rock stars are 'night owls' and spend their leisure hours in night clubs.

Once again we see how the sociologist has concentrated on human behaviour in the context of a social group. Sociologists emphasise the way that patterns of behaviour are learned from society while biologists and psychologists often argue that we inherit many of our characteristics and abilities. These differences of outlook are reflected in the 'nature versus nurture' debate.

3   Nature versus nurture

The **nature** versus **nurture** debate concentrates on the question of how far our ability is fixed at birth by our inborn 'nature':

> There once was a man who said, 'Damn,
> I suddenly see what I am.
> I'm a creature that moves
> In predestined grooves,
> I'm not even a bus, I'm a tram!'

The following case study suggests that the course of our lives is, to a certain extent, determined at birth; that is, we move in 'predestined grooves'.

Case study: the 'Jim Twins'

James Lewis and James Springer were identical twins who were separated in the first year of life and brought up separately. They never met again until they were reunited as adults by Thomas Bouchard, the professor of psychology at Minnesota University. Bouchard traced them as part of the Minnesota Study of Twins Reared Apart and he discovered an amazing number of coincidences about the separate lives which the 'Jim Twins' had led:
– both had married women called Linda,

– both had been divorced and had then married women called Betty,
– one twin had called his first son James Allan and the other had called his James Alan,
– both had had a dog that they had named Toy,
– both had spent their holidays on the same small beach in Florida,
– both drove a Chevrolet,
– both built white benches round the trunk of a tree in their gardens,
– both bit their fingernails to the quick.

Identical twins

An important point about the Jim Twins is that they are identical or monozygotic twins. In other words, they first became separate entities when a zygote or fertilised ovum divided in their mother's womb.

Most twins are dizygotic or fraternal and they result when two ova are discharged simultaneously into the fallopian tube and then fertilised independently by different spermatazoa. All cells contain **chromosomes** which control the characters of living things. Since each ovum and each sperm contain a unique, randomly determined selection of twenty-three single chromosomes, fraternal twins are therefore as different as any brothers and sisters.

We are all genetically unique apart from identical twins who have the same genetic inheritance. But it must be recognised that identical twins normally lead very different adult lives. The differences between the Jim Twins no doubt outnumbered the similarities.

Delegates at a congress of twins held in Memphis, USA.

Genes

All cellular organisms inherit characteristics from their parents via the **genes** which are contained in chromosomes and this applies to microbes, insects, cabbages and kings. In human beings the genes inherited from parents determine:

1   physical features such as colour of eyes, hair and skin and shape of facial features;
2   certain genetic diseases such as haemophilia, muscular dystrophy, thalassemia and sickle-cell anaemia which are carried from one generation to another;
3   anatomical traits such as height and weight – to a certain extent!

In the last case we must sound a note of caution and say that body form and structure are also shaped by non-hereditary influences: your friends might be tall and heavy because they have inherited this from their parents or because of the diet and exercise they have had during their upbringing.

Nature and nurture

The idea that humans are determined by these two influences dates back to the Ancient Greek philosopher Protagorus who, in the fifth century BC, compared 'physis' (nature) and 'nomos' (tradition). *Nature* refers to a person's genetic inheritance or inherited characteristics. *Nurture* refers to the influences on a person from environment and upbringing. It is, however, difficult to unravel the separate influences of nature and nurture. If the children of musically talented parents are themselves musically gifted, is it because of genetic inheritance (nature) or because they grew up in a musical environment (nurture)?

To ask which of these two factors is most important is a bit like asking which is the more important ingredient of an omelette: is it the eggs, or the filling and flavouring, or the skill of the cook, or the heat in the pan? Clearly the eggs are essential but it is arguable whether they are more important than anything else.

In 1969, an American psychologist, Jensen, claimed that only 20 per cent of the variation between people's intelligence is due to their environment and experience while 80 per cent is fixed from birth by genetic inheritance. The case of the Jim Twins might lead us to agree that genes are more influential but this matter is very controversial. Sociologists emphasise the importance of nurture rather than nature.

Case study: the Skeels experiment

The importance of nurture was shown in a famous experiment by H. M. Skeels on two groups of orphans who were thought to be of low intelligence.

The first group
These were thirteen two-year-old orphans who were transferred to an institution where they were paired with older, subnormal girls who acted as 'substitute mothers', loving them and playing with them.

The second group
These were twelve two-year-olds who were left in the unstimulating environment of the orphanage until adoption.

The result
After two years the first group were returned to the orphanage or were adopted; their average IQ (intelligence quotient) had risen from 64.3 to 92.8. In other words, their measured intelligence had risen from the level of 'mentally retarded' to not far off the average score for all four-year-olds which is 100. In contrast, the second group's average IQ scores had fallen from 86.7 to 60.5. These gains and losses in IQ were found to have persisted when both groups were tested again at the age of twenty-two.

Activities

1   Can you suggest why the intelligence of the first group improved while that of the second group deteriorated?

2   Why do you think that some would see the Skeels experiment as morally wrong?

'Breeding' and social policy

Most modern social scientists emphasise the importance of nurture but in the nineteenth century many believed that genetic inheritance effectively shaped the course of our lives and these beliefs led to a number of proposals:

1 In nineteenth-century Italy, Lombroso claimed that criminality was shown by certain physical features and was inherited. This idea led to the proposal that the population should be examined to track down all criminal types. (We discuss Lombroso's discredited idea in Chapter 12.)

2 In 1934, the British psychologist Cyril Burt concluded that intelligence 'is inherited, or at least **innate**, not due to teaching or training' and he proceeded to develop the IQ tests used in the 11+ examination. (The controversy which surrounded the 11+ examination is discussed in Chapter 10.)

3 In 1883, Galton invented the idea of **eugenics**. He was influenced by his cousin, Charles Darwin, and he was applying Darwin's ideas of evolution and natural selection, together with Mendel's science of genetics, to the human race. Eugenics means studying methods to improve the human race by selective breeding. By the 1930s this idea had led many states in the USA to adopt laws for the compulsory sterilisation of 'defective' humans and in Nazi Germany the idea of breeding a pure Aryan master-race led to the gas chambers of Hitler's death camps.

4 Socialisation and social control

Isabel Quaresma and her mother in 1980.

Case study: the Portuguese 'chicken girl'

Isabel Quaresma is ten, but cannot talk, and is only now learning to eat with a spoon. She is a 'wild child' who has only recently been brought into regular contact with human beings. . . . Since birth the child has lived in a chicken coop. Her mother is a mentally deficient rural worker living in poverty. . . . The mother works in the fields all day and soon after Isabel's birth confined her to the chicken coop, where she was thrown pieces of bread and shared the chicken-feed with the fowls. Neighbours had gossiped about this scandal for years but had done nothing, not wanting to interfere with a family matter. At last, however, a district hospital radiographer at Torres Vedras Hospital approached local institutions to accept Isabel. After a string of refusals, the radiographer took her into her own home, but could not cope. Isabel's contact with humans had been minimal and she could neither talk nor was she toilet trained – in the chicken coop she had lived in her own excrement. Her gestures and sounds resembled those of the fowls she had lived with since infancy. She scratched food up with her hands.

Isabel is now at a private clinic for severely handicapped children in Lisbon. . . . The most striking thing about her appearance is her severely stunted body. She has a tiny head, and the stature of an infant. X-rays have shown her skull structure to be sound. Her dwarfed form is almost certainly due to a life of malnutrition. One eye is clouded with a cataract, thought to be the result of a scratch from the hens she lived with. She communicates in repetitive calls and beats her arms and drums her feet to express emotion – actions probably imitative of her only living companions.

Dr João dos Santos is optimistic about her chances of social awakening. But, he explains: 'It all depends on whether we can build warm human contacts which will move her to want to speak and communicate with us.'

(Source: Jill Joliffe in the *Guardian*, 12 June 1980)

Activities

1   Describe the ways in which Isabel Quaresma differed from a normal ten-year-old.
2   Imagine that immediately after your birth you were raised by apes in the forest. If this had happened you would lack certain skills necessary for living in human society, such as the ability to talk a human language and the knowledge of customs like queuing for buses.
    (a)   List some other social skills that you would lack.
    (b)   What skills might you have gained?

Culture, norms and socialisation

All societies have a **culture**, or common way of life. A society's culture includes the following aspects:

- language;
- customs, such as birthday celebrations;
- a shared system of values, such as the belief that each man should have no more than one wife;
- social **norms** – these are patterns of behaviour which are accepted as normal and right, for example, queuing for buses.

During our lives we learn the culture of a social group. That is, we learn to think and behave in ways that are acceptable to a particular group. This learning process is called **socialisation**.

There are three stages of socialisation:

1   Primary socialisation   This stage involves the socialisation of the young child in the home. For example, a child may be taught by its parents to always say 'please' and 'thank you'.

2 Secondary socialisation This describes the influences outside the home. Children may learn how to behave from formal organisations such as the Church and the Cubs or the Brownies. We are also subject to informal influences, such as our **peer group**, that is our friends of the same age. Other agencies of socialisation are schools and the **mass media**, meaning TV, radio, comics and books. The next chapter looks at how these influence our ideas of what is considered to be appropriate masculine and feminine behaviour.

3 Adult socialisation Primary and secondary socialisation may teach us that it is wrong to tell lies or to use foul language, but we cannot be fully prepared during childhood for adult roles such as being a parent or a doctor. Medical students are gradually taught how doctors should behave by, for example, joining senior consultants on their rounds of the hospital wards. From their observations the students may learn what is thought to be a good bedside manner with patients.

Deviance, social control and social change

Social control refers to the means used by society to maintain order and stability. One way we learn norms of behaviour is through the sanctions and punishments reserved for those who deviate from the norms of society. A clear example is theft. This may be dealt with in one of two ways:

1 Informal social control If children are sent to bed without a meal for stealing, then the parents of those children are acting as informal agencies of social control.

2 Formal social control Action may also be taken against thieves by more formal agencies of social control, for example when shoplifters are dealt with by the police, the courts and the prisons.

These formal institutions would have immense difficulties imposing the law on a community if there was not a widespread willingness to obey the law in the first place. This consent is brought about by informal agencies of social control. As we have seen, the family teaches the values of a society to the young and trains them to act in socially acceptable ways.

Our next case study describes a situation in which disagreement arose concerning the definition of one type of **deviance**. Changing attitudes about standards of behaviour can lead to a change in the law.

Case study: bathing on Spanish beaches

From 1939 to 1975 Spain was ruled by General Franco, a dictator, who controlled Spanish life very strictly. In the 1960s Spain developed numerous Mediterranean resorts for foreign tourists. Many foreigners were surprised to find that bikinis were banned on Spanish beaches. In this instance Spain's strict religious traditions coincided with Franco's dislike of modern fashions. Since the death of Franco, Spain has become a more relaxed society. This has been partly due to the influence of ideas and fashions portrayed on TV. Spain now allows not only bikinis but also topless sunbathing.

A teenage Spanish girl who has had a strict religious upbringing and who then bathes topless on the beaches is no longer committing an illegal act and will no longer incur the penalties of the law. But, although she is not punished by the official agencies of social control, she may have performed a deviant act according to the standards of her family. If this is the case, her parents can punish her with a number of informal sanctions such as refusing to allow her to visit the beach again and by withdrawing their affection for her.

Activities

1   Why do you think that the laws about swimwear on Spanish beaches have been relaxed?

2   Give three examples of norms in other societies which differ from norms in British society.

3   Give three examples of norms in British society which have changed since the nineteenth century.

4   Complete the chart on the right by adding more examples of behaviour which are generally seen as deviant in modern Britain:

Behaviour seen as deviant in Britain	*Informal sanction*	*Formal punishment*
A child is cruel to a family pet	Pocket money withheld	—
Murder	Disowned by family	Life sentence

5   Describe how norms would vary in the following situations:
(a)   a doctor's waiting room;
(b)   a party;
(c)   a school assembly.

---

5   The work of a sociologist

When Paul Rock was studying sociology at university, he became interested in criminology, the study of crime. His ideas for his doctorate, in the 1960s, included observing the work of a police station and looking at life in a women's prison. These were original and promising ideas since, at that time, neither of these subjects had been investigated by British sociologists. His supervisor, however, advised him that both areas of research would present many practical difficulties.

It then struck him that studies of prisoners had ignored those who had been through the civil rather than the criminal courts. His book, *Making People Pay*, looks at how debtors can end up in prison if they fail to repay their creditors. The methods he used in this research included observation in county courts and interviews with creditors, solicitors and bailiffs as well as debtors in prison.

Paul Rock has since written several books on theories of deviance and he lectures on the sociology of deviance at the University of London. He defines sociology as 'the disciplined study of events in the social world'. When asked 'What is the point of studying sociology at school?', he replied that sociology is very useful because it helps us to make sense of the social world in which we live. It does this by making us confront a whole range of ideas and real problems, such as the problem of law-breaking and the theories put forward to explain it.

Why might it be difficult to conduct a sociological study of life in a police station?

Looking for the unexpected

Sociologists should be objective and unbiased. They should critically evaluate all sorts of evidence and look at issues from every angle. Paul Rock also claims that curiosity and patience are needed when studying people in social contexts. His most recent book, *A View from the Shadows*, is a study of policy-making in Canada's Ministry of the Solicitor-General. He started this research because he wanted to find out about the Canadian equivalent of Britain's Home Office Research and Planning Unit. He patiently observed meetings and conferences and he found that it was an advantage being a foreigner because he had an excuse for asking people 'dumb' questions about their roles in the Canadian legal system.

He says that he embarked on the research without even knowing the questions, let alone the answers. This suggests that sociologists must be willing to go beyond their original ideas and be ready to look at human situations in new ways. Eventually, a sociologist comes to focus on particular questions and a research agenda emerges.

When sociologists study social institutions such as the police, the family or the mass media, they often concentrate on the way that these interrelate or how and why they are changing. In doing this sociologists are like historians who study the recent past in order to understand the society in which we now live. The work of a sociologist shows us how we fit into society by explaining how society fits together and changes.

Activities

1 What problems might Paul Rock have had in carrying out his first two research ideas?

2 What advantages might sociologists derive from being outsiders when studying social institutions in their own society?

GCSE question from London and East Anglian Group 1988

Culture and Society

It is from their environment that, using their abilities and potential, children learn the language, behaviour, customs, attitudes and mannerisms of their particular society. A child brought up in an igloo by an Eskimo family in Alaska will learn a totally different way of life from a child raised in a floating reed bed by marsh Arabs in Iraq. Similarly, a child who learns the middle-class lifestyle of a suburban family in Kent will have had a very different social environment from a child brought up in a coal miner's family in the Welsh valleys.
(from *Examining Sociology* by J.L. Thompson, Hutchinson, 1980)

(a) What is the name given to the process of learning culture in a society?   (1)
(b) Describe *two* examples of behaviour based on culture.   (4)
(c) Explain why culture is important in all societies.   (4)
(d) Choose any group in society and explain how its culture is passed on.   (6)

GCSE question from Northern Examining Association 1988

1 What does a sociologist mean by 'nature'?   (3)
2 What does a sociologist mean by 'nurture'?   (3)

3 (a) Describe an investigation to test the relative importance of nature and nurture in the way people grow up.   (2)
   (b) Name a major problem in setting up such an investigation.   (2)

GCSE question from London and East Anglian Group specimen paper

What we think of as normal can vary from time to time and from place to place:

For example, the table manners which we generally expect of people today are very different from those which were acceptable during the Middle Ages.

Today some countries permit a man to take several wives. In Britain it would not only be considered unacceptable and deviant, but would be against the law.
(from *Deviance*, by Beecham et al, George Harrap)

(a) Explain the terms 'normal' and 'deviant'.   (4)
(b) After looking at the examples above, give *two* further examples of behaviour which some people would accept as normal but which would be thought deviant by others.   (6)
(c) How are we brought up to distinguish between normal and deviant behaviour?   (5)

CHAPTER 2

Sex role stereotyping

1 Traditional gender roles

There are two sorts of difference between men and women:

1 Sex differences refer to the different biological attributes of men and women.

2 Gender differences refer to the different masculine and feminine roles which men and women are expected to perform in society. Sociologists stress the extent to which gender roles are learned rather than inborn.

In British society, tradition gives us fixed images of the characteristics and the roles which are suitable for each gender.

Traditional gender characteristics

Some of the characteristics traditionally associated with masculinity and femininity are:

- *Masculine* hard logical brave aggressive unemotional independent
- *Feminine* soft illogical timid passive emotional dependent

Traditional gender roles

The roles in life that have in the past been set aside for the two sexes follow on from the qualities of character each sex is supposed to possess. Men have been expected to fulfil the 'important' positions of life such as businessman, lawyer, surgeon, government minister, general: the type of position that requires resourcefulness, skill, expertise, coolheadedness and courage. Also, men have been expected to take up those occupations such as builder, miner or firefighter which require strength and the willingness to face danger.

Women, on the other hand, have traditionally been expected to play a different part in society. Essentially, what has been required of women is not that they lead or build or create but that they serve others. Thus an important job for a woman has been that of housewife and mother. Typical female occupations, such as nurse, typist, or junior school teacher, have also involved serving others.

Sexism: prejudice and discrimination

Some people use these traditional ideas of masculinity and femininity to pre-judge the abilities of women and to argue that women should remain unequal because they are inferior to men. This type of **prejudice** is 'sexism' and when it leads to unfair treatment for women we would call that **sexist discrimination**. The following experiment will show you how far the traditional ideas of gender roles are changing.

Activity: sex roles experiment

This experiment requires the co-operation of an English teacher and some male and female pupils. You ask the teacher to set the following homework: Write an essay beginning 'Today is my eightieth birthday and I look back to the day I left school . . .'

You then compare the male and the female pupils' answers. When this exercise was tried with grammar school girls in 1968, most described lives in which their roles were limited to being housewives.

In 1983 the experiment was repeated with 190 third-year pupils and 50 sixth formers, half boys and half girls. The following differences emerged:

Girls
87 per cent described marriage (compared to 60 per cent of the boys) and most saw marriage and motherhood as the main focus of their lives. Many spelt out the number of children they imagined having, their sex, names, age gaps between them and *their* future lives. Thirty-three per cent even wrote about grand- and greatgrandchildren.

Boys
They saw marriage as providing a backdrop against which to play out the drama of their careers. Eight times as many boys as girls referred to world events (rather than personal events) such as nuclear war or political changes.

You could also look at two studies which have investigated the ambitions of teenage girls: *'Just Like a Girl': How Girls Learn to be Women* by Sue Sharpe and *Losing Out: Sexuality and Adolescent Girls* by Sue Lees.

Nature, nurture and stereotypes

Male and female pupils might explain their different views of their future lives by stressing the importance of *nature* and saying that a woman's womb naturally equips her for a life centred on the home and focused on child-rearing.

Sociologists, however, point to the importance of *nurture* or the process of socialisation. They stress how our upbringing prepares us for our sex roles and how the portrayal of these roles in comics and on TV offers us **stereotypes**.

A stereotype is an over-simplified image which distorts reality. For example, we might hold the view that all young football supporters are hooligans. 'Big boys should never cry' is a sex role stereotype. When stereotypes of social groups are exaggerated, they can easily lead to blind prejudice.

Breaking down gender barriers

The next three parts of this chapter look at some of the ways in which the different agencies of socialisation mould us into traditional sex roles. Although we are largely steered towards narrowly defined masculine or feminine categories, we do have some choice in this matter. We can only belong to one of the two biological sex categories, but we can choose from a wide spectrum of gender attributes for different activities.

These two sex symbols were teenage pin-ups in the mid-1980s. Were they also gender models for teenagers to copy?

If enough fathers push prams then it no longer deviates from masculine norms and eventually our culture will be rewritten so that pram-pushing becomes a masculine, or at least a 'gender-neutral', activity. One example of the way that traditional gender barriers have broken down is the 'unisex' fashions dating from the 1960s, such as both sexes wearing denim jeans and T-shirts. And the mid-1980s saw the 'gender-bender' phenomenon: for example, women competing at body-building and male pop stars such as Boy George and Marilyn wearing female make-up.

While a person's sex is biologically determined, their gender is socially constructed. That is to say, our ideas of what is feminine and what is masculine depend on our culture. In many cultures women perform activities that our society would traditionally see as masculine or unfeminine. For example, women are not allowed to serve as active combat troops in Britain but women have joined in front-line fighting in many societies, such as modern Israel.

2   Sex role stereotyping in the home

From birth we start to learn the appropriate gender roles for both sexes in our culture. Our primary socialisation (see page 8) gives us our first lessons in sex roles in the following ways:

- parents' role models,
- the way we are dressed as toddlers,
- games and toys,
- rules about appropriate behaviour.

Parents' role models

One of our main lessons in sex roles comes from the example which our parents set us in the way they divide up tasks around the house. Even when wives are going out to work, they still tend to find that their husbands leave most of the domestic chores to them. This is shown in the following survey:

The domestic division of labour in households with working women

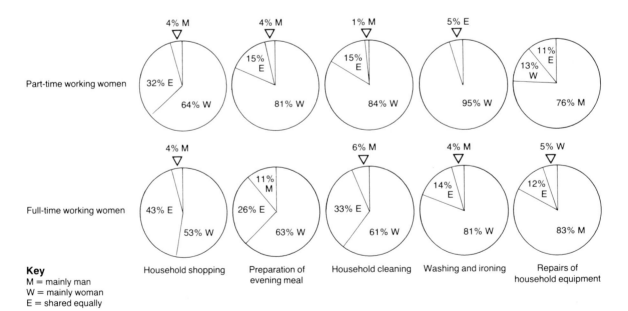

Key
M = mainly man
W = mainly woman
E = shared equally

(Source: *British Social Attitudes: the 1985 Report*)

10

Peter likes to help.

He sees Daddy go up.

He wants to help Daddy.

I want to help you,
he says.

Please can I help you?

Yes, says Daddy, you can
help me.

help sees Daddy

20

Here we are at home,
says Daddy.

Peter helps Daddy with
the car, and Jane helps
Mummy get the tea.

Good girl, says Mummy
to Jane.

You are a good girl to
help me like this.

Good good girl

Some pages from Boys and Girls *(Book 3b in the Ladybird Key Words Reading Scheme) – published in 1964 but still being purchased by some schools and libraries in the 1980s.*

Data-response exercise: the domestic division of labour

1 When wives are working full time, in what percentage of households do husbands equally share household cleaning?

2 Which domestic task is most likely to be done by men?

3 Which domestic task is most likely to be equally shared between men and full-time working women?

4 Using the figures on page 16, explain the following statement: 'When young children notice who cooks each day, they are learning a role model.'

5 How far do the figures support the claim that domestic chores are now jointly shared, especially when wives are working full time?

Clothes, games and toys for toddlers

When researchers from the State University of New York observed babies at shopping centres, they guessed the babies' sex and then checked by asking the parents. The pairs of observers rarely disagreed and mistakes in guessing the babies' sex were even rarer. It turned out that 77 per cent of the girls wore pink and 79 per cent of the boys wore blue.

Activities

1   An interesting piece of research is to look through the toddlers section of a clothing catalogue and count the number of items which are clearly designed (a) for girls, (b) for boys, in comparison with those that are (c) 'unisex' and suitable for either.

2   Look at a sample of advertisements for children's toys in a toy catalogue or on children's TV. Make three lists for toys which are shown (a) mainly used by girls, (b) mainly used by boys, (c) for either sex.

Rules about appropriate behaviour

The Equal Opportunities Commission has produced a booklet called *An Equal Start ... Guidelines for those working with the Under-Fives* which says:

> There is a time in every child's life for tranquillity and a time to release aggression and let off steam; there is a time to be docile and a time to be assertive; a time to cry and a time to shout. None of these characteristics is determined by the sex of the child and none should be regarded as inappropriate for either a girl or a boy.

Some of the ways that parents tend to lay down different rules for girls have been described in a survey of children in Nottingham called *Seven Years Old in the Home Environment*. This survey found that in comparison with boys, seven-year-old girls were:

- twice as likely to be fetched from school,

- more likely to be told they must say where they are going before going out,

- much more likely to be stopped from 'brawling in public' with their brothers and sisters although fighting in the home was often tolerated,

- more likely to be given the responsibility of looking after a younger brother or sister,

- far less likely to object to displaying affection in public, such as kissing their parents goodbye at the garden gate as they set off for school. The book describes how Bartholemew sits on his mother's lap in the evening and insists on his bedtime kiss; but he refuses even to wave her goodbye in the morning if anyone is watching. The **taboo** on male tenderness is thus enforced by the peer group: Bartholemew is afraid to appear a 'cissy' in front of his friends.

3   Media images

Stereotyped images of girls and women are often projected by the mass
media. These mass media include comics, advertisements and TV. If you
look for children's birthday cards in your local newsagents you will probably
find that very few are 'unisex' and suitable for either sex. Some cards show
girls in frilly dresses with fluffy dogs while others show boys playing football
or driving railway engines.

Women in textbooks

A 1983 Report called *'Pour Out the Cocoa, Jane': Sexism in Children's
Books* describes the following analysis of science textbooks: twenty-three
popular chemistry books contained 258 pictures of males and only twenty-
six pictures of females; 80 per cent of illustrations in physics books showed
only men and when women did appear they were 'in a bathing suit, in
a bath, as a nurse, with a vacuum cleaner'.

Women on TV

The findings of a survey of twenty-four TV companies in nine EEC countries
were presented in 1985 at an EEC Seminar on *Women in Television*. Only
14.5 per cent of TV journalists who appeared on the screen were women.
None of these seemed to be over fifty and none wore glasses, although
33 per cent of male TV journalists wore glasses on screen.

   Similar figures can be found in K. Durkin's *Television, Sex Roles and
Children* which claims that:

- males generally outnumber females by seven to three on TV,
- women are the main stars of only 14 per cent of mid-evening programmes,
- about 90 per cent of voice-overs on advertisements are performed by
  men,
- the background music of commercials aimed at boys is usually loud
  and dramatic, while for girls it is often soft and melodic.

Mirror Woman

WHY COMICS AREN'T A LAUGHING MATTER

THERE HE IS AGAIN, THAT DISHY GARY. OH GOSH, HOW CAN I GET HIM TO NOTICE ME...

Is YOUR daughter being brainwashed?

JACKIE, Britain's top teenage girls' magazine, celebrated its 1,000th issue this week.

Almost every young girl reads it at some time, and one in three have bought it over two decades.

That makes it very influential indeed.

"Twenty Years On and Still at the Top!" blares the Press handout.

But what has happened to Jackie readers? Twenty years on they're still at the bottom.

Girls, even in 1983, are lagging behind in almost every field at school and work despite attempts on their behalf to be more enlightened about education and provide equal opportunities.

Prey

Times have changed, but girls' images of themselves haven't. And where do they get those from? You've guessed it......

Comics have an enormous influence on children. A survey has shown that a staggering 47 per cent of Britain's youngsters choose them as their favourite reading matter. And naturally they are affected by the contents.

In Jackie they learn that trendy girls don't do their homework. They're too busy dreaming about boys.

But the fun really starts when the prey is caught. Jackie advises: "If he still fusses about wanting to play darts with the lads when you've insisted he takes you to the disco, deal with him firmly. This is best done by bursting into tears..."

Picture stories follow the same line. They usually start with a pretty

PARTY TIME: This week's issue of Jackie

girl dropping her shopping or losing her pet dog in the hope that some handsome boy will come to the rescue.

It's the traditional image of girls in a nutshell: pretty, helpless, petulant and dumb.

"No wonder girls never get anywhere when they

continually see themselves in this role," says Rosemary Stones, a researcher at the Children's Rights Workshop.

"The teenage comics are the very worst. They took off in the Sixties with Romeo and Valentine and were full of handsome men with chiselled chins and girls with luxurious curls and six-inch eyelashes.

> *Get with a swish hairdo and a snazzy dress*

JACKIE'S celebration issue carries, by way of a joke, the answer to an early reader's problem on how to get a boyfriend.

"Easy," reads the answer. "Get with a swish hairdo and a snazzy dress, slosh on lots of perfume and go where the boys are." But flick back a few pages and you'll see that nothing has

changed. Under an article headed "Train your boyfriend the Jackie way," is the immortal advice:

"Remember, boys are timid creatures who tend to panic easily if they think they're being hunted. But they tend to respond to smiles and sidelong glances."

Must take note of that.

by MARGARETTE DRISCOLL

"Boys go from Hornet and Hotspur to DIY or car magazines, or even Playboy, I suppose.

"Girls are left in a soppy, romantic dreamland, where their one interest in life is to get—and keep—a man.

"Boys are taught teamwork, to stand together. Girls are told implicitly that other girls are spiteful, not to be trusted."

In a quick survey of girls' comics like Judy, Debbie and Mandy, we found typical stories like Wee Slavey, about a cruelly abused servant girl from the 18th century, and Educated Edith, the tale of a talented girl who has to skimp on her schoolwork to look after her poor, sick father. But it isn't only girls who get a stereotyped image.

Working-class kids are loud, scruffy and insolent. Middle-class kids are creepy and wet. Upper-class kids are snobbish and brutal.

Nicholas Tucker, a psychologist who specialises in children's literature, says: "Images in comics help children to back up the judgments and prejudices they see around them.

Shake

"The whole world of girls' comics needs shaking up and bringing up to date."

Jackie is looking forward to another steady twenty years' sales.

By that time there might be a few more bright young girls around. And maybe, just maybe, they'll stop buying it.

The good girl's guide

A ROUND-UP of the comics showed that girls who might be even slightly brainy always have dull names like Edith—and usually spots and glasses too.

The four basic schoolgirl types are: the wistful ballerina, the jolly hockey-

sticks sporty type, the helpless unfortunate and the hapless swot.

The only girls who ever step out of line are the ones who act like boys. Beryl the Peril and Minnie the Minx are quick-witted and inventive. But they're also dirty, destructive and rude.

An article from the Daily Mirror, *7 March 1983.*

4 Girls in school

Do silent girls get ignored?

Research has shown that teachers are involved in as many as 1,000 exchanges with pupils each day. These **interactions** can range from questions or praise and encouragement to negative comments disapproving of a pupil's behaviour. Some pupils may receive as many as 120 of these direct contacts during the day and others have been observed to receive as few as only five, two being their names called out at morning and afternoon registrations! This kind of research frequently shows that:

- male pupils are most active, assertive and demanding of teachers' time and attention,
- boys receive more praise than girls and usually dominate class discussions,
- many teachers take longer to get to know the names of the girls they teach.

One girl in *Invisible Women: the Schooling Scandal* said, 'I think he thinks I'm pretty mediocre. I think I'm pretty mediocre. He never points me out of the group, or talks to me, or looks at me in particular when he's talking about things. I'm just a sort of wallpaper person.'

Activities

1 If you are at a mixed school, then the next time a teacher has a session of asking questions round a mixed class, count how often boys are asked compared to girls. You could also see if there is a difference between male and female teachers in how fairly their attention is distributed.

2 Why might girls in mixed science groups be less willing than boys to volunteer spoken answers in class?

3 Why is it argued that girls used to get more individual attention and better science results when more of them attended single sex schools?

4 Why might higher numbers of girls opt to do science subjects in single sex schools?

5 How far are male or female teachers concentrated in particular subject departments at your school or college?

Examination results

It has long been recognised that girls generally perform better than boys in examinations – when they are entered. Girls had to be marked more harshly in the old 11+ examination in order to adjust the results so that equal numbers of both sexes got to mixed grammar schools.

In 1985, for the first time, more girls left school with A-level passes than boys:

Qualifications of boy and girl school leavers in 1985

	Girls (%)	Boys (%)
18-year-olds with at least one A-level	18.5	17.9
16-year-olds with 5 or more O-levels	11	9.1
Leavers with no examination passes at all	10.3	14

Girls enjoying a craft lesson.

Inequalities in educational achievement can be seen in three areas:

1   options chosen,
2   examination subjects taken,
3   entry to higher education – 8.6 per cent of boys go on from school to do university degrees compared to 6.3 per cent of girls.

Options in the fourth and fifth years

It has been estimated that only 2 per cent of girls opt for technical crafts. When a Croydon school refused to allow Helen Whitfield to take a craft course, she took the school to court claiming 'less favourable treatment' under the Sex Discrimination Act. In 1979 the (male) judge ruled against her, saying that she had 'acted throughout under her mother's influence and was used as a weapon, or perhaps an ally, in her mother's campaign for women's rights'.

If your school or college is mixed, an interesting exercise would be to compare the numbers of males and females opting for different subjects.

A-Level passes and degrees taken

The figures on page 23 suggest that many academic subjects are 'sex stereo-typed'. The figures are from the Equal Opportunity Commission's *Women and Men in Britain: A Statistical Profile*.

In 1987, 46 per cent of undergraduate students were women, compared to 25 per cent in the early 1960s, and 38 per cent of postgraduate students were women. These figures show that there are increasing proportions of women in higher education, although only a very small percentage of professors are women.

Females as a percentage of A-level passes, summer 1983, England and Wales

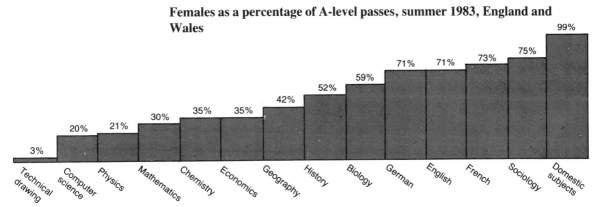

Women as a percentage of full-time undergraduate university students, 1983 (GB)

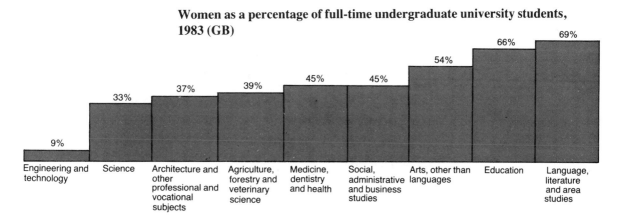

5 Women in 'his-story'

An important point to realise in any discussion of sex role stereotyping is how far things have changed in recent years. For example:

- Many publishers and librarians now give priority to children's stories with girls in active and adventurous roles.
- Many advertisements now feature 'liberated women' such as career women who drink Guinness.
- Many schools campaign against sexism. This new philosophy can be found in PE departments which encourage mixed sports with girls joining in football games and boys joining modern dance classes.
- In 1972 women were allowed to run in races further than 400 metres in the Olympic Games.
- In 1970 General Motors in the USA introduced an **affirmative action programme** to promote greater opportunities for women. The company increased the proportion of female students at its engineering college from 0.6 per cent in 1970 to 32 per cent in 1977.
- A few similar attempts, called **positive discrimination**, have been tried in Britain. For example, some Labour councils actively recruit women into manual jobs with trade apprenticeships, such as electrician or carpenter. Also, the Equal Opportunities Commission has launched a programme called WISE (Women into Science and Industry).

Activities

1 Carry out a survey to compare the career
   ambitions of males and females.
2 Time how long it takes you to list twelve
   famous men, excluding royalty, from
   British history before 1900. Now time
   yourself again, this time listing twelve
   famous women, excluding royalty, from
   British history before 1900.

If we look back in British history, we find that few women had influential
roles in society. Very few women ever became political leaders or famous
writers, artists or scientists. A useful book on this topic is *Hidden from
History* by S. Rowbotham.

The progress towards greater freedom for women and more equality
between the sexes has taken many years. Some of the landmarks are shown
in the following date chart.

Steps on the road towards equality between the sexes

1792   Mary Wollstonecraft wrote *A Vindication of the Rights of Women*,
       inspired by Tom Paine's *Rights of Man*.

1849   Queen's and Bedford Colleges were established for women at the
       University of London.

1874   Girton College for women was set up at Cambridge, but they were
       not allowed full degrees until 1948.

1888   The TUC passed its first resolution for equal pay and women were
       given the vote in county council elections.

1889   Annie Besant led the Bryant and May match-girl strikers to victory.

1905   Annie Kenney, a trade unionist and **suffragette** (a woman campaign-
       ing for women's right to vote), submitted a written question on
       behalf of 96,000 female cotton workers asking 'Will the Liberal Gov-
       ernment give votes to women?' at an election rally. Winston Chur-
       chill, candidate for N.W. Manchester, chose to ignore the question
       and, after she had heckled him, she was dragged from the meeting
       with Christabel Pankhurst who spat at a policeman to get herself
       arrested. After refusing to pay fines, they became the first suffra-
       gettes to be imprisoned.

1914   500,000 women went to work in the 'war effort', for example in
       munitions factories.

1918   Women over thirty were given the vote in general elections and
       the first women joined the police.

1919   Nancy Astor became the first woman MP and the Sex Disqualifica-
       tion (Removal) Act opened up the professions to women.

1928   Women over twenty-one were given the vote. They now had the
       same entitlement to vote as men.

1941   Britain became the only country to introduce conscription for women
       (if they were unmarried and aged twenty to thirty).

1958 The first women peers were allowed in the House of Lords.

1969 The Women's Liberation Movement held their first demonstration, disrupting the 'Miss World' contest at the Albert Hall with smoke bombs and bags of flour.

Women demonstrating against the Mecca Miss World Contest in 1971.

1970 The Equal Pay Act gave women the right to the same wages as men if they were doing broadly similar work for the same employer and the Matrimonial Proceedings Act gave wives the right to an equal share of a couple's assets (e.g. the value of their house) on divorce.

1972 The feminist magazine *Spare Rib* was launched. Erin Pizzey set up the first refuge for battered wives. By 1980 there were ninety-nine Women's Aid Groups and 200 refuges.

1975 The Sex Discrimination Act was passed and the Equal Opportunities Commission was set up to help enforce this law against treating women less favourably than men in areas such as: education and training; recruitment advertising and getting a job; buying a house and getting a loan.

1976 The first Rape Crisis Centre was opened by feminists in London. The Domestic Violence Act allowed victims of marital violence to get their spouse excluded from the marital home by court order.

1980 Women Against Violence Against Women held their first national conference in Leeds – where the Yorkshire Ripper had just murdered his thirteenth female victim.

1982 NALGO, the union for council office workers, printed and distributed 250,000 pamphlets against sexual harassment at work.

1984   The Equal Pay Act was amended so that either sex could now ask an Industrial Tribunal to award equal pay if their work was of 'equal value' in terms of effort, skill, decision-making and other demands.

1984   Scotland Yard set up an Equal Opportunities Unit after it was disclosed that it had been running an illegal quota system which restricted recruitment of women to 10 per cent. (In 1988, 30 per cent of Metropolitan Police recruits were women.)

1986   The 1975 Sex Discrimination Act was amended with an equality clause which relates to retirement, dismissal and demotion as well as access to opportunities for promotion, transfer and training.

1989   The Employment Act ended many restrictions on the employment of women, such as for work in mines and quarries.

1989   Barbara Harris became the first ever woman bishop in the Anglican Church (in Boston, in the USA).

However, women still have a long way to go on the road to equality with men. This is indicated by the following points:

- Most junior bank staff are women but most bank managers are men. In his book called *The Brotherhood*, Stephen Knight claims that promotion to management depends very largely on joining the Freemasons, a secret society with male only membership.
- In 1986 only 13.5 per cent of hospital consultants and 19.6 per cent of GPs were women.
- In 1987 only seventeen of Britain's 465 judges were women.
- In 1981 23 per cent of new computer science graduates were women. But by 1986 this proportion had fallen to 13 per cent. (Have computers become 'toys for the boys'?)

Activity: do you agree with this feminist conclusion?

The important question is not how and why women come to mother our children, but how and why men do not. The issue is not just 'nature' or socialisation experiences, but social control and power. Men don't rear children because they don't WANT to rear children. By leaving childcare to women, men are free for activities outside the home which bring status and power. Parenting is a time-consuming and unpaid occupation. This explains why parenting brings lower status, less power and less control of resources.

(adapted from 'Women in the Family: Companions or Caretakers' by Diana Leonard and Mary Anne Speakman in *Women in Britain Today*, 1986)

GCSE question from Southern Examining Group 1988

(a)   Girls and boys often choose different subjects in schools. Identify and explain *three* reasons for their subject choices.   (6)

(b)   How have legal and social changes helped to improve the status of women in our society during this century?   (6)

CHAPTER 3

Childhood and youth culture

Introduction: the evolution of childhood

When a class of six-year-olds in a London infant school were asked to draw pictures of adults and children, their pictures showed adults working and children playing. This separation of the adult world of work and the childhood world of play has only occurred in the last few hundred years.

During the middle ages children were dressed exactly like adults and joined in grown-up activities. In 1212, 20,000 French children and 30,000 German boys and girls were led by two twelve-year-olds to go and fight in the Holy Land. This Children's Crusade is not so surprising when you realise that children were allowed to wear a sword from the age of five and join the army from the age of eleven.

As late as the 1600s, Heroard's diary about Louis XIII of France shows how he joined in dances at the royal court from the age of three and at five was practising archery and watching bear-baiting. By the time little Louis was seven, he was riding, hunting and enjoying entertainments such as wrestling, jousting and bull-fighting.

Daniel Defoe said, in 1724, that all children over the age of four or five could earn their own bread. Apprenticeships, teaching the skills of a craft, started between the ages of seven and twelve. But in the seventeenth century (1600 to 1700) an increasing number of merchants sent their sons to grammar schools. The development of schooling was one of the factors which reflected the changing status of childhood.

1 The changing status of children and teenagers

Three important factors which have helped to give childhood its modern character are:

1 schooling,
2 exclusion from adult paid work and
3 laws which protect children and define their status.

This painting by François-Hubert Drouais shows how children in the eighteenth century were dressed as 'mini adults'.

Schooling

This was made compulsory up to the age of ten in 1880 and the school leaving age was raised as follows:

1880 – 10 years old
1893 – 11 years old
1899 – 12 years old
1902 – 13 years old
1914 – 14 years old
1947 – 15 years old
1972 – 16 years old

Exclusion from adult paid work

During much of British history the rich arranged the marriages of their children to create alliances between powerful families while the poor exploited the labour of their children by making them work. In 1761, a woman called Anne Martin was sentenced to two years in Newgate Prison for blinding children so that she could use them for begging. More commonly, children in the early nineteenth century were forced to work the same eleven- or twelve-hour day as their parents.

In 1842 the First Report of the Commission on the Employment of Children and Young Persons in Mines was presented to Parliament. This report quoted an eight-year-old girl, Sarah Goodber, who described her working day operating 'the trap', a lever to control the air supply, in a Yorkshire coal mine: 'I'm a trapper in the Gauber Pit, I have to trap without light, and I'm scared. I go at four and sometimes half-past three in the morning and come out at five and half past. I never go to sleep. Sometimes I sing when I've light, but not in the dark: I dare not sing then.'

This report resulted in Lord Shaftesbury's Mine Act of 1842 which stopped underground working in pits for all girls and for boys under the age of ten. Numerous Factories Acts have restricted the hours which young people can work. Under the 1973 Employment of Children Act, paid work is not allowed under the age of thirteen except for doing light farm work for one's parents or taking part in films or stage shows with a special licence. Pupils aged between thirteen and sixteen may only work for two hours on a school day, between 7 and 9 a.m. and 4.30 and 7 p.m.

Laws which protect children and define their status

Crime   Up to 1780 there were 200 offences which carried the penalty of death by hanging and children were held by law and custom to be adult, and therefore responsible for their crimes, over the age of seven. Thus a seven-year-old girl was hanged in Norwich for stealing a petticoat and in one day alone, in February 1814, five children were condemned to death at the Old Bailey courts. Their crimes were burglary and theft and they were aged between eight and twelve.

Today, the age of criminal responsibility in England and Wales is ten. Below this age you cannot be charged with a criminal offence, although you can be arrested, cautioned and held under a 'place of safety' order. Between the ages of ten and fourteen the prosecution has to prove that a child knows the difference between right and wrong.

When teenagers under the age of seventeen are arrested, the police must inform their parents or guardians and they should not be interviewed without them, or another adult such as a social worker, being present.

Crimes involving young people under seventeen are normally dealt with in a juvenile court. If you are found guilty of an offence for which an adult could be sent to prison, then at fourteen you can be sent to a detention centre, at fifteen you can be sent to a borstal and at seventeen you can be sent to an adult prison.

Sex and marriage   A girl cannot legally consent to sexual intercourse with a man until she is sixteen. Before 1885 the age of consent was twelve and it was raised to sixteen in 1929. In the event of 'underage sex' between a man and a girl aged fifteen or under, it is the man rather than the girl who can be prosecuted for an offence.

Between the ages of sixteen and eighteen a girl (or should we call her a young woman?) may only marry with her parents' consent. A girl under seventeen who goes to live with her boyfriend may be given a supervision order or a care order by a juvenile court if her parents, the police or the social services regard her as in 'moral danger'.

It is unlawful for two consenting males to commit homosexual acts in private unless they are both over twenty-one.

Other age limits   The list on page 30 shows some of the activities which are only allowed past a certain age:

Age	Activity
14	Own an air rifle.
15	Possess a shot-gun under supervision.
16	Sell scrap metal.
	Ride a motor bike.
	Buy wine or beer with a meal.
	Join the armed forces if male.
17	Join the armed forces if female.
	Drive a car.
	Buy or hire fire arms.
18	Buy alcoholic drinks in a pub.
	Pay the Community Charge (the Poll Tax).
	Vote in parliamentary or council elections.
21	Stand for Parliament.
	Hold a licence to drive a lorry or a bus.

These laws change from time to time. You can check them in the reference section at your local library. A good book is *First Rights* published by the National Council for Civil Liberties.

Case study: adolescence in a hunting and gathering society – initiation to adulthood among the !Kung

The !Kung were traditionally a hunting and gathering people in the Kalahari Desert of Namibia in southern Africa. Girls were often married at the age of seven or eight to young men at least twice their age. But they were not expected to live with their husbands until after their first menstruation. This landmark called for far greater ritual celebration than the actual marriage ceremony.

Initiation to adulthood for a !Kung boy came at about fourteen once he had proved himself as a hunter by killing a large antelope on his own.

As Van der Post and Taylor have described,

> On his return to the camp he must stay apart from everyone else, especially women. The animal, once killed, must be cooked on a special fire which the women must avoid; and he himself must not partake of the meat. After this he was scarified by his male relatives with a series of short, vertical incisions on his face, arms, chest and back.

After this ritual the boy would be regarded as a man and a hunter, ready for marriage.

Activities: test yourself on some legal age limits

1 How old do you have to be to:
   (a) buy cigarettes and smoke in public?
   (b) claim Income Support?
   (c) enter a betting shop and place bets?
   (d) enter a pub?
   (e) buy fireworks?
   (f) change your name without your parents' consent?
   (g) work your own market stall?
   (h) choose your own doctor and give consent for treatment?
   (i) use a pawn shop?
   (j) make a will?
   (The answers to this quiz are at the end of the chapter.)

2 Describe any celebrations, ceremonies or rituals in modern British society which you think mark the end of childhood or the start of adulthood.

2 The ideas of youth and youth culture

Youth

Young people's legal rights vary as they go through their teenage years. There is a gradual transition to adulthood between the ages of fourteen, when they start paying full fares on public transport, and eighteen, when they can give blood and sit on a jury. At eighteen parents no longer have custody over their children who are no longer 'minors' but have reached the age of 'majority'.

The raising of the school-leaving age could be seen as extending childhood further into adulthood. Or one might argue that a recent social category has arisen called youth, meaning the period between childhood and adulthood.

Youth has expanded in both directions:

1   Youth starts earlier than in the past because the average age of sexual maturity has been falling. One explanation for this is our improved diet and rising standard of living which has also caused a rise in people's average heights from one generation to the next. The average height for ten- to fourteen-year-olds has increased by about $2\frac{1}{2}$ cm every decade since 1900: are you taller than your parents?

2   Youth also ends later than before because an increasing proportion of those in their twenties are still partly dependent on their parents. Many are at college or university and many remain living at home due to housing and job shortages. These young people are extending their youth into their twenties before becoming fully independent adults.

We now turn to the question of how far young people have a distinct culture of their own. Many adults find it difficult to understand features of the teenage world, such as GCSE and YTS, discos and skateboards, which never existed when *they* were young. Teenyboppers' 'flavour of the month' pop idols and fast changing fashions seem to give young people a way of life which is alien and closed to most adults. While most teenagers enjoy this **youth culture**, some join particular youth groups with distinct lifestyles.

What is meant by youth subcultures?

In looking at post-war youth cults such as teddyboys and punks, sociologists have asked whether such groups are **subcultures**. For sociologists, culture means a way of life of a society. A subculture therefore refers to a way of life shared by a minority which is different in important respects from the life pursued by the majority of the population. For example, travellers have a subculture because they have their own distinctive patterns of behaviour and different values and beliefs from the rest of society. Therefore, when a group of young people lead a distinctive way of life with their own attitudes, values and modes of behaviour, we can call this a **youth subculture**.

Hippies at a 1967 'Flower Power' gathering in Hyde Park.

Case study of a youth culture: the hippies

In the late 1960s some young people developed a 'hippy' life-style which, by our definition, would qualify as a youth subculture. Their **alternative value system** can be seen in some of their well-known slogans. 'Peace and Love' shows a rejection of militarism and violence. The message 'Tune In, Turn On and Drop Out' means take 'mind-expanding' drugs and reject the 'rat-race' of the conventional career ladder.

One approach to understanding youth cults is called **semiology** or **semiotics**. This means the study of signs and symbols. If we look at the outward styles of the hippies we can interpret their meanings and so try to 'read' their subculture:

1   Long hair for men indicated a rejection of the discipline of school, work and the army which dictated 'short back and sides' haircuts; and rejection of traditional ideas of masculinity in favour of the freedom of 'unisex' hairstyles.

2   Wide, flared trousers indicated a rejection of the narrow trousers with turn-ups of the 'straight' world of office workers.

3   Necklaces of beads with bells and loose, smock-like shirts called kaftans indicated an identification with Eastern mysticism; and, like the bell-bottomed trousers, this loose clothing symbolised a free and easy, casual approach to life.

Reasons for post-war youth cults

Some sociologists have emphasised that youth cults are a post-war phenomenon. As well as the raising of the school-leaving age, the following reasons are usually given for the emergence of youth culture:

1   Affluence: in the 1950s advertisers began to talk about the spending power of the youth market because teenagers had more money to spend than previous generations.

2   Leisure: modern teenagers not only have more money to spend than previous generations but they also have more free time in which to enjoy discos, films, records, fashions and so on.

3   The mass media: two sorts of influence can be seen:
(a) the record industry, TV, radio and magazine publishers have expanded to cater for the teenage market;
(b) the mass media as a whole have stimulated interest in new youth groups. The popular press often seem obsessed with the new, 'way out' styles of the young.

It is undoubtedly the case that these factors have had an effect on young people's lives and since the 1950s a series of youth cults have emerged with their own styles of dress and music. But while 'pop music' emerged from the new rock-and-roll of the 1950s, youth groups can nevertheless be found further back in history. Therefore it is a mistake to think that youth culture only arrived after the Second World War. The next two parts of this chapter look at two youth groups: one from the 1890s and the other from the 1930s.

3   The Edelweiss Pirates in Hitler's Germany

The Hitler Youth

Nazi Germany was a **totalitarian state**. In other words, Hitler's Nazi Party tried to control, by persuasion and terror, all the important areas of an individual's life. The Nazis demanded total loyalty and service from the German people and the young were trained to become good Nazi citizens by the Hitler Youth organisation. The activities of the Hitler Youth took place after school or work and at weekends. These activities included hiking and camping, along with military drill and instruction in Nazi beliefs.

The Edelweiss Pirates

In 1939 the Hitler Youth was made compulsory up to the age of eighteen. This was by no means popular and a number of alternative, anti-Nazi youth cults spontaneously appeared. Upper-middle-class youth in Germany formed the Swing Movement and upset the Nazis by dancing the 'jitterbug' to the music of American jazz bands. Also, a working-class youth subculture arose around the Edelweiss Pirates who took their name from their badges. These metal badges were worn on their collars and were the shape of edelweiss flowers or the skull and crossbones. The Edelweiss Pirates started in the west of Germany but groups, such as the 'Roving Dudes' of Essen, sprang up across the country and all saw themselves as 'pirates' – rebels outside of the law.

The activities of the Pirate groups

The Edelweiss Pirates usually wore checked shirts, dark short trousers and white socks. Although it was wartime, the different Pirate groups were able to enjoy a wide range of similar activities. The sexes were segregated in the Hitler Youth but the Pirates took girls along on their weekend camping trips into the country and girls joined them when they met in parks in the evenings. They wanted freedom and their resentment of the Nazi system was shown in two of their activities: beating up members of the Hitler Youth and singing Nazi tunes with anti-Nazi lyrics.

The Nazi crack down on the Edelweiss Pirates

The Pirates were mainly youths who had left school at fourteen for fairly well-paid factory jobs and who resented having to belong to the Hitler Youth up to the age of eighteen. They were also joined by conscript soldiers on leave and by 1944 their activities had escalated from defacing Nazi posters to hiding army deserters and escaped prisoners. In Cologne, they

Group hanging of twelve Edelweiss Pirates, Cologne-Ehrenfeld, 1944, for taking part in underground anti-Nazi activities such as sabotage and arms raids.

even killed the local chief of the Gestapo. The Nazis stepped up their response from warnings, arrests and shaving the heads of Pirates to rounding up thousands, sending many to concentration camps and hanging their 'ringleaders'. In fact they had no real leaders.

The Edelweiss Pirates are a good example of a youth subculture. They were rebels with their own values and styles of dress and music which were alternatives to those of the dominant, official Nazi way of life.

4   The original hooligans of the 1890s

Violent youth in Victorian London

In 1974, the Conservative cabinet minister, Sir Keith Joseph, said: 'For the first time in a century and a half, since the great Tory reformer Robert Peel set up the Metropolitan Police, areas of our cities are becoming unsafe for peaceful citizens by night and some even by day.' This issue of law and order was a key part of Mrs Thatcher's election campaign of 1979. In fact, nineteenth-century Londoners going through their badly lit streets at night were frequent prey to young ruffians armed with cudgels. It has been estimated that a Briton in the early 1980s had a 25 per cent lower chance of being murdered than in the 1860s.

Flogging, which had been abolished in 1861, was reintroduced in the 1863 Garotters' Act after a wave of street robberies in which victims were choked. *The Times* of 10 June 1863 observed that this new peril of the streets had created 'something like a reign of terror' in which 'whole sections of a peacable city community were on the verge of arming themselves against sudden attack'.

The first 'Hooligans'

In 1899 there were 3,444 cases of assault on London's 13,213 police constables and *The Times* complained: 'The pickpocket is dying out, the Hooligan replaces him.' As Pearson has noted,

> The word 'hooligan' made an abrupt entrance into common English usage, as a term to describe gangs of rowdy youths, during the hot summer of 1898. 'Hooligans' and 'Hooliganism' were thrust into the headlines in the wake of turbulent August Bank Holiday celebrations in London which had resulted in unusually large numbers of people being brought before the courts for disorderly behaviour, drunkenness, assaults on the police, street robberies and fighting.

Various new recreations of working-class youth were blamed at the time. These developments in popular culture which were condemned included the music halls, professional football, the 'penny dreadful' comics, Bank Holiday excursions to seaside resorts and then the moving-pictures of the early cinema. One solution was seen to be the growing Christian boys organisations, such as the Boys' Brigade, the Church Lads' Brigade and, after 1908, the Boy Scouts. Baden-Powell, the founder of the Boy Scouts, called the Hooligan 'the best class of boy'.

The uniform of the Hooligan: 'All of them have a peculiar muffler twisted round the neck, a cap set rakishly forward, well over the eyes, and trousers very tight at the knee and very loose over the foot.'

Summary

We can note four aspects of the late nineteenth-century urban delinquents:

1   Affluence   As was noted at the time, the Hooligans were not the very poorest slum-dwellers. They were well-shod and often had enough money in their pockets to pay their fines as well as afford their own special styles of clothing. Their money came from their jobs as 'handy lads' in factories, errand boys, messenger boys or delivery van boys.

2   Leisure   Groups such as the 'Peaky Blinders' or 'Sloggers' in Manchester and the 'Somers Town Gang' or 'Chelsea Boys' in London had enough free time to hang around the streets and create their own gang subcultures.

3   The temporary delinquent career   A correspondent in the *Daily Graphic* of 1900 noted: 'It is a mistake to confuse the Hooligan with the habitual criminal – the man whose living is crime. The Hooligan works . . .

The Hooligan, as he gets older, generally settles down into a respectable, if a humble, member of society.'

4   The mass media   J. Davis has shown that the London Garotting Panic of 1862 resulted in increased arrests because a media panic lead to greater police vigilance. Thus the 'crime wave', such as it was, can be seen as having been created by the actions and reactions of the press, the public and various government agencies. It did not reflect any significant increase in actual criminal activity in the streets.

Policing the Crisis by S. Hall and others has similarly concluded that the Mugging Panic in 1973 was stirred up by the press. It is to the effects of the media on post-war youth culture that we now turn.

Activities

1 Interview some teenagers of different ages and find out whether they belong to any youth organisations. If they do, ask them to describe the aims and activities of their organisations.

2 What does the Hooligan phenomenon at the turn of the century have in common with any of the post-war youth cults?

---

5   Youth culture and the media

Some observers argue that youth culture has emerged because of post-war affluence, extended schooling and the unclear position in which modern youth find themselves. But sociologists such as Stan Cohen have stressed the way in which youth subcultures are partly the creation of the mass media.

Mods and rockers and moral panics

Cohen has looked at how the press reported events at Clacton on Easter Sunday 1964. On this particular bank holiday, it was very cold and wet and there was some fighting between young people who had gone to the coast for a day of fun. A few youths ended up throwing stones at each other and breaking windows and some of these belonged to groups of motorbike riders called rockers or scooter riders called mods. The papers chose to report these disturbances as 'riots' and 'battles'. Cohen argues that they exaggerated events for two reasons:

1   The press often have little news to report over a bank holiday and there is also a natural tendency for reporters to overdramatise events in the sensationalist, popular papers.
2   The press tend to take the same view as the police, magistrates and parents when there is seen to be a threat from gangs of youths. They overreact and amplify people's fears.

When society is undergoing rapid change, people feel insecure. The media

Daily Mirror

Scooter gangs 'beat up' Clacton

'WILD ONES' INVADE SEASIDE—97 ARRESTS

3d.   Monday, March 30, 1964   No. 18,746

By PAUL HUGHES

THE Wild Ones invaded a seaside town yesterday—1,000 fighting, drinking, roaring, rampaging teenagers on scooters and motor-cycles. By last night, after a day of riots and battles with police, ninety-seven of them had been arrested.

A desperate S O S went out from police at Clacton, Essex, as leather-jacketed youths and girls attacked people in the streets, turned over parked cars, broke into beach huts, smashed windows, and fought with rival gangs.

Police reinforcements from other Essex towns raced to the shattered resort, where fearful residents had locked themselves indoors.

By this time the centre of Clacton was jammed with screaming teenagers. Traffic was at a standstill.

Fought

The crowd was broken up by police and police dogs. Several policemen were injured as the teenagers fought them.

A number of arrests had already been made. Addresses had been taken, and messages sent to parents.

And worried mothers and fathers were beginning to arrive from the London area to bail out their sons and daughters.

The harassed police were glad to see them go. For the cells at Clacton police station were crammed with youngsters under arrest.

By last night the score of arrests and charges — still incomplete — included:

Thirty for assault on police and civilians; thirty for creating disturbances and fighting; ten for theft; and at least twenty for other offences, including drunk and disorderly, malicious damage and using obscene language.

Rough

Police said the court hearings would begin on April 27.

The Wild Ones—this was the title of a Marlon Brando film in which teenaged motor-cyclists terrorised a town—have caused trouble in Clacton before. But not on this scale.

They began arriving on Friday and Saturday and many slept rough on the beach, under the pier, in promenade shelters, and in beach huts they broke open.

Others spent the night roaring round the town on their scooters and motor-cycles.

Youths in leather jackets help a police officer making inquiries last night into the rampage by gangs of teenagers at the seaside resort of Clacton. A police dog stands by.

This report of the 'riots and battles' of the Mods and Rockers, in Clacton on Easter Sunday in 1964, was typical of the press.

can provide a focus for their general fears and bewilderment by inspiring **moral panics** about threatening groups such as mods and rockers. These groups then become **folk devils** or scapegoats who can be blamed for causing the 'collapse of society'.

The media amplification spiral

Each of the seven stages in the **media amplification spiral** leads on to the next:

1 **Initial problem** Bored youths seek excitement.

2 **Initial solution** Youths go in groups to the seaside on bank holidays for fun.

3 **Reaction from the media** Media exaggerate the activities and appearances of the gangs. They create popular stereotypes of mods and rockers and they predict more trouble.

4 **Moral panic** The public become increasingly anxious about the aggressive mods (short hair and parka coats) and rockers (greasy hair and leather jackets).

5 **Reaction from the forces of law and order** More police are drafted into bank holiday resorts; confrontations with youths lead to more arrests; courts give out stiffer sentences.

6 **Isolation of the deviant groups** Those young people who identify with the 'folk devil' groups feel persecuted and anti-police. They become more isolated from the rest of society and develop more cohesive subcultures.

7 **Confirmation of stereotype** Members of youth cults see themselves as troublemakers and live up to their label or media image.

The further reaction of the media ensures that the process then continues by a repetition of stages 3 to 7. This spiral can be described as a **self-fulfilling prophecy**: that is, a prediction which leads people to act in such a way that their actions make the prediction come true. In this case the media's original moral panic creates troublemakers who may try to live up to their sensationalised reputation.

Case study: defusing the threat posed by the punks

In 1976 a new youth subculture emerged: the punks. We can trace two sorts of response from the media:

1 **Punks and moral panic** Cohen believes that the threat posed by the early mods and rockers was exaggerated out of all proportion by the media. The early punks were given similarly lurid and sensational coverage. Yet the punks largely looked for this sort of reporting since they aimed to outrage and shock the public: they wore Nazi swastikas and ripped T-shirts, they stuck safety pins through their nostrils and they revelled in anti-social public activities such as spitting, vomiting and glue-sniffing.

2 **Incorporating the punks into mainstream fashions** It was not long however before the press turned away from portraying punks as 'folk devils'. Punks were soon shown to be 'the kids next door' who enjoyed some amusing fancy dress at weekends. Rebel music groups on independent labels were soon given big contracts by major record companies. High street chain stores soon adapted punk styles and within a few years many smart young office workers, male and female, had bright orange hair, shaved at the back and sides.

Conclusion

Childhood and youth are social categories. They are defined differently in different societies and at different stages in history. Most young people generally follow the conventions of their parents and for those who do have contact with a youth subculture, it is usually a brief flirtation. Many sociologists conclude that youth culture has a positive function. It helps adolescents through a period of uncertainty and stress when they are searching for their own identity.

Answers to the test on legal age limits

(a)	16	(d)	14	(g)	17	(i)	14
(b)	18	(e)	16	(h)	16	(j)	18
(c)	17	(f)	18				

Case study: girls in youth subcultures

Angela McRobbie has asked why girls have been absent from studies of Teds and Mods and Skinheads. Were girls really absent from the subcultures (and if so, why)? Or were they ignored by male sociologists?

Her research found that girls *are* members of youth subcultures but in marginal, 'feminine' positions that reflect the normal sexual expectations of boys. Girls are defined as 'girl friends', for example. Female skinheads and punks are certainly rebelling against the mainstream culture of femininity, but within the subcultures themselves traditional working-class gender divisions still seem to hold.

McRobbie also suggests that there is really no such thing as a female subculture, a way in which working-class girls can resist dominant cultural norms collectively, as a group of girls.

Teenage girls do share a 'teenybopper' or 'bedroom' culture: friendship groups based on the home, on magazines like *Jackie*, on pop stars and pin-ups. But as girls grow older these friendships become less significant and their lives become defined by their marginal status in subcultures or by the commercial culture of femininity.

(adapted from *The Sociology of Youth* by Simon Frith, 1984)

Activity

It is claimed that girls do not enjoy the same freedom from parental control as boys and that this explains why girls are far less prominent in youth groups. Compose a questionnaire on parental supervision and give it to a sample of male and female teenagers.

GCSE question from Midland Examining Group 1988

(a) Describe *three* ways in which the position of children in modern Britain has changed since the early nineteenth century.   (6)

(b) What reasons have sociologists given for the rise of post-war youth subcultures? (For example, the Teddy Boys, Hippies and Punks).   (8)

The family as a social institution

CHAPTER 4

Do we need families?

1 The universal functions of the family

Many sociologists argue that the family is the most basic and enduring of all social arrangements because it satisfies basic and enduring needs. We begin this chapter by identifying these needs. Next, we look at family life in a Kenyan tribe and in the Israeli kibbutz. Finally, we examine the development of the British family.

The three basic needs which the family fulfils

1 A society must have new members to replace those that have died, otherwise it will become extinct. **Procreation**, having children, is the obvious method of acquiring new members. Producing babies is not however enough; the children need to be cared for after birth. It is possible, of course, for birth to take place outside a family grouping. Babies could be produced by a couple who were not united in any way and then be looked after by one parent alone or by an institution that society had created for that purpose. But the family seems to have always been a natural grouping to meet the basic need of procreation and child-rearing.

2 A society needs its new members to be socialised into its values and patterns of behaviour. This job of **socialisation** could be left entirely to professional child-minders but throughout history the family has had the essential responsibility of preparing the young for membership of society. The natural bonds of affection between parents and children make the family unit an effective and readily available agency of socialisation. This, then, is the second basic need that the family fulfils.

3 Most of us have a need for stable and intimate relationships with another person or a small group of people. The family makes this possible and so provides us with **emotional support** and psychological satisfaction.

A toddler's play is part of the process of socialisation.

These are the three basic functions that the family performs and they explain why the family is a grouping which has persisted throughout history. We now look at an example of a **pre-industrial society** where the family had a wide variety of functions.

2   The family in a pre-industrial society

In the 1930s Jomo Kenyatta was an African student in London. Within thirty years he was the first President of the independent republic of Kenya. His book, *Facing Mount Kenya: the Tribal Life of the Gikuyu* (1938), describes, from first-hand experience, his people's traditional way of life before it was disrupted by European missionaries, white farmers and colonial administrators. It gives us a clear picture, from the inside, of a pre-industrial society in which the family had a wide range of important functions. Some of these are described below.

The functions of the traditional Gikuyu family

1   Procreational functions

The Gikuyu tribal custom requires that a married couple should have at least four children, two male and two female. The first male is regarded as perpetuating the existence of the man's father, the second as perpetuating that of the woman's father. The first and second female children fulfil the same ritual duty to the souls of their grandmothers on both sides. The children are given the names of the persons whose soul they represent.

2 Religious functions The Gikuyu have ceremonies for communing with the spirits of their ancestors. They also worship the god, Ngai, who is the creator and giver of all things.

> . . . religion is interwoven with traditions and social customs of the people. Thus all members of the community are automatically considered to have acquired, during their childhood teachings, all that is necessary to know about religion and custom. The duty of imparting this knowledge to the children is entrusted to the parents.

So the parents act as both priests and teachers.

3 Educational functions

> The education of very small babies is . . . carried on through the medium of lullabies. In these the whole history and tradition of the family and clan are embodied and, by hearing these lullabies daily, it is easy for the children to assimilate this early teaching.
>
> When the child is able to speak, he can answer many questions which are asked gently and naturally to test how much he has learnt. Such questions as these might be asked: What is your name? Who is your father? What is your age-group? What is the name of your grandfather? And your great-grandfather? . . . Why are they given such-and-such names for their age-groups?
>
> Peer groups are named after events, such as battles and droughts, which occur at the time of their initiation into adulthood. In the late 19th century one age-group was called 'gatego' meaning Syphilis. This enables a tribe with no written records to remember historical events such as the arrival of European illnesses.
>
> When the children are very young they are left at home minding small babies, or are taken to the field where they are allowed to play in the corner of the cultivated field. . . . As soon as they are able to handle a digging-stick they are given small allotments to practise on. . . . Parents help them to plant seeds and teach them how to distinguish crops from the wild plants or weeds.
>
> To test the boy's power of observation and memory, two or three herds from different homesteads are mixed, and the boy is asked to separate them by picking out all that belong to his herd.
>
> The girl's training in agriculture is the same as that of the boy. The mother is in charge of the co-education of her children. In the evening she teaches both boy and girl the laws and customs, especially those governing the moral code and general rules of etiquette in the community. The teaching is carried on in the form of folklore and tribal legends. At the same time the children are given mental exercises through amusing riddles and puzzles which are told only in the evenings after meals, or while food is being cooked.

It can be seen that the family is the major unit of socialisation and social control in Gikuyu society.

*Women preparing food in
an African village.*

4   Economic functions

The chief occupations among the Gikuyu are agriculture and the rearing
of livestock, such as cattle, sheep and goats. Each family, i.e. a man,
his wife and their children, constitute an economic unit.

Children join in farming work from an early age and tasks which are shared
equally between the sexes include planting, weeding, harvesting, beer-
brewing and trading at the markets. Everyone's life is based on agriculture
and the ownership of farms is organised according to bonds of kinship:
the family is the basis of land tenure.

5   Political functions   Organisation of the tribe is clearly based on the
family unit:

The Gikuyu customary law of marriage provides that a man may have
as many wives as he can support, and that the larger one's family the
better it is for him and the tribe. ... In Gikuyu the qualification for
a status to hold high office in the tribal organisation is based on family.
... It is held that if a man can control and manage effectively the affairs
of a large family, this is an excellent testimonial of his capacity to look
after the interests of the tribe.

In the Gikuyu system of government elders are linked through village and
district councils where judges are elected. In all this

the starting point was the family. From the governmental point of view
members of one family group were considered as forming a family council, with the father as the president.

Conclusion

A number of further functions are to be found within the family or within the grouping of several families known as a **clan**. These functions include care of the old and sick and recreational activities such as dances. Kenyatta concludes that a Gikuyu's personal needs, physical and psychological, are satisfied 'while he plays his part as a member of a family group, and cannot be fully satisfied in any other way'. The family in pre-industrial Britain was similar to the traditional Gikuyu family in so far as it carried out a similarly broad range of functions.

Activity

The modern **welfare state** includes payments from central government such as pensions and unemployment or sickness benefits. It also includes local government services such as council housing, schools and social workers.

List those functions of the typical pre-industrial family which have been partly or completely taken over by the welfare state in modern Britain.

---

3   An alternative to the family: communal living on a kibbutz

Zionism was a movement founded in 1897 to re-establish a Jewish nation in Palestine. In 1909 seven young Jewish pioneers, recently arrived in Palestine from Europe, set up a farm in which they each had an equal say in making decisions. Living in tents with few resources, it made sense to share all that they had. Collective settlements also offered defence against hostility from local Arabs. There was a great need for labour because large tracts of land had to be reclaimed from the malarial swamps in the Jordan Valley. For this reason, women came to work alongside men, while the children were raised in large groups by child-minders.

This was the beginning of the kibbutz movement. By 1980 there were about 230 kibbutz villages (**kibbutzim**) in Israel. Some were inspired by socialist ideas of equality of income and equality between the sexes. A guiding principle has been that property is shared and work is organised collectively.

Life in the average modern British family compared with collective life on a typical kibbutz

1   The average British family is supported by one or both parents earning a living and the family is a unit of consumption with the family budget determining a family's standard of living. On a kibbutz the community as a whole is the unit of consumption; there is no family budget, only a community budget. This offers collective provision for individual needs; members are equally rewarded for their labour not with wages but with housing, food, clothing and all the necessities of life as well as some pocket money.

2   The members of an average British family are dependent on one another. In a kibbutz wives are not dependent on husbands, husbands are not dependent on wives and children are not dependent on parents: all are dependent on the community.

3   Mothers in average British families are often full time housewives. In the economy of the kibbutz wives share an equal role with their husbands.

4   Average British families eat, sleep and live together in self-contained units with parents having almost sole responsibility for their children. Kibbutzniks eat in a communal dining room. Their children are weaned at six months and then live in separate children's houses where they are looked after by **matapelets** ('metapel' means 'to take care'). The children visit their parents in their bungalows or flatlets for about two hours in the early evening each day and for longer periods on the Sabbath.

Communal upbringing on the Kabri Kibbutz in Israel.

The Children of the Dream

This was the title of a study published in 1969 by Dr Bruno Bettelheim, an American expert in child psychology, who visited many kibbutzim. In comparing upbringing on the kibbutz with conventional family life he came to the following conclusions:

Advantages

1   All children are given opportunities and no child has better clothes or more pocket money than any other.
2   There are no signs of problems such as battered babies, bullying, serious mental illness or sex crimes.
3   There is little jealousy, rivalry or possessiveness.
4   No one feels neglected, lonely or abandoned.

5 There are few educational failures and pupils are not plagued by the pressures of ambitious parents.

6 Kibbutzniks are hard workers renowned for their loyalty and bravery. Although they were less than 4 per cent of Israel's population in 1967, they provided 25 per cent of the casualties in the Six-Day War and many of the army's heroes.

Disadvantages

1 The same kibbutznik officers were said to lack flexibility in making rapid, spontaneous decisions on the battle-field. During socialisation, the pressure to conform stifles the adventurous individuality and originality which is needed for creative intellect. Bettelheim observed that if a kibbutznik expressed a personal opinion and then found that others were not supporting him, he always either backed down immediately or else pretended that he was only joking.

2 Because they are deprived of warm, close, intimate contact with others, kibbutzniks tend to be shy outside of their group, emotionally undemonstrative and unable to establish really deep, loving relationships.

3 One major advantage of family life is that it offers children the chance to be themselves, to rebel against their parents and to explore negative feelings. But while outbursts of temper offer relief to adolescent confusions and frustrations in normal homes, teenagers on the kibbutz are expected to suppress any anger.

4 They also have to suppress any sexual arousal while sharing mixed dormitories up to the age of eighteen. And they dare not question the doctrines of the system. As one kibbutz psychiatrist told Bettelheim, 'The result of all this repression is that our children are ashamed to be ashamed, are afraid to be afraid. They are afraid to love, are afraid to give of themselves.'

It should be recognised that other social scientists have come to different conclusions about kibbutz life and so have criticised Bettelheim's study.

Recent developments

In the first kibbutzim shared child-rearing was seen as a key part of creating collective loyalty. There was a strong tendency to emphasise the community and so to downgrade the importance of the family. In recent years however there has been a reaction to this and many parents want to play a greater part in bringing up their own children. It used to be the custom that parents did not visit their babies in the kindergarten during the day but now parents tend to visit whenever they like and many mothers resent the influence which the child-minders have over their children.

When kibbutzim were being set up, personal housing was given low priority and a couple often only had a two room flatlet (a bit like at a Butlin's holiday camp). Most would watch TV or read the papers in the kibbutz club rather than in private. But families on more modern kibbutzim are likely to have bungalows with their own kitchens and in 1974 children slept in their parents' quarters in 10 per cent of kibbutzim.

This re-emergence of the traditional family unit perhaps shows that the communal way of life on the kibbutz is not a real alternative to the family. There seems to be a vital need for family affiliation and it seems that close relations between members of a community, as exists in a kibbutz, are perhaps not an adequate substitute for family ties.

Activity

Bearing in mind the conclusions of Bettelheim's research, give reasons why you would or would not like to experience living in one of the following social units:

(a) an Israeli kibbutz,
(b) a boarding school,
(c) a hippy comune,
(d) an oil rig or a battleship,
(e) a monastery or a convent.

---

4   Extended and nuclear families

Before we look at family life in Britain, we need to make clear the distinction between the **nuclear** and the **extended family**.

The nuclear family

A nuclear family consists of the unit with just two generations: parents and their children. In the family tree of the modern Royal Family we can see that Prince Charles grew up in a nuclear family consisting of his mother, his father, his sister and his two brothers. Following his own marriage he has formed his own nuclear family with his wife and children.

The extended family

This term was originally used to describe a social unit living under the same roof in which a nuclear family is joined by other relatives. An example would be J. R. Ewing living at Southfork Ranch (just outside Dallas in Texas) with his wife Sue Ellen, his mother Miss Ellie, his brother Bobby, his sister-in-law Pam and his sister Lucy. Since such an arrangement involves several nuclear families living together, it is also called a joint family. Another example from a TV series is *The Waltons* household.

In describing the evolution of the typical British family, sociologists have stressed the way in which **industrialisation** and **urbanisation** (the movement of people to large towns) in the nineteenth century led to widespread poverty among the urban working class. Since there were few of today's welfare services, people needed help from their extended families who often lived in nearby streets. If we use the term in this sense then we can say that most of us have an extended family because most of us have relatives outside our immediate nuclear family.

The term 'extended family' does not therefore refer only to a situation in which a nuclear family lives with other relatives in the same household. It refers to all the relatives of a nuclear family. There are, of course, wide variations in the closeness of contact between relatives and sociologists are interested in identifying the reasons for these variations.

Four generations of the British Royal Family on the occasion of Prince Henry's christening in December 1984.

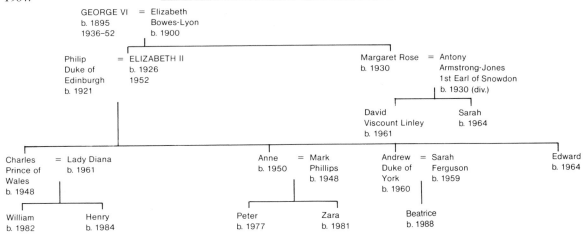

Activities

1 Draw a family tree for the main characters in your favourite TV soap opera such as *East Enders* or *Coronation Street* OR draw your own family tree and show the two nuclear families to which your mother or father belong.

2 Contacts within the extended family often bring mutual support. For example, grandparents might regularly babysit with their grandchildren and grandchildren might often do the shopping or the gardening for their grandparents.

   (a) which relatives in your extended family have you seen during the last twelve months?

   (b) How often do you usually see each of these relations?

   (c) What are the different reasons for your contact with them?

   (d) In what ways do you maintain indirect, rather than face-to-face, contact with them?

3 Imagine that your are married with two children. Your parents propose that they join you in buying a large house so that you can all live together. What would be the main advantages and disadvantages of this arrangement to all involved?

Case study: the extended family in the East End of London in the 1950s

In 1954 and 1955, Peter Townsend and Peter Marris studied *The Family Life of Old People* in Bethnal Green by interviewing a random sample of 203 pensioners. They found that:

... fifty-eight per cent of the old people belonged to a three-generation extended family in the sense that they saw relatives of the two succeeding generations every day or nearly every day and shared much of their lives with them. The group of relatives varied in size from six to over twenty. Generally it was built around grandmother, daughter, and grandchild, but variations were introduced by the sex and number of surviving children, the marital status and degree of incapacity of old people, and the distances at which the relatives lived.

Mrs Knock, aged sixty-four, lived with her husband, a single son, and a granddaughter of eight years old. Her eldest daughter lived in the next street and her youngest daughter in the same street. She saw them and their children every day. They helped her with the shopping and she looked after the grandchildren when they were at work. Money was exchanged for these services. Her youngest son, recently married, lived two streets away and called every evening. Her two daughters had the midday meal with her and she sent a meal to her youngest son because his wife was at work in the day.

(Source: *The Family Life of Old People* by P. Townsend, Penguin, 1963)

Data-response exercise: the extended family in the East End of London in the 1950s

1 Name two ways in which Mrs Knock helped her daughters.
2 Name two ways by which the daughters repaid Mrs Knock for these services.
3 The above study concluded that the majority of pensioners in Bethnal Green belonged to a three-generation extended family. On what data was this conclusion based?
4 What criteria, or standards, were used to determine whether or not a pensioner belonged to a three-generation extended family?
5 Explain the meaning of following statement: 'The extended family often provides reciprocal, or mutual, support between generations.'

5   The evolution of the 'typical' British family

In *The Symmetrical Family* Michael Young and Peter Willmott have argued that the family in Britain has gone through four stages of development:

1 the pre-industrial nuclear family,
2 the industrial extended family,
3 the modern nuclear family,
4 the managing director family.

Stage one: the pre-industrial nuclear family

Before the Industrial Revolution and the introduction of the factory system, a typical family operated as a **unit of economic production**. This means that husband, wife and children all worked together, for example, in farming or a cottage industry such as manufacturing textiles in the home. The average family lived as a small nuclear unit, like many modern families. This occurred because couples often married late (in their late twenties) and their own parents often died early (in their early forties), with only a few years between the two events. This meant that few families had surviving grandparents to join those few children who survived infancy and so create three-generation extended family households. Laslett has estimated that from 1564 to 1821 only 10 per cent or so of homes contained kin beyond the basic nuclear family; this figure was about the same in 1966.

Stage two: the industrial extended family

The factory bell and compulsory education split up the family which had previously worked together as an economic unit. By the end of the nineteenth century adults were commonly earning wages outside the home while children had to attend school.

The lack of welfare provision by the government meant that the extended family offered important support to the poor. Anderson has studied the 1851 census statistics for Preston, in Lancashire, which at that time was a rapidly growing town of textile mills. The figures show that 23 per cent of households contained extended kin such as grandparents or orphaned nephews and nieces who needed to be cared for.

Family units became larger because (a) five or six children often survived in the Victorian family, (b) adult life expectancy also increased so that more grandparents survived, (c) relatives often lived nearby or in the same household. Willmott and Young's study of Bethnal Green, in East London, in the 1950s showed how the extended family of the nineteenth century had continued in traditional, urban, working-class communities. They found that many young couples started their married lives in one of their parents' homes; the generations then stayed in close contact.

The Demeter Tie   In one of the Greek myths Demeter searches for years for her lost daughter, Persephone. The mother is tied to her daughter by a strong bond. In traditional working-class communities this tie is recognised in this rhyme:

A son's a son until he gets him a wife,
but a daughter's a daughter all her life.

In stable communities such as pit villages, where sons followed fathers down the coal mine, there was little **social mobility** between the 1850s and the 1950s. Few sons moved up in the world to non-manual jobs and few moved away to other areas. Male relatives could 'put in a good word' with employers and landlords to help young men get jobs and homes, but it was often young wives who were most in need of help from the extended family.

Tunstall's survey of *The Fishermen of Hull* found that trawlermen would leave their wives while they went on month-long voyages but they would forbid their wives to go out to work. Isolated with their children, the wives would turn to their female relatives for companionship. Since the burden of raising families in poverty has usually been shouldered by women, they have often depended on the support of relatives. And so the extended family has been called an informal trade union of women.

The Bethnal Green survey found that the households of mothers and their married daughters were in many ways merged: 60 per cent lived within two or three miles of each other, 80 per cent had seen each other within the previous week and 50 per cent visited daily.

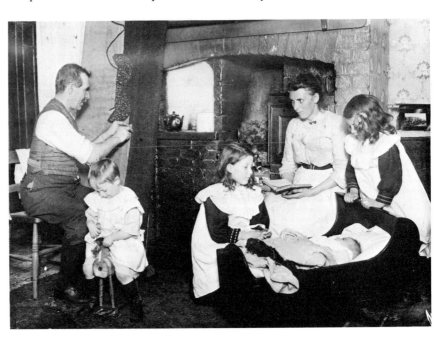

A miner's family at home in 1912.

Marital roles   The industrial extended family was partly **patriarchal**, which means that the father was the dominant authority. Yet it was also **matriarchal** in the sense that wives often organised all the practical aspects of family life, such as putting money by in different jars to pay the bills and equipping children for school or work.

Willmott and Young have talked of husbands being squeezed out of the warmth of the female circle and taking to the pub in their defence. One could also say that the women defended themselves from poverty while their husbands spent a lot of their incomes on alcohol. The late Victorian working man's home was often cold, damp, gloomy and over-crowded; many men preferred to spend their evenings in the welcoming comfort of the Victorian pub with the luxury of its engraved glass windows, upholstered seats, gas lamps and coal fires.

Stage three: the modern nuclear family

In this stage the family has the following characteristics:

1   **Conjugal roles** are joint rather than segregated. This means that marital roles and family decisions are more equally shared. Therefore there is greater symmetry or balance between husband and wife than in the stage two family.

2   The husband's leisure is more **privatised** and **home-centred** with activities such as D-I-Y and watching TV.

3   Smaller nuclear families (with only two or three children, like stage one) operate as self-contained **units of economic consumption**; with **child-centred recreation**, such as outings to the Alton Towers theme park.

4   There is more isolation from the extended kinship network because families are more geographically and socially mobile, moving house and changing job. They are also more self-reliant as a result of affluence and the welfare state.

The process of transition to stage three family life is vividly illustrated by the young East Enders who left the close-knit communities of the Bethnal Green slums in the 1950s. They moved out to the overspill estates and the Essex New Towns such as Basildon and Harlow. Here husbands could dig the garden of their new 'semi' and could dare to push the pram down the street.

The principle of stratified diffusion   Willmott and Young use the idea of stratified diffusion to explain the process by which family life has evolved. The idea means that patterns or styles of life filter down from the upper to the lower classes. Here are four examples:

1   Foreign holidays were once only for the upper classes but by the 1970s cheap package holiday flights allowed many working-class families to enjoy Mediterranean holidays.

2   Female education and ideas of equality in marriage enabled the working class of the 1930s to follow the middle class of the 1880s in using birth control to plan for smaller families.

3   By the 1960s many working-class homes were enjoying the luxuries of consumer durable goods such as TVs, washing machines and refrigerators as well as telephones and central heating.

4   More and more working-class families have also copied the middle class in switching to stage three nuclear patterns of family life.

The idea of stratified diffusion implies that we can predict the next stage for the average family of the future by looking at the upper-middle-class family of today. As far as the material aspects of home life go, we might expect that continued economic growth will allow more families to enjoy wall-to-wall carpets, double-glazing, patio doors, dishwashers and second telephones, second TVs, second cars and second toilets.

Stage four: the managing director family

Young and Willmott predict a shift from the stage three family which is centred on the home to a future where life is centred on work and on leisure based outside the home. In this family of the future (which is claimed to be already spreading from the professional classes) both husband and wife have interesting technical careers and a range of leisure pursuits such as sailing, squash, golf, jogging, riding and hang-gliding. Such activities are not necessarily shared: on a Tuesday evening father goes straight from a conference to the badminton club, mother dashes from a business appointment to her evening class in car maintenance, while teenage son and daughter fix meals in the microwave oven before heading off to the roller-disco and the sub-aqua club.

Young and Willmott found signs of this new type of **work-centred** and less cohesive family life in their survey of London in the early 1970s. Signs included:

- more work satisfaction and a decline in unrewarding, low skill jobs;
- more shiftwork;
- more women leading independent lives alongside their roles of wife and mother;
- new trends such as flexi-time and home-working via computer terminals;
- men and women increasing their commitments outside the home, in both work and leisure, as their education and standards of living rise.

Activities

1   How far do recent developments, such as growing unemployment and increasing poverty, contradict Young and Willmott's optimistic predictions?

2   What predictions would you make concerning family life in Britain in the early twenty-first century? How far do your predictions match those of Young and Willmott?

Conclusion

Young and Willmott try to encompass all family life in Britain over the last few hundred years in just four stages or patterns. While it is useful to identify broad trends in the development of the family, it would be misleading to fail to recognise the diversity of family life in modern Britain. Some indication of this variety is given in the next chapter, together with a more detailed account of changes such as falling birth rates and rising divorce rates.

GCSE question from London and East Anglian Group 1988

Explain the ways in which families fulfil their functions in any *one* society.   (15)

GCSE question from Midland Examining Group 1988

(a)   Explain *two* differences between *nuclear* and *extended* families.   (4)

(b)   Explain three reasons given by sociologists for the growth of the nuclear family in Britain today.   (6)

CHAPTER 5

Recent patterns of family life

1   Has family life become better or worse?

Recent changes in family life have provoked both optimistic and pessimistic responses. Some believe that the family in modern Britain is declining and that the centuries-old social arrangement called 'marriage' is no longer working. The opposite view argues that family life is in many ways better than ever before. A number of points in this debate are listed below.

1   The loss of functions   A negative view of the modern nuclear family sees it as stripped of many of the functions which it used to fulfil in the past. The positive view argues that the welfare state now offers support, ranging from child benefit payments to leisure centres, which enables the family to make a better job of its different basic functions.

2   Mobility and isolation   Does family life suffer if the mobile nuclear family moves away from the warmth of stable local kinship networks and a friendly community? Family life is not necessarily worse on a new housing estate or in a tower block of flats. Many families now enjoy increased choice about where to live and which neighbours or relatives to visit. The 1976 Hunt survey found that 50 per cent of pensioners with living relatives received a visit from them at least once a week and almost a third 'several times' a week.

3   Child abuse and 'latch key children'   There has been some concern at the neglect of children who return home from school to an empty home because parents are at work. The press have also highlighted recurring cases of severe cruelty to children. But standards of child-care are far higher than, say, 150 years ago. Also families with working mothers may be materially and emotionally better off than those with housebound 'captive wives'. Housewives without paid jobs may be depressed by money worries and by the isolation of being trapped at home all day with toddlers.

4   The decline in popularity of marriage?   Marriages seems less popular among those in their early twenties. In Sweden, for example, married couples in the eighteen to twenty-four age group are outnumbered by **cohabiting** couples who are living together outside wedlock. After falling since Victorian times, the average age for first-time brides and grooms has recently risen. But the continuing popularity of marriage can be seen in two sets of figures: firstly, over 90 per cent of women and over 80 per cent of men get married by the age of thirty; secondly, 80 per cent or so of divorcees aged under thirty remarry within five years of divorce and current trends suggest that 20 per cent of the population will have been remarried by the year 2000.

5   The increase in divorce and broken homes   We cannot conclude that the rise in divorce means that there has been an increase in marital breakdown. In the past many **empty-shell marriages** continued, long after any loving relationship had died, merely because divorce was so difficult to obtain. Broken homes and orphans were more common in the last century when families were often disrupted by the early death of a parent due to illness or an accident at work, or by the disappearance of fathers due to desertion, migration or war.

This chapter focuses on some of these issues, such as the rise in divorce and the increase in mothers going out to work. We also go in search of that elusive phenomenon: 'the typical British family'.

2   The roles of working mothers

The rise in the proportions of children with mothers who go to work has been one of the major changes affecting family life since the war.

The increase in mothers going out to work

In the stage one pre-industrial family, wives were economic partners in home-based production. After the Industrial Revolution, wives were far less likely than their husbands to join factory-based work. Out of 1,382,000 factory workers in the 1841 census only 8,789 were women. The 1851 census shows that only 25 per cent of married women went out to work. Very few of these were middle-class wives and those working-class mothers who were employed in places like textile mills were increasingly 'squeezed out' by men protecting scarce jobs and by new laws which regulated women's hours and conditions at work. The result was that only 10 per cent of married women went out to work in 1911.

The two wars temporarily brought women back into the labour force but the dramatic increase in mothers at work has occurred since the 1950s. In 1961 30 per cent of married women were 'economically active' and by 1987 this had risen to 66 per cent. Much of this increase has been due to the recent trend for mothers to return to work more quickly after having a baby. In the early 1950s the average time of return was $7\frac{1}{2}$ years after the latest birth but by the 1980s it was an average of $3\frac{1}{2}$ years. Also, many women are now returning to work between births.

Reasons for the increase in working mothers

We can list some of these reasons under two headings: motivating factors and enabling factors.

Motivating factors

1   A mother's income can be essential for financial survival. The 1978 DHSS Report *Wives as Sole and Joint Breadwinners* estimated that three or four times as many families would be in poverty if it were not for the earnings of working mothers. The 1980s have seen economic recession

with more fathers out of work and with husbands on low wages finding fewer opportunities of boosting their pay by working overtime. There has also been an increase in one-parent families, 90 per cent of them with mothers rather than fathers.

2   A mother's motivation for returning to work might be to raise the family's standard of living so that they can afford a bigger mortgage in order to buy a better house, or so that they can afford foreign holidays.

3   If you lack a waged occupation then society gives you a comparatively low status. This is true of housewives in the same way as it applies to pensioners, children, students and the unemployed. More women want a separate identity apart from the roles of wife and mother. Margaret Thatcher is an example of a career-minded woman who saw motherhood as a threat to her independence and ambitions. In 1953 she had gained a Chemistry degree at Oxford and was studying law when her twins, Carol and Mark, were born. Her own mother helped to look after them so that, four months later, she was able to successfully sit her final law exams. She has since said: 'I thought that if I didn't do something quite definite then, there was a real possibility that I'd never return to work again.'

4   Many mothers are attracted by the sociable adult company of the workplace as well as the satisfactions of involvement in interesting jobs. They are keen to escape from the boredom and depression of being an isolated *Captive Wife* – the title of Hannah Gavron's study of mothers who were housebound with small children.

Margaret Thatcher's twin children did not prevent her from starting a political career.

CONSERVATIVE WINNER

BOROUGH OF FINCHLEY

FRIERN BARNET

MARGARET THATCHER FOR WESTMINSTER

Enabling factors

1   Industry has increased its demand for female labour which is often employed at low wages and on a part-time basis. (Only 31 per cent of working mothers are in full-time jobs.) Vacancies have expanded particularly in **service sector jobs** such as catering, cleaning, shops and offices. A number of employers have developed flexi-time and job-sharing schemes as well as workplace crèches (nurseries for toddlers).

2   Women now have better educational opportunities as well as a fairer deal at work due to the Equal Pay Act and the Sex Discrimination Act.

3   Mothers now have smaller families than previous generations.

4   Husbands are far less disapproving of their wives going out to work and modern research has argued against Bowlby's 1951 report which suggested that children of working mothers suffered from maternal deprivation.

5   Household gadgets such as tumble-dryers, freezers, microwave ovens and food processors as well as convenience foods have helped to reduce the time and labour of housework and child-care. Sue Sharpe's research in *Double Identity: the Lives of Working Mothers* also found that sons, as well as daughters, were fairly often given generous pocket money for helping around the home.

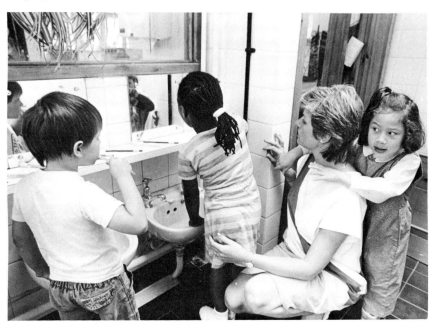

A few employers provide workplace crèches for the children of their employees.

Average hours spent: (per week, in 1988)	in paid employment	doing household chores
women in part-time jobs	20	37.5
women in full-time jobs	39.7	27.5
men in full-time jobs	44.5	12

Women and their families have benefited in all sorts of ways from the increased numbers of mothers going out to work but wives have also suffered from an overload of work tasks, few of which are truly shared by their husbands. You can see this by referring back to the chart on the domestic division of labour on page 16.

In view of such findings, conclusions about shared, joint or **symmetrical roles** in the modern, stage three family have been overstated. Indeed Young and Willmott themselves found, in their 1973 study, that married men spent an average of only ten hours per week on household tasks. This compared to twenty-three hours for women employed full-time and thirty-five hours for wives in part-time jobs.

The 1974 Swedish Parenthood Law is an example of an attempt to establish more symmetry in domestic roles. This law gives either parent the right to fifteen days leave per year to care for sick children and the right to nine months leave on 90 per cent of normal earnings when a baby is born. But in only 10 per cent of cases has this baby-care leave been taken by fathers rather than mothers.

Activities

1   Conduct a survey of a number of mothers to find out how many have full-time or part-time jobs and how many pay their children for help around the home.

2   Interview four working mothers and ask them for their reasons for returning to work. Then see how far the reasons which

they have given match the motivating factors given above.

3   Interview some full-time housewives and ask them why they do not go out to work.

4   Ask some men about their attitudes to wives going out to work and young mothers pursuing full-time careers.

---

3   What is the typical family like?

The 'cereal packet norm'

Next time you watch the advertisements on TV see how far this picture is true: the typical adman's family shows mother seeing off her two children to school and her husband to work in the morning and then getting on with cleaning the floor and putting the dirty clothes in the washing machine. Her two children are ideally one of each sex and the boy is preferably the eldest. They return home to find her cutting sandwiches or getting in her brilliant white washing from the line.

Advertisements for products such as breakfast cereals and washing powders have for many years featured such stereotypes and sociologists have asked how far this 'cereal packet norm' really applies to the average family. The first part of this chapter has already shown that the typical modern mother goes out to work. We now look at some of the ways that families and households vary.

The four phases of the family life-cycle

1   **'Nest-building'**   The average length of time between a couple's marriage and the birth of their first baby is just under three years and about

90 per cent of couples in their first marriage have children. This first, home-making stage of the new family is shorter for the 30 per cent or so of teenage mothers who get pregnant while single and then get married before their first child is born.

2   Child-rearing   This 'whole families' phase lasts from the birth of the first child to when the first child leaves home. During the last century many women died in early middle age, in their forties or early fifties. Since the average number of children was six, this meant that the typical wife in the nineteenth century spent most of her married life rearing children.

3   Dispersal   In first-time marriages the average groom is aged twenty-four and the average bride aged twenty-two. The average twenty-two-year-old bride is twenty-five when her first child is born and so will be only forty-three when this child becomes an adult. With her offspring now 'leaving the nest' and dispersing to set up their own households and families, our average mother can now look forward to another thirty-five years of life in a shrinking family unit.

4   Elderly couple   With their children grown up and 'dispersed', our average couple now approach retirement in a two-person household – like the nest-building phase. The average wife can expect to spend her last years alone as a widow. This is because the average wife has a husband who is two years older than herself and because the average male life expectancy is some six years less than that of females.

Figures from the census reveal that families in the second, child-rearing phase are outnumbered by the families in the other phases of the family life-cycle.

Types of households

No family	1961 (%)	1987 (%)
One person under retirement age	4	9
One person over retirement age	7	16
Two or more people	5	3
One family		
Married couple only	26	27
Married couple with one to two dependent children	30	23
Married couple with three or more dependent children	8	5
Married couple with independent child(ren) only*	10	9
Lone parent with at least one dependent child	2	4
Lone parent with independent child(ren) only	3	4
Two or more families (joint family household)	3	1
	100%	100%

* An 'independent child' is a son or daughter who is over sixteen and no longer in full-time education but who is still living at home.
(Source: Office of Population Censuses and Surveys)

According to the census, a 'household' is a group of people who live and eat together. Between 1961 and 1981 the population of Britain grew by less than 7 per cent but the proportion of households grew by 20 per cent. This means that average household size has fallen. The average number of people per household fell from 3.09 in 1961 to 2.59 in 1984. The figures on page 60 show that in 1987 a quarter of all households consisted of people living alone.

We can also see that the common picture of the average home as a two-parent family with two school-age children is true of less than a quarter of all households.

Types of families

In 1981 there were 19.5 million households in Britain. Of these households 22 per cent consisted of single people and 2.8 million of these were pensioners living on their own. Some 13 million households consisted of families (defined as married couples, with or without children) and 1.6 million households consisted of one-parent families.

Types of married couple families, 1983

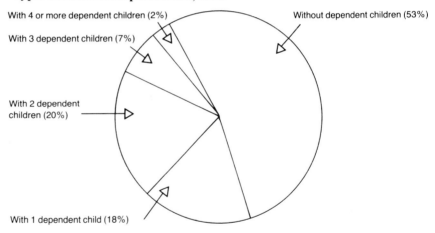

(The average number of dependent children was 1.9.)

(Source: *The General Household Survey*, 1983)

Data-response exercise: types of households and types of families

1 From the table showing the percentages of different types of households,
   (a) what percentage, in 1987, were single person households?
   (b) which type of household increased the most between 1961 and 1987?

2 From the pie chart showing the proportions for different types of married couple families, in 1983,
   (a) what percentage of families had no dependent children?
   (b) what percentage of families had more than two dependent children?

3 What is meant by 'dependent children'?

From these figures we can conclude that the typical number of children is two but that the majority of married couple families have no children living at home. The typical family is the couple whose children have grown up and left home while the 'cereal packet norm' family of two parents and two children in fact only exists in one fifth of two-parent families. Instead of a family stereotype it is more useful to think in terms of a diversity of types of family.

The one-parent family

In 1986, 14 per cent of dependent children in Britain lived in one-parent families; almost twice the proportion of 1972, the earliest year for which General Household Survey data are available. One reason for this is the increase in **illegitimate births** (23 per cent of all births in 1987 as against 6 per cent in 1961) with unmarried mothers far less willing to put their babies forward for adoption. In fact, 70 per cent of such births are registered in joint names (compared with 38 per cent in 1961) and many are later legitimised by marriage.

The one-parent family may have a parent who is single, separated or widowed (and some 14,000 wives have husbands in prison) but the most common situation, in about 40 per cent of one-parent families, is that the parent is a divorced mother. Our next section looks in detail at divorce.

Activities

1   Draw two bar charts, one for the typical woman of the 1880s and one for the average modern woman. The lengths of the bars represent the number of years they live. Divide these bars so that they show the number of years at school, at work before marriage and in the four phases of the family life-cycle. (The average Victorian bride was aged twenty-six.)

2   Most of us will belong to two basic forms of family: our **family of origin**, which we grow up in, and our **family of destination**, the family of marriage which we create with our spouse (husband or wife). Explore the options involved by describing your idea of either (a) the ideal type of family to grow up in, or (b) the ideal family you would like to create when you get married. Mention aspects such as the number and sex of children and the age differences between them; the domestic division of labour and the amount of contact with relatives.

---

4   The rise in divorce and the reconstituted family

Some 20 per cent of the marriages of 1974 ended in divorce within ten years, compared to less than 2 per cent of 1926 marriages. We can attempt to explain this increase by looking firstly at general factors which have affected most couples and secondly at factors affecting particular groups who get married.

General reasons for the rise in divorce

1   Changes in the law   In the 150 years before the 1857 Matrimonial Causes Act there were only about 250 divorces granted: in other words

An increasing number of children grow up in one-parent families: this father is bringing up his son on his own .

less than two per year. Divorce did not really become accessible to the average couple until the 1949 Legal Aid Act. In the 1960s the law still obstructed the easy termination of unhappy, 'empty-shell' marriages. This was partly because the partner petitioning for divorce had to prove the other partner's guilty conduct. It has been estimated that less than half of all marital breakdowns appeared in the divorce statistics.

The 1969 Divorce Reform Act has, since 1971, simplified procedures so that divorce is now obtainable on the grounds of **irretrievable breakdown of marriage** which can be due to separation, desertion, adultery or 'unreasonable behaviour'. In 1984 the law was changed to permit divorce after one year of marriage (not three years as before).

The majority in the 1986 Irish Referendum voted against new laws which would have allowed divorce in Eire.

2   Changing attitudes   Reform of the divorce laws reflects society's changing norms. Some believe that the declining influence of the church (**secularisation**) means that people attach less value to marriage; so it has become another disposable item in our 'throwaway culture'. Others maintain that the media's emphasis on romance and personal happiness gives us all higher ideals than our grandparents had: we expect higher standards in our marriages and so it is perhaps inevitable that an increasing number of marriages will fail to come up to the mark.

3   Other 'opportunity-increasing' factors   Even if unhappy wives in the past had not faced an uphill struggle against obstructive divorce laws and **social stigma** (disapproval and condemnation of divorcees), they would still have faced practical problems such as finding work, finding new housing and finding new partners. Women today are more likely to be independent: with a decent education, fewer children and a job where they can meet new partners. The 1970 Matrimonial Proceedings Act gives wives an equal right to ownership of the home and the development of the welfare state has made council flats and supplementary benefits available.

Particular groups who are more divorce-prone

1   Teenage marriages   In 1901 only 1.6 per cent of men married as teenagers. In 1971 the figure was 10 per cent of men and 30 per cent of women. On current trends, 50 per cent of these teenage brides and almost 60 per cent of these teenage husbands will see their marriages end in divorce. Apart from immaturity, a number of factors can be listed: many teenage brides are pregnant, many face housing difficulties and financial problems, many are married to unskilled manual husbands who are five times more likely to get divorced than husbands with professional occupations.

2   Mismatched partners   It could be argued that all partners who get divorced were mismatched but sociologists tend to concentrate on conflict generated by social factors such as mobility. If a husband receives rapid promotion at work, he may feel that he has 'left his wife behind', even though they both have the same social origins. Difficulties can also arise when a person marries someone outside his or her social group, for example a partner from a different ethnic or religious group.

Another cause of incompatibility is homosexuality. This must affect a certain number of marriages since 90 per cent of us get married while 12 per cent or so of us are homosexuals. Also, about 10 per cent of us will also face the tensions caused by infertility problems.

3   Groups with a reduced commitment to marriage   Partners who have failed to have children, or spouses in the dispersal phase of the family's life-cycle, may be less committed to their marriages than those in the honeymoon stage of home-building. Those who have parents or close relatives who are divorced also tend to be more prone than average to get divorced.

4   Certain occupational groups   Some jobs carry a higher risk of divorce. Obvious examples are long-distance lorry drivers, sailors and professional criminals. In 1983 the divorce rate for husbands in classes I and II was 7 per 1,000 compared to 28 per 1,000 among classes IV and V and 34 per 1,000 for the unemployed. (These categories of social class are explained in Chapter 9.)

Serial polygamy and the blended family

Polygamy means marriage between a member of one sex and two or more members of the opposite sex. Our laws restrict us to **monogamy**: marrying only one partner. The traditional Christian wedding ceremony unites bride and groom ''til death us do part' but in America divorce and remarriage have become so common that a new pattern of marriage has been called **serial polygamy**. This means that each spouse marries a series of partners.

Estimates in 1989 suggested that 37 per cent of marriages will end in divorce. It is increasingly common for children to see their parents' marriage break up. Since two-thirds of divorcees remarry, many of these children will only temporarily belong to one-parent families. They can usually expect to gain a step-father from their mother's remarriage and they may also gain step-brothers and step-sisters (step-siblings). This **reconstituted family**, created from two previous marriages, has been called a **blended family**. One of the characteristics of such a step-sibling family is that it is unplanned so that all of the children may be of similar ages or, by contrast, they may be separated by an unusually large number of years.

The last section of this chapter looks at the way families in three ethnic minorities also diverge from the nuclear family of the 'cereal packet norm'.

Activity

The American anthropologist George Murdock has estimated that there have been 4,000 separate societies since the dawn of mankind. In examining studies of a sample of 250 societies, he found the family to be a universal institution and 75 per cent of these societies practised **polygyny**. This is the form of polygamy in which each man has more than one wife.

Among societies such as the Gikuyu, men
(a) had a life expectancy little beyond their thirties,
(b) set great store by having sons and
(c) married late, after they had accumulated the necessary cattle to pay the brideprice (the opposite of a dowry).
Why do these factors make polygyny a sensible arrangement?

---

5   Family life in ethnic minority cultures

The Asian family

The cultural differences between Punjabis, Tamils, Pakistanis and Bangladeshis are as great as their similarities. Sikhs, for example, have freer attitudes to the social position of women than Muslims. Nevertheless, Asian families in Britain tend to follow a common pattern of maintaining traditional loyalties with multi-generation, extended networks of kin. The strengths and flexibilities of the Bengali kinship system are symbolised by the fact that in Bengali there are fifty-three different terms for a relative while in English we use a basic dozen terms.

Case study: the Biraderi and Pakistani families in Britain

The word 'Biraderi' is derived from Biradar, brother, and it means the clan of men who can trace their relationship to a common ancestor. As Muhammad Anwar has written, in *The Myth of Return: Pakistanis in Britain* (1979):

> From the point of view of residence, job selection, reciprocal services and other related matters in Pakistani families, the Biraderi networks play an important role. In fact the whole way of life of Pakistanis is directly or indirectly related to this institution.

In his survey of Pakistanis in Rochdale, Lancashire, Anwar was told by Mr M.S. how he was 'sponsored', or helped, by his relatives:

> 'I did not do anything, my relative Mr A.A. arranged my ticket through agents in Pakistan. He arranged my accommodation, food and job in the mill where he had worked for three years. Later my brother came to join us along with other relatives. We live like a Biraderi, as an extension of our Biraderi in Pakistan. This is the only way to be safe, successful and happy in this strange country.'

Almost 90 per cent of the Pakistanis interviewed in Anwar's survey had found their jobs with the help of a friend or relative.

Almost 80 per cent had obtained help from friends or relatives either to pay the whole price of a house or to pay a substantial deposit to bring down the size of the monthly mortgage repayments. Relatives have an obligation to help in order to maintain the *izzet* (prestige) of their Biraderi. Further examples of the way that the kinship network of the Biraderi offers support are also given by Anwar:

> . . . a daughter of one person in the Biraderi is treated as a daughter of the whole Biraderi and this feeling is shown particularly at the time of marriage ceremonies. . . .

In Pakistani communities, there appears to be an order of preference for appeal for help: family, Biraderi, fellow villagers, friends, neighbours, other Pakistanis and the rest of society. For example, if one needed to fill in an official form or go to an office for some reason, one would look to one's family first. If nobody was able to help, one would consider the Biraderi members, and so on.

When a Kenyan Asian and a Pakistani stood as Labour and Liberal candidates in the 1972 local elections in Rochdale, both candidates used the Biraderi organisation to mobilise support.

A Hindu family in Bradford.

The Greek Cypriot family

Greek Cypriot families in Britain also tend to show a closeness within the extended kinship network. When a daughter marries in Cyprus, her parents traditionally provide accommodation for the newly weds, often by building a flat above the parents' bungalow. A second daughter can be provided for by building a second storey. This wedding gift is not quite like a dowry since the property is owned by the daughter.

Many Greek Cypriots in Britain continue the pattern of married daughters living near their parents. And, although relatives do not always live nearby or work in the same businesses, close contact is often maintained by grandparents looking after the children of working mothers. Life in the Greek Orthodox Church also keeps extended families in regular contact. Apart from meeting at weekly worship and festivals like Christmas, Easter and the Feast of the Assumption, families often meet at annual memorial services for close relatives. Also, they usually have 'open house' for aunts, uncles and cousins on 'name days' – the saint's day of the saint who a person has been named after is as important as that person's birthday.

Even if Greek Cypriots in Britain have not returned to Cyprus for many years, they will almost certainly find many relatives eager to offer generous hospitality when they visit. It would bring dishonour on the family if anyone was reluctant to fulfil the obligation to entertain even quite distant relatives. The honour of the family's name can also be threatened if there is a hint of a daughter getting a bad reputation. Although marriages are not exactly 'arranged', suitors are often carefully selected from 'good Greek families'.

The West Indian family

While 12 per cent of all British families with children are one-parent families, the 1984 *Black and White Britain* survey found that the comparable figure among West Indians in Britain was 31 per cent and concluded,

> West Indians tend to wait longer in life before setting up married or cohabiting partnerships: this is evidenced by the fact that overall 40 per cent of West Indian households contain a single adult alone or a lone parent with children under 16. It is not uncommon for West Indian women to have children in their late teens and twenties and to wait until much later to establish a marital or cohabiting household. It would be wrong, however, to characterise lone parents as predominantly young. Four-fifths of West Indian lone parents are aged 25 or over.

This pattern of family life is common in Jamaica where in 1960 the average age at marriage was thirty-one for women and twenty-five for men. Studies of Jamaica in the 1950s found only a quarter of households based on a formal marriage with another quarter consisting of common-law marriages or **consensual unions** where the partners live together without being legally united by a formal marriage. This leaves half of all households falling into a third category, called **female-dominated**. Here children may live with their mother in a single-parent family or, while mother goes out to work, female relatives may take on the roles of both missing parents.

Four factors have been suggested to explain the Caribbean tradition of families with absentee fathers:

1   The African slaves brought to work on the plantations in the West Indies were usually forbidden to marry. A slave's children automatically became the property of the mother's owner.

2   These slaves brought West African cultural traditions of **matrifocal extended families** in which family life was focused on the mother.

3   Since the ending of slavery, men in the West Indies have often lacked stable and regular employment. They have been unable to offer adequate economic support to their partners and many have had to migrate to find work. This has made them reluctant to enter into settled marriages and so adult males have been 'marginal' to the family. In Barbados in 1921 male migration meant that there were only 526 males for every 1,000 females.

4   A fourth factor is the way that our welfare system works. If an unmarried mother cohabits with her child's father, or any other man, then he is assumed to be supporting her and she loses her entitlement to supplementary benefit payments. This same pattern in the USA, where 36 per cent of the black population is in poverty, has led Farley to talk of the 'feminisation of poverty'. His 1984 figures show that black Americans have a 56 per cent illegitimacy rate with 47 per cent of US black households headed by females. He concludes that the welfare payments of the Aid to Families with Dependent Children actually encourage desertion by fathers.

Conclusion

The family persists. But when we look more closely at this enduring social institution we find a diversity of family types. For example, a special minority of families not so far mentioned are those with fostered or adopted children: over 20,000 children are adopted each year and over 20,000 are temporarily placed with foster parents.

Among the many types of family, the extended family is by no means dead. Mutual support between generations at times of birth, marriage or death, or when raising funds for a first mortgage, is so common that the modern family has been described as a **modified extended family**.

Smaller families mean fewer uncles and aunts. Greater life expectancy and younger marriage mean that young grandparents, in their late forties or early fifties when their first grandchildren are born, can expect to live to see their great-grandchildren. These four-generation families mean that **kinship networks** become 'narrower but deeper'.

Reconstituted families offer the chance to widen this narrow kinship network. Remarriage creates a form of blended family so that an additional extended family can appear overnight with the arrival of a step-parent.

In 1984, 35 per cent of all marriages involved partners who had been married before. This popularity of remarriage supports the numerous surveys which show that marriage generally increases one's happiness. Married people are much more likely to say that they are happy than single people.

GCSE question from Midland Examining Group 1988

'The most striking feature of modern families in Britain is that they are similar.' To what extent do you agree or disagree with this view? Give reasons.   (8)

CHAPTER 6

Population

Changes in the population.

Definitions

This chapter is about **demography**: the study of the size, structure and development of human populations. Before we focus on the ways that Britain's population has changed, we need to define some important terms:

Birth rate   The number of live births per 1,000 persons of all ages in one year.

Fertility rate   The number of births per year per 1,000 women of child-bearing age (fifteen – forty-four).

Death rate   The number of deaths per 1,000 living members of a population per year.

Rate of natural increase   The birth rate minus the death rate.

Infant mortality rate   The number of deaths of infants under one year old per 1,000 live births per year.

Burden of dependency   This refers to the total numbers in non-working age groups compared to the numbers in working age groups.

Emigration   People leaving the country to go and live in another country.

Immigration   People coming to live in the country from another country.

Net migration   The number of people immigrating minus the number of people emigrating.

1   Population growth and the census

It took from 'the beginning' until about 1830 for the human population to reach its first thousand million. By 1930 there were 2,000 million people in the world; by 1960 3,000 million and by 1975 4,000 million. In 1985 the world's population was put at 4,800 million and the United Nations forecasts that it will reach 6,100 million by the year 2000 and eventually stabilise at 10,200 million in the year 2110.

At present the world's rate of population growth is about 1.7 per cent per year. This is twice as fast as in the first half of this century but slower than the peak rates of 2 per cent in the early 1960s. By 2025 it should be back below 1 per cent. But the UK's population has already virtually stabilised to a position of 'zero growth': it only grew from 56,224,000 to 56,448,000 between 1974 and 1984.

A page from the 1871 census.

The four stages of population growth

The changing birth and death rates explain the way Britain's population has grown in the following four stages:

Stage	Years	Birth rate	Death rate	Population growth
1	to 1750	high	high	slow, to 8 million
2	1750–1880	stable	falling	fast, to 26 million
3	1880–1930	falling	falling	slower, to 40 million
4	1930–1985	low	low	slow, to 56 million

Changes in the UK's total population size are caused by three factors: numbers of births, numbers of deaths and net migration. The numbers entering and leaving the country are monitored and all births and deaths have to be registered. This creates a running total of the size of the population. A further check is made every ten years when the whole population is counted in the census.

The census

The 1981 UK population figure of 56,379,000 is the number who were present when the 1981 census was conducted. This survey has been held every ten years since 1801 (except 1941) and since 1951 it has been taken on a Sunday evening in April. This time of year has been chosen because few people are away on holiday in April, yet the weather is not too bad for those who have to walk from door to door collecting the census forms. Each household has to fill in a form giving details about those in the house that night. Those in hospitals, hotels, prisons and boarding schools are also counted and the police try to find all those sleeping rough out of doors.

The figures are very useful to the government who have to forecast how much will need to be spent in the future on providing benefits such as pensions and facilities such as maternity hospitals. The pages of past census returns can also give us a good picture of changes in family size and patterns of **geographical mobility** (internal migration from one part of the country to another).

Eleven children was not uncommon in a Victorian family.

Case study: the 1871 census

The following transcript is taken from the 1871 census for Osborne Road in Hornsey, North London (at that time part of Middlesex):

House number	Name and surname of each person	Relation to head of family	Age	Rank, profession or occupation	Where born
9	Charles Walkden	Head	27	Rail Clerk	Wiltshire
	Harriet Walkden	Wife	30		Hertfordshire
	Percy Walkden	Son	2		Middx
	Harriet Walkden	Daughter	1		Middx
	George Hunt	Boarder	22	Rail Clerk	Hampshire
	Eliza Parker	Servant	15	General Servant	Hertfordshire
11	John McMillan	Head	31	Tea Merchant	Scotland
	Elizabeth McMillan	Wife	29		London
	Arthur McMillan	Son	8 m		London
13	Richard Bullimore	Head	39	Accountant	Lincolnshire
	Louisa Bullimore	Wife	25		Middx
	Richard Bullimore	Son	8	Scholar	Middx
	William Bullimore	Son	6	Scholar	Middx
	Marion Bullimore	Daughter	5	Scholar	Middx
	Annie Bullimore	Sister	28	Farmer's daughter	Lincolnshire
	Mary Hayward	Servant	26	Domestic Servant	Hampshire
15	John Davison	Head	27	Commercial Clerk	Middx
	Alice M. Davison	Wife	21		Middx
	Alice S. Davison	Daughter	1		Herts
	Amy Richardson	Servant	22	Nursery Governess	Essex
	Elizabeth Dowdell	Servant	21	General Servant	Wilts

Data-response exercise: the 1871 census

1   How old was Harriet Walkden at the time of the 1871 census?
2   How many children lived at 13, Osborne Road, Hornsey?
3   How old was Louisa Bullimore when she gave birth to her first child?
4   What evidence is there that middle-class people lived in Osborne Road?
5   What evidence is there to show the extent of migration to London from other parts of the country?

2   Reasons for the fall in average family size

From 1871 to 1931, the birth rate more than halved from thirty-three to sixteen. In the 1970s it fell to twelve. The average number of children per family fell as follows:

1860s	6.16
1880s	4.81
1900s	3.30
1930s	2.06

By 1944 there was anxiety that the birth rate had fallen too low and so a Royal Commission on Population was set up. One of its recommendations was to encourage more births by giving mothers a family allowance, now called child benefit. The Commission's 1949 report included the following survey figures which clearly show how family size fell first among the middle classes:

Husband's occupation	*Number of live births per woman first married in:*	
	1900–1909	*1920–1924*
Professional	2.33	1.75
All groups combined average	3.53	2.42
Unskilled labourers	4.45	3.35

We now look at four of the major reasons for the fall of the birth rate in Britain over the last hundred years.

The availability of birth control

The intra-uterine device was invented in ancient times when pregnancy in camels was prevented by placing pebbles in their wombs. The ancient Egyptians described many methods of contraception and in the seventeenth century Cassanova used sheaths or condoms made from the intestinal membrane of the cow.

In the nineteenth century, the new discipline of economics was christened 'the dismal science' because of the gloomy predictions of *Essay on the Principle of Population*. This was written by Thomas Malthus in 1798 and claimed that population grows by **geometric progression** (that is 2, 4, 8, 16, 32) while food production can only increase by **arithmetic progression** (that is 2, 4, 6, 8, 10). One effect of the ideas of Malthus was the ending of Parish Relief. These handouts to the destitute dated from the Elizabethan Poor Laws but they were seen as encouraging large families and so they were replaced by Victorian workhouses. In these institutions husbands were separated from their wives and children and forced to work.

Malthus only recommended later marriage as a means to avoid overpopulation but during the 1820s and 1830s a number of leaflets and books were published advocating pessaries (vaginal sponges) and douching (flushing of the vagina) with mixtures of chemicals such as salt, zinc sulphate, vinegar, alum, quinnine, tannin, opium, prussic acid, iodine, alcohol, carbolic acid and strychnine.

Some of the landmarks in the history of birth control in the last 150 years are:

1843 Vulcanised rubber was introduced for the sheath and cervical cap.

1877 A banned contraceptive advice pamphlet was republished by two radical reformers, Annie Besant and Charles Bradlaugh, MP. They deliberately invited prosecution to create publicity about birth control and they succeeded. Their trial and appeal attracted national press coverage with public donations paying their £1,000 legal costs.

1880s The vaginal diaphragm, or Dutch Cap, was given wide circulation in clinics in Holland.

1914   Marie Stopes wrote the first of several family planning booklets. Called *Married Love*, half a million copies were sold by 1924 and Stopes went on to set up the first birth control clinics in Britain.

1950s   The oral contraceptive, 'the pill', and the modern intra-uterine device, the IUD or 'coil', were introduced.

1974   Contraceptives became free on the National Health Service (NHS) to all women, married or single.

1970s   A new trend was that by the age of thirty-five one or other partner in 30 per cent of all couples was opting for sterilisation by vasectomy or the closing of the fallopian tubes.

1983   90 per cent of sexually active people said that they used some form of contraception.

The falling infant mortality rate

The infant mortality rate is the number of deaths per 1,000 live births before the age of one. It has fallen as follows:

1851	1891	1901	1921	1941	1951	1961	1986
154	153	128	72	49	30	22	9

Between the 1840s and the 1890s, the mortality rate for children aged five to nine halved from 9 to 4.3. There was less risk that a child in each family would fail to survive to adulthood and so parents no longer needed to allow for such risks by having 'extra' births.

Economic motivations

Early pioneers, such as Annie Besant, tried to popularise birth control among working-class women as a means of reducing poverty. However, before compulsory education, child labour meant that each additional child could bring in extra income to the household. And, before the development of pension schemes and welfare services for the elderly, children were seen as an insurance policy: a means to provide for their parents' old age.

Children are now an economic liability rather than an asset to their parents. A study in 1985 estimated that the typical mother can expect to lose £49,000 in life-time earnings as a result of raising two children. This figure is based on the average mother who loses nine years of full-time work, partially offset by three years of part-time earnings, and who also falls behind in promotion prospects.

In *Prosperity and Parenthood*, J. A. Banks has argued that the middle classes were first to adopt widespread family limitation in the 1880s because of economic factors such as the rising costs of school fees and servants combined with an economic depression. The next big slump occurred between the wars when unemployment rose to 20 per cent and by the 1930s working-class families had also adopted similar habits so that over 60 per cent of the population was using birth control.

Social motivations

Changing social attitudes and norms which have affected couples' decisions on family size include secularisation, the child-centred family and **feminism**, the belief in equal rights for women. Feminism has meant that wives are better educated and more likely to want a career. Secularisation means that the church has a declining influence. When over 60 per cent of couples were using birth control in the 1930s, this was despite the disapproval of the churches: the Methodists did not approve of contraception until 1939; the Church of England finally sanctioned its use in 1958 and in 1968 Pope Paul VI firmly restated the Catholic opposition to artificial birth control.

If increasing numbers no longer believe in religion then what do they believe in? Many parents see the whole point of their lives revolving around doing their best for their children and improving their standard of living. These child-centred and materialist values motivate couples to want only two or three children. After all, what's the point in having a nice new car and a smart, three-bedroomed semi-detached house if neither is big enough for all the family?

3   Britain's ageing population

Increasing life expectancy

Increasing life expectancy in the UK in years

	1901	1931	1951	1971	1988
Males	48	58	66	69	72
Females	52	62	71	75	78

Life expectancy figures show the average future life-span that new born babies can expect to have if the death rates at the time of their birth continue. The average age of a population will rise if death rates fall (and/or birth rates fall): this produces an ageing population, with an age structure characterised by increasing proportions in older age groups. Between 1861 and 1961 the death rate in Britain halved from twenty-four to twelve.

The twentieth century has seen the introduction of penicillin and antibiotics, the development of vaccines and immunisation as well as dramatic improvements in diagnostic and surgical techniques. Free personal health services for all started in 1948 through the NHS. However, the death rate had already taken its most dramatic fall during the Victorian era of public, rather than personal, health measures. Environmental health was improved by better drains and water supplies and better conditions at work, while ill-health in the home was also prevented by higher standards of diet, housing, hygiene and education.

The burden of dependency

The figures on page 76 show that the proportions of the population who were of working age were the same in 1871 and 1971. This 58 per cent

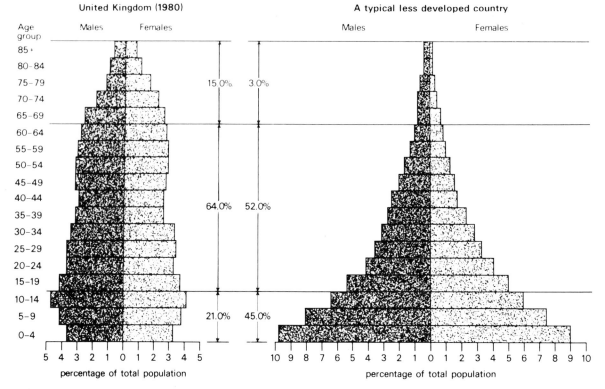

Above: a nation's age distribution changes from fir-tree-shaped to barrel-shaped as an economy matures.

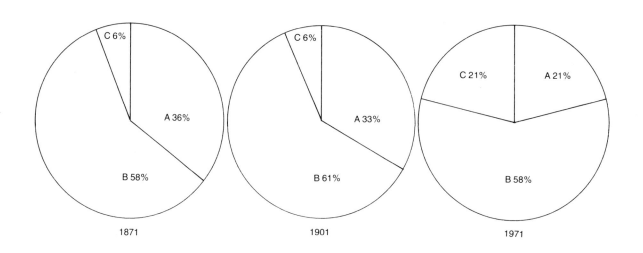

Key

A = 0 to school-leaving age
B = Working age to 60 for women and 65 for men
C = Over retirement age

had to provide the income tax, national insurance contributions and growth in economic output to support the 42 per cent of children and pensioners. Two further points need to be made:

1   The actual number employed, out of a working-age population of 35 million in 1987, was only 25 million. This is because ten million sixteen to sixty-five-year-olds were not earning: these include full-time housewives and students, the sick and disabled, the unemployed and the early retired.

2   An increasing proportion of the dependent population are pensioners rather than children and an increasing proportion of these pensioners are very elderly. In 1951 there were 141 British centenarians (people over 100 years old) but in 1985 1,819 received a telegram from the Queen on their hundredth birthday. Future trends are very important for planning government spending: provision of health and social services for a person over seventy-five costs seven times more than for the average person of working age.

Trends in the age structure

Case study: getting mothers and the elderly back to work

The over-fifties are the only section of the population that will continue to grow into the next century. The sharp decline in teenagers, because of the fall in the birth rate in the 1970s, is already creating problems. (The fall in seventeen to twenty-one-year-olds from 4.7 million in 1981 to 3.4 million by 1996 has been called **the demographic time bomb**.)

A few years ago, employers were worried about how to encourage older employees to take early retirement to create jobs for school-leavers. Now the over-fifties are in demand. Tesco, which started the trend with a small advert for the over-fifty-fives in a paper in Crawley, Sussex, last August, already has 2,500 recruits.

Because of labour shortages in the South-east, British Rail has been trying to woo back drivers who have retired. Dixons, the high-street store chain, has pioneered term-time working for mothers with school-age children.

'It is an astonishing turn-around', said Malcolm Wicks, director of the Family Policy Studies Centre. 'A few years ago, there were too many young people and too few jobs. The government invented the Youth Training Scheme. Women were encouraged to stay at home and look after their children. Now it's all changed.'

(adapted from *The Sunday Times*, 5 March 1989)

Case study: progress and poverty among the old

Changes in the life-styles of the elderly, 1959–1982

	1959 (%)	1982 (%)
Women aged over 65 living alone	33	46
Women aged over 65 retiring from paid jobs	9	25
Percentage of over 65s carrying out D-I-Y jobs – males	36	74
Percentage of over 65s carrying out D-I-Y jobs – females	21	45
Percentage of over 65s possessing a:		
telephone	9	64
refrigerator	12	88
car	16	36
washing machine	22	70
TV	55	96
Foreign holiday in previous year	4	11
Percentage of over 65s who are non-smokers	62	73

	1959	1982
Average weekly total expenditure		
OAP households	£5.16	£44.86
all households	£15.50	£125.41
Average weekly spending per person		
OAP households	£3.71	£32.32
all households	£5.03	£45.96

(Source: *Social Trends*, 1984)

The problems of the elderly

While the majority of pensioners enjoy a far higher standard of living than most pensioners in the past, there is a sizeable minority who suffer from a number of conditions:

- 571 old people died in their homes from hypothermia in 1985,
- 1,800 were the victims of violent crime,
- 189,000 could not get in and out of bed unaided,
- 695,000 could not cope with stairs,
- 757,000 could not bath or shower without help,
- 1,056,000 could not walk unassisted,
- almost 500,000 had no living relatives,
- 1,000,000 had no regular visitors.

500,000 out of the 1,100,000 dwellings in the UK which are 'unfit for human habitation' are inhabited by elderly people.
Nearly 2,000,000 old people depend on supplementary benefit.

(Source: Help the Aged, 1986)

Data-response exercise: progress and poverty among the elderly

1   What percentage of over sixty-fives did *not* have telephones in 1982?

2   To what extent did the percentages of over sixty-fives carrying out do-it-yourself jobs change between 1959 and 1982?

3   (a) How many old people in 1986 were estimated to have no regular visitors?
(b) Where does this estimated figure come from?

4   What proportion of UK dwellings 'unfit for human habitation' are occupied by pensioners?

5   How far is it true to say that 'old people live longer, healthier and better lives than ever before'? Use the above information to support your answer.

Occupational therapy in a geriatric hospital.

4   Internal migration patterns – urbanisation

The main reason for changes in the **geographical distribution** of the population is migration from one part of the country to another. The main shifts in the last 120 years can be described in three phases:

1851–1911: Rural depopulation – the drift to the cities

In 1851 9 million people, or 54 per cent of the population of England and Wales, lived in towns and cities. By 1911 28 million, or 80 per cent of the population, was concentrated in urban areas. The mechanisation of farm work meant a fall in demand for agricultural workers. To escape unemployment or low wages, many people left villages and moved to industrial areas.

The main parts of the country to lose population in the second half of the nineteenth century were all rural areas: the northern Pennines, the Yorkshire Wolds and the Vale of York, most of Wales outside the coalfields and a belt across the middle of England from the South-West, through the South Midlands, to East Anglia.

Apart from London and the ports of Humberside and Merseyside, the main urban areas to attract rural migrants were in South Wales, the West Midlands, South Lancashire, West and South Yorkshire, Northumberland and Durham: all fast-growing industrial areas based on coalfields.

1911–1951: The growth of suburbs and the drift to the South

Some rural areas continued to lose population in the first half of this century. These included Exmoor, central Wales, northern East Anglia, the Fens, rural Lincolnshire, the Vale of Pickering, the North York Moors and the northern Pennines. But other rural areas, close to **conurbations** (or sprawling cities), gained population with the development of **dormitory suburbs** for commuters.

Areas of traditional heavy industry were hardest hit by the high unemployment of the 1930s slump. Many people left areas such as South Wales, Lancashire and North-East England as jobs disappeared in industries such as textiles, coalmining, shipbuilding and heavy engineering. Those who moved from these declining regions headed for the Midlands and the South where the growth industries between the wars included electrical engineering; the manufacture of cars, aircraft and consumer durables such as radios and refrigerators; paper making and printing; and food processing, as well as banking, finance and insurance. It has been estimated that 80 per cent of the new manufacturing plant in Britain between the wars was built around London, such as the factories of Heinz and Hoover, Firestone and Ford.

1951–1985: Regional policy and de-urbanisation

The South-East's population rose from 7 million in the 1930s to 17 million in 1985. Government **regional policy** has tried to reverse the drift to the South by encouraging industry to locate in the northern and western **Celtic Fringe** and other areas of high unemployment. This can be seen if one looks at the car industry. Between the wars this was based in the Midlands and the South. But when Ford wanted to expand close to their Dagenham plant near London, the government persuaded them to build new factories in Halewood, Liverpool and Bridge End, South Wales instead. Similarly, Rootes Motors were persuaded to build a plant at Linwood in Scotland and Leyland at Bathgate in Scotland. More recently, governments have given millions of pounds to attract Delorean Cars to Belfast and Datsun to North-East England. When Datsun advertised 420 vacancies for production line jobs at their new factory at Washington, Tyne and Wear in 1985, they received 15,000 applications.

Government policy has also encouraged **de-urbanisation** from major cities by the post-war development of New Towns, such as Stevenage, Crawley, Bracknell and Harlow beyond London's Green Belt. The following cities have seen a marked fall in population:

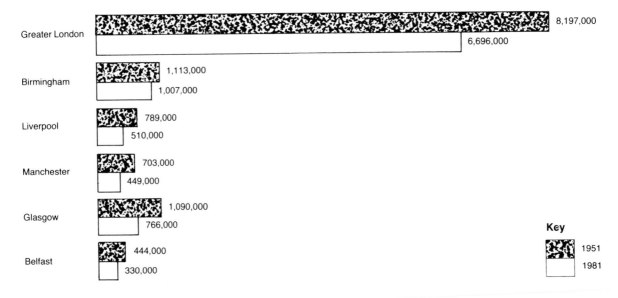

	1951	1981
Greater London	8,197,000	6,696,000
Birmingham	1,113,000	1,007,000
Liverpool	789,000	510,000
Manchester	703,000	449,000
Glasgow	1,090,000	766,000
Belfast	444,000	330,000

Key

1951

1981

Between 1971 and 1981, the biggest changes of population were in London (down 10 per cent) and East Anglia (up 12 per cent). Apart from 'overspill' population moving to New Towns, this **flight from the cities** has been most marked for the location of factories and the trend of pensioners to move to coastal resorts. In 1981, over a third of those living in Worthing and Eastbourne were over retirement age. From 1959 to 1975 the changing location of manufacturing jobs was most marked in London (down 38 per cent) and other conurbations (down 16 per cent), while employment in manufacturing rose by 29 per cent in country towns and 72 per cent in rural areas.

Case study: 'Contours of the Nation's Great Divide'

Research in 1985 concluded that the following towns were top and bottom of a 'prosperity scale':

	Unemployment rate	Change in jobs 1976–1981	Households with two or more cars
Winchester, Hampshire	5%	+7%	25%
Consett, Co. Durham	25%	−33%	11%

Both the north–south and urban–rural divides emerge clearly. Forty of the top fifty towns came from south of a line drawn from the Wash to the Bristol Channel. Market or new towns that have prospered in a belt round the north, west and south of London make up the top 10.

After Winchester at number one come Horsham, Bracknell, Milton Keynes, Maidenhead and Basingstoke. Their prosperity, which has been stimulated by motorway corridors along the M4, M3 and M23 motorways, will be given an added impetus by the completion of London's orbital M25 motorway . . .

Aberdeen is the first area from outside this belt, at number 19, and this is a special case where prosperity has been fuelled by North Sea Oil development. The other prosperous areas in the north are the market towns of rich farming or tourist areas such as Kendal (37) in the Lake District, Matlock (49) in the Peak District or Harrogate (39) on the edge of the Yorkshire Dales . . .

Only five of the bottom 50 areas are south of the Midlands. But Scotland, Wales and the north-east have well over half these low-placed towns between them. The M62 motorway linking Merseyside to the Humber, in contrast to the M25 prosperity belt, has proved to be a ribbon of depression . . .

Of the bottom 20, seven areas are shipbuilding centres . . . four are mining communities . . . seven are steel centres.

(Source: Philip Beresford in *The Sunday Times*, 29 September 1985)

Activity

Half of all families in the USA move house every five years. Conduct a small-scale survey to find out how frequently a group, such as fellow students, have moved house. Ask the respondents to list their reasons for moving and the disadvantages which they have experienced as a result of moving.

This man had spent all his working life at the East Moors steelworks in Cardiff and now he has been employed to help demolish it.

5 External migration patterns

What is meant by 'the English'?

For many centuries the population of England has included numerous surnames of Irish, Welsh and Scottish origin. The earliest English towns attracted migrants from the north and west, from the Celtic Fringes of the British Isles. Successive waves of settlers also came from the south and east, from across the Channel and the North Sea.

The last time that England was successfully invaded was in 1066 by the French led by William the Conqueror, Duke of Normandy. But before the Normans, invaders included Saxons from Germany; Vikings and Danes from Scandinavia; and soldiers from all over the Roman Empire, including most of the countries around the Mediterranean.

Many people would consider that the Royal Family is one of the most English of institutions. But the 'English' monarchy has included kings and queens from France, Scotland, Holland and Germany. Queen Victoria's husband was German and the present Queen's husband was born in Greece. It is sometimes said that Richard III, who lost his throne to the Welsh Tudors, was the last English king.

Push and pull factors and refugees

It could be argued that all English people have immigrant ancestors since everyone left England around 70,000 BC, at the start of the Ice Age, leaving no population at all until seasonal hunting groups 'immigrated' around 40,000 BC. Settlers have continued to arrive over the centuries. Most have been attracted by economic prospects – the chance to improve their standard of living (**pull factors**); some have been refugees escaping from economic desolation, such as famines, or driven from their homes by religious and political persecution (**push factors**).

In the 1980s refugees to Britain included exiles fleeing from persecution under the new regime in Iran and Tamils escaping from the civil war in Sri Lanka. Another refugee group, over many different years, has been the Jews.

Jewish immigrants

Most of the Jewish community in Medieval England followed the Norman invaders from France. After terrible persecution, all 16,000 Jews were expelled from England in 1290. The first to return in the seventeenth century were Sephardic Jews escaping from the Catholic Inquisition in Spain and Portugal. By 1800, 4,000 or so of these had been joined by some 20,000 Ashkenazi Jews from Eastern Europe who were mainly poorer and spoke Yiddish – a mixture of Hebrew and German.

At this time Britain provided a haven for nearly 80,000 refugees from the civil war in France which followed the French Revolution. This began a tradition, which continued throughout Victorian times, of Britain providing a safe refuge for many political exiles, such as the German revolutionary, Karl Marx. This reputation for providing asylum for victims of persecution was severely tested when Jewish refugees arrived again in 1882. By 1914 120,000 destitute Jews had arrived from the Russian Empire where they had been the victims of anti-semitic progroms – campaigns of terror against Jewish communities. Many of these settled in the slums of London's East End where, in the 1930s, they were to face street battles with the 'blackshirts' of Oswald Mosley's British Union of Fascists Party.

Britain's tolerant 'open door' policy began to change with the Aliens Acts of 1905 and 1920. These restrictive laws meant that a special case had to be made to allow in 4,000 Basque children in 1937 (victims of the Spanish Civil War) and 10,000 Jewish children in 1938 (victims of the German Nazis). Many of these children left behind parents who perished in Fascist atrocities.

The history of Jewish immigration to Britain illustrates the combination of push and pull factors which can cause migration. Many were 'pulled' by Britain's 'open door' and most were 'pushed' by persecution – like the 50,000 Huguenots (French Protestants) who sought refuge from Catholic victimisation in the 1680s and like the 5 million Irish (half the population of Ireland) who were forced by starvation to emigrate, mainly to England, Scotland or America, between 1820 and 1920.

Emigration from Britain

Despite the thousands of arrivals mentioned above, nineteenth-century Britain had an outward flow of net migration (immigration minus emigration). Between 1881 and 1921, for instance, there was a net loss of population of between 2 and 3 per cent a year. Most of the 2,278,000 British emigrants who left between 1861 and 1911 went to the USA, South Africa and the **Old Commonwealth** colonies which became self-governing dominions in 1931, such as Canada, Australia and New Zealand.

In these countries the white settlers often took the lands of the native peoples such as the Eskimos, Zulus, Aborigines, Maoris and Native

Americans. Except in South Africa, the whites came to form the majorities in these lands. One Maori has estimated that if the white descendants of these British emigrants were suddenly 'repatriated' and sent back to the British Isles, then 20 million people would arrive at Heathrow airport. (In the USA alone, 40 million Americans give their ethnic origin as Irish.)

The larger part of the British Empire developed into the **New Commonwealth**: the colonies mainly in Africa, the West Indies and the Indian sub-continent where the white soldiers, missionaries and plantation owners only formed a small part of the population. After bitter struggles, these nations gained independence following the Second World War – many not until the 1960s.

'The Last of England' by Ford Madox Brown (City Art Gallery and Museum, Birmingham). The subject of this painting, for which the artist used himself, his wife Emma and their child as models, was suggested by the departure of Thomas Wooler as an emigrant to Australia in 1852.

Recent patterns of net migration

The net outward flow of the nineteenth century continued into the twentieth, as these figures for net civilian migration show:

1901–1911	−82,000
1911–1921	−92,000
1921–1931	−67,000
1931–1951	+25,000
1951–1961	+ 6,000
1961–1971	−28,000
1971–1981	−45,000

In 1984 there was a net inflow of new residents (defined as those who, having lived abroad at least a year, now intend to stay in Britain at least a year). But from the following categories we can see that 47 per cent of these new residents were in fact British emigrants returning to Britain:

New residents in UK and departing residents, 1984

	British	*NCWP**	*Old C'wealth*	*EEC*	*Other foreign*	*Total*
Arriving	95,000	35,000	15,000	15,000	41,000	201,000
Departing	103,000	16,000	10,000	8,000	28,000	165,000

(*NCWP = New Commonwealth and Pakistan)

Post-war immigration from the New Commonwealth

Immigrants from the New Commonwealth have included refugees from Cyprus and students from West Africa, but the largest groups have come from the West Indies and India and Pakistan. The pattern of immigration of these largest groups can be described in three phases:

1 Push and pull factors in the 1950s The obvious push factors were the poverty and unemployment that many people experienced in the Caribbean and the Indian sub-continent, while a strong pull factor was the large number of unfilled job vacancies in Britain. Additional factors included:
(a) West Indian emigrants were restricted from their first choice of destination, the USA, after 1952;
(b) the partition of India in 1947 split border areas, such as Punjab, with Pakistan. This disruption encouraged many to leave;
(c) in the heyday of the British Empire, a quarter of the world's population were British subjects and so, automatically, were also British citizens. The 1948 Nationality Act confirmed that Commonwealth citizens remained British;
(d) very low unemployment in Britain in the 1950s created a labour shortage so that recruiting teams were sent to Jamaica, Barbados and Pakistan from London Transport, hospitals, textile mills, restaurants and hotels.

2 The peak in the early 1960s By the 1960s, British politicians began to decide that they could no longer welcome unlimited immigration to the 'Mother Country' from the coloured New (rather than white Old) Commonwealth. While Acts were passed outlawing racial discrimination in 1965, 1968 and 1976, many claim that British governments were, at the same time, blatantly racist themselves: they introduced Immigration Acts in 1962, 1968, 1971 and 1981 which were basically designed to take away the rights of British passport holders if they were black rather than white. It was the rush to enter before the first restrictions were imposed in 1962 which caused the peak in the immigration figures in 1961.

3 The falling flow of dependents Entry vouchers for workers coming to Britain, introduced by the 1962 Commonwealth Immigration Act, were reduced so much in the 1960s that by 1973 90 per cent of New Commonwealth immigrants were wives, children and older parents joining men already here. This flow of dependents has since fallen.

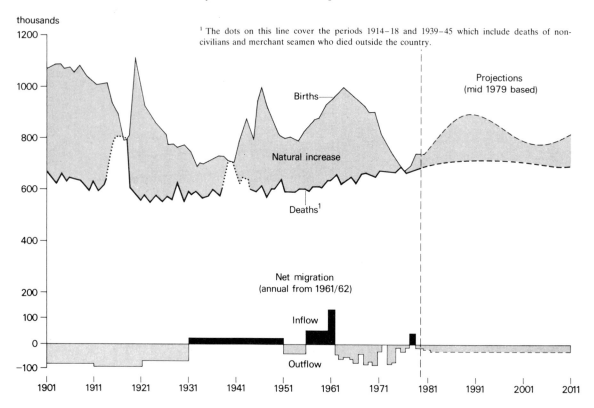

The changes and projected changes of the UK's population in the twentieth century (source: Social Trends, *1986).*

Some people have referred to 'the problem of coloured immigrants'. It is more accurate to refer to the problems created by the racial prejudice of the host population. We take a closer look at the ethnic minorities within the UK and the issue of racism in our next chapter.

GCSE questions from London and East Anglian Group 1988

1 In 1951 there were 11 per cent of the population beyond retiring age; in 1981 there were 17 per cent. Examine the causes and effects of this ageing population.   (15)

2 Outline the changes in social relationships that may occur as a result of people moving away from conurbations and cities.   (8)

GCSE question from Southern Examining Group 1988

(a) Identify and explain *two* reasons why the infant mortality rate is lower in Social Class 1 (e.g. top managers) than in Social Class 5 (unskilled workers).   (4)

(b) Identify and explain *two* reasons for the fall in the size of the rural population of Britain this century.   (4)

CHAPTER 7

Ethnic minorities and racism

The spectre of prejudice is lying in wait.

Throughout history societies have been divided and human beings have persecuted and oppressed each other for a variety of reasons. Religion, sex, social class, age, nationality and race have all been, and indeed still are, the grounds upon which one group inflicts suffering on another.

One might be tempted to think that human beings are cursed with the inability to get on with one another and that the desire to persecute others simply because they are different in some way is a fixed part of human nature. Such a conclusion would, however, be mistaken for human nature is not something which is fixed, that does not allow for growth and change. Thus, some forms of persecution and oppression that existed in the past have to a certain extent been eliminated from our society. For example, the idea that women are inferior has been challenged. And homosexuals are another group that now experience far less persecution than in the past.

One type of persecution and oppression which is still the cause of tremendous suffering is racism. We begin this chapter by attempting to define racism and explain its causes.

1 What is racism?

We can define **racism** as prejudice or discrimination which is determined by the belief that one race is superior to other races. We now look more closely at three aspects of this definition.

Prejudice

Prejudices are prejudgements which people will not modify in the light of new experience. For example, someone might hold a mentally rigid view that all young football supporters are hooligans. If this person then met a large number of polite, well-behaved young football fans but was unwilling to shift from his or her original view, then we could call this person prejudiced. A typical prejudiced viewpoint is that 'all women drivers are awful'.

Discrimination

When people, such as club doormen, are racially prejudiced and use their power to the detriment of particular groups, for example refusing admission to black youths, then they are discriminating. **Racial discrimination** occurs when a racist idea becomes a racist action. **Racial prejudice** is sometimes called 'passive racism'. Active discrimination may be on an open, individual level or it may operate on a hidden institutional level.

Institutional racism

This is found where institutions such as firms and schools maintain practices and procedures which discriminate. An example is the administration of justice in the USA where blacks comprise 11 per cent of the population but account for 50 per cent of state prison inmates. As Pinkney has commented: 'They serve longer sentences than whites for the same offence, and capital punishment has been virtually reserved for the black man.' An example of a victim of harsh sentencing is George Jackson who, at the age of eighteen, was given a sentence of 'one year to life' for stealing $70 from a petrol station. He spent ten years in jail for this offence, seven and a half of them in solitary confinement, at the Soledad and San Quentin prisons in California. His experiences made him one of the foremost black radicals of the 1960s and he was shot dead in a prison riot in 1971.

Racism and Nazi Germany

To understand fully the meaning of racism it is helpful to look at an historical example of a society which was openly racist and which took racism to an extreme conclusion.

The racial doctrines of the Nazi Party   Nazi ideas rested on the belief that races are fundamentally unequal and that superior races have the right to oppress and enslave inferior races. They believed that the Jews were one of the lowest races while the Germans were part of the Aryan master race. As is the case with racists, the Nazis created physical and cultural stereotypes of races. The Northern European Aryans were supposed to be tall, blond-haired and blue-eyed. It was claimed that they were superior because they were responsible for all the great cultural achievements of mankind.

The Jews, on the other hand, were stereotyped in a completely negative and unappealing manner. Physically, they were caricatured as deformed, dirty and ugly. Culturally, they were presented as destroyers of civilisation. The Nazis believed that the Aryan race would only retain its superiority if it avoided intermarriage with other races and if it conquered the inferior races.

The racist laws of the Nazi Government   When the Nazi Party, led by Hitler, took over the government of Germany in 1933, it immediately set about the systematic persecution of the Jewish people. Jews were banned from government jobs and all Jews were made to wear badges. Jewish shops and businesses had the Star of David painted on them and Germans were encouraged to boycott them.

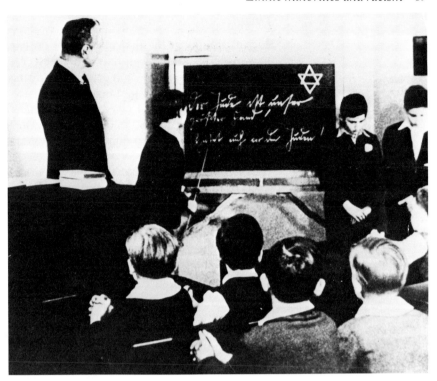

A classroom in Nazi Germany. While two Jewish boys face their class, another pupil reads from the blackboard: 'The Jew is our greatest enemy. Beware of the Jew!'

In 1935 the Nuremberg laws were passed which took away all the rights of the Jews in Germany. They were deprived of German citizenship, forbidden to marry non-Jews, banned from serving in the army or practising medicine. Jews could not be teachers, farmers, journalists, lawyers or artists. By 1938 20,000 Jews had been placed in concentration camps.

The 'Final Solution'   The next and last step in the persecution of the Jews was what Hitler called the 'Final Solution'. This took place during the Second World War and involved the extermination not only of German Jews but Jews living in all the countries that the Nazis had conquered. The intention was genocide, the deliberate destruction of a people, and 6 million Jews died in the Nazi 'Holocaust'.

It must also be remembered that the Nazi invasion of Russia, which led to the death of at least 10 million Russian soldiers and a further 10 million Russian civilians, was partly prompted by the Nazi belief that the Slavic races were inferior and ought to be enslaved by the Aryans. The Nazi experience horrifically illustrates what racism can lead to.

2   Four causes of racism

Different groups have suffered from racism for different reasons and this makes it difficult to generalise about the causes of racism. We therefore concentrate on the racism that one group, black people, have experienced and continue to experience. We now look at four different views of the origin of racism.

The idea of racial differences

Racism springs in the first place from the view that there are basic and unchangeable differences between races. This view gained widespread acceptance in the nineteenth century following the ideas of scientists, such as the Swedish zoologist Linnaeus. He divided mankind into Caucasian, Mongoloid and Negroid races. Such classifications were based on observable physical variations, colour being the most important one. Linnaeus thought that the cultural differences between races could be explained by their physical differences.

Other writers concluded that the 'superior' culture of the West was a result of the superior physical and mental features of the European races. Black people were seen as members of a biologically inferior race. While some people still hold these views, the modern science of genetics has made the idea of race meaningless. Our physical make-up depends on more than 100,000 genes and over 90 per cent of these are similar for all human beings. Physical differences between so-called races are few and superficial compared to physical similarities. A French person may be biologically more similar to an Eskimo, for example having the same blood group, than to another French person.

Race is not really a scientific category. Race is more truly a social label. In some cultures ideas of race are passed on by socialisation. Sociologists prefer to use the term **ethnic group**. We all belong to an ethnic group and our membership may be based on shared physical attributes, such as skin colour, or it may be based on shared cultural attributes, such as customs concerning clothing.

Colonialism and slavery

The notion that races were unequal became popular at the same time that Europeans were settling in territories all over North and South America, Asia and, later, Africa. By the eighteenth century, Britain had larger colonies than any other empire in the history of the world and the British were transporting at least half of the 15 million West African slaves who were taken across the Atlantic Ocean. This trade in slaves flourished because of the demand for cheap labour in the West Indies and North America where huge profits could be made from cotton, tobacco and sugar plantations.

One view of racism sees it as a European invention which served to justify the slave trade and the colonising of Africa. Slavery and colonialism were held to be good things: they helped to civilise inferior black people by bringing them into contact with the superior way of life of the white man. In spite of the success of the popular campaign which abolished British slavery in the 1830s, racism remained a deeply entrenched part of British culture.

Scapegoating

In biblical times a ritual took place each year which involved loading a goat with objects which symbolically represented the sins of everyone in

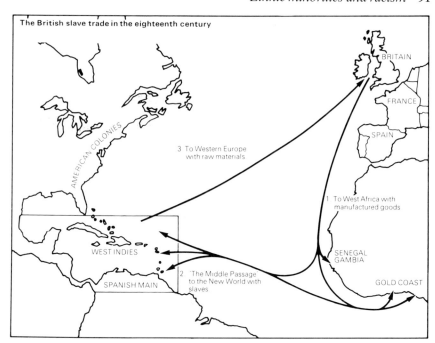

The British Slave Trade in
the eighteenth century.

the community during the previous twelve months. The goat was then
driven out into the wilderness and everyone felt better.

When a society is faced with difficult problems that threaten its stability,
there is a tendency to blame distinctive and powerless minorities. In anxious
times of crisis, people may readily accept simple but irrational explanations
for complex problems. Blame may be easily directed at a minority because
its distinctiveness arouses suspicion and its weakness prevents effective re-
taliation to hostility from the majority.

In the 1930s the Nazis made the Jews into scapegoats and succeeded
in convincing millions of Germans that the Jews were the cause of their
unemployment problem. Hitler knew that the Jews were not really to blame
for Germany's economic problems but they provided a simple explanation
which helped him to gain power by suggesting a simple cure – namely,
the destruction of the Jewish community.

It is a familiar tactic for unscrupulous politicians to create scapegoats.
In Britain, political parties like the National Front have tried to gain support
by blaming black people for social ills such as unemployment, crime and
poor housing.

Stereotypes and the media

To a certain extent, the media have had a harmful effect on race relations
in Britain by reinforcing stereotyped attitudes about black people and by
presenting them in a negative way; that is, the media tends to define black
people as a problem.

A **stereotype** is a fixed image of a group of people and stereotyping
is a process which involves the following stages: (a) taking some easily
grasped features that a group is supposed to have; (b) making these features
the dominant characteristics of the group; (c) suggesting that all members

TO BE SOLD & LET
BY PUBLIC AUCTION,
On *MONDAY the 18th of MAY*, 1829,
UNDER THE TREES.
FOR SALE,
THE THREE FOLLOWING
SLAVES,
VIZ.
HANNIBAL, about 30 Years old, an excellent House Servant, of Good Character.
WILLIAM, about 35 Years old, a Labourer.
NANCY, an excellent House Servant and Nurse.
The MEN belonging to "LEECH'S" Estate, and the WOMAN to Mrs. D. SMIT

TO BE LET,
On the usual conditions of the Hirer finding them in Food, Clothes and Medical.
THE FOLLOWING
MALE and FEMALE
SLAVES,
OF GOOD CHARACTERS.
ROBERT BAGLEY, about 20 Years old, a good House Servant.
WILLIAM BAGLEY, about 18 Years old, a Labourer.
JOHN ARMS, about 18 Years old.
JACK ANTONIA, about 40 Years old, a Labourer.
PHILIP, an Excellent Fisherman.
HARRY, about 27 Years old, a good House Servant.
LUCY, a Young Woman of good Character, used to House Work and the Nursery.
ELIZA, an Excellent Washerwoman.
CLARA, an Excellent Washerwoman.
FANNY, about 14 Years old, House Servant.
SARAH, about 14 Years old, House Servant.

Also for Sale, at Eleven o'Clock,
Fine Rice, Gram, Paddy, Books, Muslins,
Needles, Pins, Ribbons, &c, &c.
AT ONE O'CLOCK, THAT CELEBRATED ENGLISH HORSE
BLUCHER,

This advertisement, in the West Indies in 1829, offers three slaves for sale to the highest bidder and eleven more for hire.

of the group possess these features. For example, the prevailing stereotype of Irishmen in jokes and cartoons has portrayed them as stupid.

Children's comics, stories, school textbooks and films have often stereo-typed black people in a particularly offensive way: as humble, stupid servants or as 'dumb', brutal savages. A more recent media image has portrayed black youth as muggers. In 1982, a front page headline in the *Daily Mail* read 'Black Crime: the alarming figures'. The story was based on London's 1981 figures from the Metropolitan Police. These figures claimed that 'robbery and other violent thefts' were more likely to be committed by 'coloured' than white assailants. The *Daily Mail* ignored the fact that this is one of the smallest categories of crime, only involving 3 per cent of recorded serious offences.

Most British cities have higher recorded crime rates than rural areas, including cities like Glasgow where there are in fact very few black people. It is therefore more meaningful to link crime rates to urban conditions rather than colour. Despite this obvious truth, most popular newspapers continue to reinforce prejudices against black people by suggesting that they are more criminally inclined than white people.

Parts of the media, such as Channel Four, have taken some steps towards offering a more responsible and balanced picture of black people, by, for example, showing their positive contributions to our society. However, as one assistant editor of a major newspaper has put it, 'everything to do with coloured people takes place against an underlying premise, that they are the symbols of the embodiment of a problem'.

Activities

1 Use the three stages of stereotyping described above to construct favourable or unfavourable stereotypes of several of the following groups: teachers, police officers, politicians, second-hand car salesmen, stockbrokers, dustmen.

2 Consider several TV series, such as *Mind Your Language*, *Grange Hill*, *No Problem!*, *East Enders*, and say whether the programmes you have chosen give a favourable or unfavourable picture of black people. Is it a realistic picture or a stereotype?

3 In 1986 15,000 pupils from over 500 schools and colleges took part in a survey organised by *New Society*. Forty-two per cent of whites reckoned themselves to be racially prejudiced. This prejudice was higher among boys and in the north. It was highest against Asians but lowest among Asians.

Design a questionnaire to test whether people are racially prejudiced or racially tolerant.

---

3 Who are the ethnic minorities?

The people of Britain can be divided up according to religion; regional customs, such as accent and diet; and different patterns of class behaviour. If this is done, then no single group would form a majority. And so there is a sense in which we all belong to a particular ethnic minority. Official figures, however, concentrate on ethnic minorities who have mainly established themselves in Britain comparatively recently:

Ethnic groups in Britain, 1984–86	*total (thousands)*	*% born in UK*
White	51,107	96
All ethnic minority groups of which	2,432	43
West Indian	534	53
Indian	760	36
Pakistani	397	42
Bangladeshi	103	31
Chinese	115	24
African	103	35
Arab	66	11
Mixed	235	74
Other	119	28
Not stated	691	68

(Source: *Social Trends*, 1989)

The 1985 Swann Report gives the following approximate figures for some other ethnic minorities:

Italian 200,000
Cypriot 140,000
Travellers (including gypsies) 30,000
Ukrainian 25,000
Vietnamese 17,000

In 1984 the GLC estimated that the Irish community makes up 17 per cent of London's population.

Some 6 per cent of the population is non-white and of these about 40 per cent were born in the UK. Seven per cent of the population were born outside the UK and of these over half are white.

A 1986 survey of Inner London Education Authority schools found that 20 per cent of the pupils spoke a language other than English at home. The total number of languages was 161 and the numbers of pupils speaking the most common of these languages were:

Bengali 12,000	Arabic 2,706
Turkish 4,383	Italian 2,102
Gujerati 3,831	French 2,030
Urdu 3,642	Portuguese 1,821
Chinese 3,546	Yoruba (Nigeria) 1,120
Spanish 3,210	Vietnamese 774
Greek 3,033	Tagalog (Philippines) 765
Punjabi 3,015	Twi (Ghana) 724

Asian diversity

The diversity of the ethnic minorities may be seen by focusing on those labelled 'Asian'. Those who originate from the Indian sub-continent may speak a number of different languages including Bengali, Gujerati, Urdu and Punjabi. They may belong to different religions: in 1977 40 per cent were Muslim, 29 per cent Hindu and 25 per cent Sikh. And they come from a number of countries: India, Pakistan, Bangladesh, Sri Lanka. There are also those of the East African Asian community who left Uganda, Kenya and Tanzania in the 1960s and 1970s.

The 1982 Policy Studies Institute (PSI) Survey found that 20 per cent of Asians aged over twenty-five left school before they were ten years old. These might include Muslim peasants from Pakistan who were recruited by textile mills in Bradford and Blackburn in the 1960s to come and work the night shifts. In Indian Restaurants 80 per cent of workers in fact come from Bangladesh, which was called East Pakistan until 1971. Other Bengalis work in the rag trade, cutting out and making up garments, in the Spitalfields and Brick Lane areas of Tower Hamlets in the East End of London. Another category, from the rural Indian state of Punjab, are the Sikhs. Many of these found work in the foundries of the West Midlands.

The 1982 survey found that another 20 per cent of Asians over twenty-five had stayed in full-time education past their nineteenth birthday – while less than half that proportion of whites had done the same. These Asians include businessmen and doctors. In a 1979 survey of heads of households in Greater London 21.5 per cent of Asians were in the category 'Professional, Managerial, Employers' compared to 20.8 per cent of whites and 3.6 per cent of West Indians. Over a third of all doctors in the UK were born overseas and over half of the 1,200 sub-post offices in London are owned by Gujeratis (from the Indian state of Gujerat) – many of them have the surname Patel and most are Hindus.

Question: What do all these jobs have in common: working long hours in corner shops, takeaways and the rag trade; doing night shifts in textile mills, foundries and mental or geriatric hospitals?

Answer: These are all jobs which have become unpopular with most of the population. Employers have been ready to recruit workers from ethnic minorities for these types of work.

Areas where many of the black minorities live

The 1981 census gives the following figures showing the percentages of all heads of households who were born in the New Commonwealth or Pakistan (NCWP):

Area	Caribbean	Indian	Pakistani and Bangladeshi	Total NCWP
London boroughs			*(%)*	
Haringey	11.0	2.8	1.0	29.8
Hackney	15.1	3.1	1.6	28.0
Lambeth	13.6	2.1	0.9	23.5
Tower Hamlets	4.8	1.4	9.9	20.3
Brent	12.2	8.8	1.9	33.5
Ealing	4.8	12.6	1.9	25.4
Waltham Forest	6.0	2.6	4.2	17.5
Hounslow	1.3	9.1	1.4	17.1
Districts				
Leicester	1.8	12.7	0.7	21.7
Slough	3.2	9.2	5.2	21.0
Wolverhampton	4.4	9.7	0.6	15.5
Birmingham	4.8	4.4	4.7	15.2
Luton	4.1	3.0	4.6	13.9
Blackburn	0.1	6.0	4.2	11.5
Sandwell	2.8	6.6	1.5	11.4
Bradford	0.8	2.8	6.9	11.2

4 The extent of racial discrimination

The 1976 Race Relations Act

This Race Relations Act strengthens the two previous laws of 1965 and 1968 so that every individual is legally protected against racial discrimination as a job applicant; as an employee; as a house-buyer; as a tenant; as a customer and as a pupil. The Act also outlaws 'incitement to racial hatred'

There is only one race: the human race.

and it has established the Commission for Racial Equality to give advice to complainants.

The 1985 British Social Attitudes Survey found that 35 per cent described themselves as racially prejudiced and nearly 66 per cent thought that black people are denied jobs because of their race. Despite the law, racial discrimination is still widespread in modern Britain. We now look at how widespread it is in the key areas of education, employment, housing and policing.

Education

Exam results and verbal reasoning banding of Inner London fifth-year pupils, 1986 (percentages)

Ethnic background	5 or more O-levels (grades A to C) or grade one CSEs	Verbal reasoning band	
		top	bottom
Indian	21	25	31
Pakistani	16	20	29
Greek	16	18	27
Irish	11	25	21
English, Scottish, Welsh	9	25	20
Turkish	6	8	51
Caribbean	5	14	32
Bangladeshi	4	9	57
All	10	22	25

(Source: Ethnic Background and Examination Results 1985 and 1986 – ILEA Research and Statistics Branch. 1987)

At transfer to secondary school, each of the 1986 Inner London fifth-year pupils had been placed into one of three bands. This banding was based on assessments of the pupils' verbal reasoning ability by their primary school teachers. The verbal reasoning bands are intended to correspond to the top 5 per cent (VR band 1), the middle 50 per cent (VR band 2) and the bottom 25 per cent (VR band 3). The above figures show that the ethnic groups with the poorest exam results tended to have few in the top band

and many in the bottom band.

It has been found that lower assessments in verbal reasoning ability are closely related to lack of fluency in English, poverty and social class. These are factors *outside the school* which help to explain the differences in exam results between different ethnic groups.

The 1985 Swann Report also found explanations for ethnic under-achievement *within the education system*. These factors included lack of suitable pre-school provision, lack of relevance of the curriculum to the needs of pupils and poor communication between the school and the parents.

The Swann Report also emphasised negative stereotyping and low expectations by teachers. The Report spoke of the 'unintentional racism' of teachers' attitudes and gave the following examples: 'West Indian children will be good at sports but "not academic"'; 'Asian children will be hard working and well motivated but likely to have unrealistically high careeer aspirations'; 'Chinese children will be reserved, well behaved, and likely to be "under pressure" at home from having to help in the family business in the evenings'.

Employment

Black and White Britain: the Third PSI Survey interviewed 5,001 black adults and 2,305 white adults in 1982. This survey found that across Britain the percentage of men with jobs in the sixteen to twenty-four age group was 61 per cent for whites, 48 per cent for Asians and 42 per cent for West Indians. Even where ethnic minority students stay in education, they do not necessarily get equal opportunities when qualified: 7 per cent of Asians with A-levels were found to have manual jobs compared to 2 per cent of whites with A-levels.

The survey also found that in each occupational category blacks, when compared to whites, received lower wages, were more likely to work shifts and were less likely to supervise others. The proportion reporting racial discrimination in being refused promotion was 8 per cent of Asians and 11 per cent of West Indians; in being refused a job it was 10 per cent of Asians and 26 per cent of West Indians. But how would you know that you had suffered in this way? The 1974 PEP Study used 'situation tests' in which actors from different ethnic groups applied for vacancies in a range of occupations while pretending to have very similar qualifications and experience. This research showed that black applicants suffered discrimination in 20 per cent of skilled manual vacancies, 30 per cent of non-manual vacancies and 37 per cent of semi-skilled and unskilled vacancies.

Housing

When the 1974 study conducted test applications for rented property using black and white actors, the black applicants met with racial discrimination in over 25 per cent of cases. In the 1982 survey, 49 per cent of West Indians and 39 per cent of Asians reported that they had experienced discrimination in seeking privately rented accommodation from a white landlord.

The 1986 report on the allocation of council housing in the London borough of Tower Hamlets found the following pattern over sixteen-months:

Type of housing	Percentage of offers to Asians	Percentage of offers to non-Asians
Has central heating	40	56
Built after 1969	23	34
Has access to garden	9	13
Built before 1945	10	5

The report found that housing officers tended to have unfavourable stereotypes of Bengalis and social security tenants which resulted in these groups being allocated to 'sink' or 'problem' housing estates: usually the oldest, most dilapidated and most inferior estates.

Case study: housing tenure patterns from the 1982 PSI Survey

(column percentages)

	White	West Indian	Asian (%)	Bangladeshi	Sikh
Owner occupied	59	41	72	30	91
Rented from council	30	46	19	53	6
Privately rented	9	6	6	11	3
Housing association, etc.	2	7	3	6	—

Data-response exercise: housing tenure from the 1982 PSI Survey

1 What is meant by the expression 'column percentages'?

2 What proportion of West Indian households were found to own or be buying their house or flat?

3 What proportion of White households rented public sector housing?

4 Use the figures in the last two columns to describe some of the large variations between different Asian groups.

Policing

Following the Brixton riots of 1981, Lord Scarman's report recommended more community policing and more recruitment of black police officers. By 1988 there were 1,108 British police officers from the black and Asian communities. The Scarman Report also recommended that racially prejudiced behaviour by a police officer should be a disciplinary offence normally punished by dismissal. This last recommendation has not been implemented by the police.

In 1979 the Institute of Race Relations study, *Police Against Black People*, identified seven elements of 'everyday, routine' police misconduct towards black people:

1   stop and search without reason,
2   unnecessary violence in arrests,
3   particular harassment of juveniles,
4   danger of arrest when suspects asserted their rights,
5   risk to witnesses and bystanders,
6   repeated arrests of individuals,
7   black homes and premises entered at will.

Ian Bennett, a community policeman, enjoying the St Pauls Festival in Bristol.

Researchers who spent two years carrying out participant observation with the police in London found that 'Racialist language and racial prejudice were prominent and pervasive ... racialist talk and racial prejudice are ... on the whole expected, accepted and even fashionable ... we cannot produce examples of police officers objecting to racialist language or arguing with others who express racialist views' (from the 1984 PSI Report on the Metropolitan Police).

Some see this racism as stretching to the very top of the force. In June 1982, shortly after he was appointed the head of London's police, Kenneth Newman told a journalist: 'In the Jamaicans, you have people who are constitutionally disorderly ... constitutionally disposed to be anti-authority ... It's simply in their make-up.'

5   Racial harassment and violence

The following section is adapted from *Living in Terror: A Report on Racial Violence and Harassment in Housing* (1987), *Learning in Terror: A Survey of Racial Harassment in Schools and Colleges* (1988), both published by the Commission for Racial Equality, and *Under Siege: Racial Violence in Britain Today* (1988) by Keith Tompson.

History

In 1919, there was a series of attacks on black people in the dock areas of the country where black people predominantly lived, among them Cardiff, Glasgow, Liverpool, Hull, Manchester and London.

In 1948 and 1949 there was a series of attacks in Liverpool, Deptford and Birmingham. In Liverpool, there were three nights of violence between black and white people.

The late 1950s saw attacks on blacks by racist white youths. The 1960s saw the 'paki-bashing' phenomenon led by gangs of white skinheads. The 1970s saw further attacks, with the report *Blood on the Streets* describing the racial harassment suffered by Bangladeshis in the Spitalfields area of Tower Hamlets.

The 1980s

While racial attacks are not a new phenomenon, their scale and number is new. One reason is because racial harassment is now increasingly recognised and the police, for example, to some extent, attempt to record incidents in a structured way. Previously unrecorded and effectively 'forgotten' victims of racial attack are now increasingly public knowledge.

Another reason for public recognition of the problem in the 1980s was because of the sheer horror of the attacks. In 1981, Mrs Khan and her three young children lost their lives in a firebomb attack on their Walthamstow home. In 1985, Shamira Kassam, a pregnant woman, died with her three small sons in an arson attack on her home in Ilford.

In 1987, a young Asian boy was stabbed to death by a white pupil in a Manchester secondary school. He had been defending other Asian pupils from physical assault and his death after school in the playground was the outcome of a long period of racial conflict.

For years the effect of Newham Council's housing policy has been that the south of the borough is virtually white-only and that black people have been consigned to low-grade estates north of the Barking Road divide. The white Croydon Road gang patrols the frontier between the two territories. In 1986, a sister at Newham General Hospital's emergency department said that no black person was safe on a Friday or a Saturday night along the Barking Road – every night she was sure to get a case, some so badly hurt you couldn't recognise them.

Research findings

Newham Council's 1986 survey found that one in four of Newham's black residents had been victims of racial harassment in the previous twelve months. Two out of every three victims had been victims more than once. 116 victims reported 1550 incidents of racial harassment, including:

- 774 cases of insulting behaviour;
- 188 cases of attempted damage to property;
- 175 cases of attempted theft;
- 174 cases of threats of damage or violence;
- 153 cases of physical assault;
- 40 cases of damage to property.

The Scottish Ethnic Minorities Research Unit carried out a survey of racial harassment of school children in South Glasgow in 1986. Within the sample, 25 per cent had suffered damage to property, 37 per cent had experienced personal racial attacks and 100 per cent had been subjected to racial abuse. In another Glasgow survey more than half of ethnic minority interviewees said they had suffered racist graffiti on their homes and almost half said they had been racially abused.

In 1987, the Commission for Racial Equality surveyed 107 council housing departments. Of these, 77 per cent said that they thought racial harassment was becoming a more serious problem. This was particularly the case in London, the South of England and the North, whereas the figure for the Midlands was only 56 per cent. In a well-publicised case, Newham Council evicted the McDonnell family for racial harassment of other tenants. A number of councils are now including a clause in their tenancy agreements which states that those who carry out racial harassment may be evicted.

The 1986 Runnymede Trust report *Racial Violence and Harassment* concludes by saying:

> Few areas in Britain can now be regarded as safe for black residents. As the section on arson showed, racial attacks have taken place in areas such as middle-class Hendon, North London and in Shrewsbury in rural Shropshire.

Conclusion

In 1986, the government announced that visitors to the UK would in future need to get a visa if they came from certain countries. These countries were India, Pakistan, Bangladesh, Nigeria and Ghana. The acquisition of a visa was by no means automatic and, even when agreed, could take months to get.

Hundreds of families from the Indian subcontinent had been planning to visit relatives in Britain. They were now alarmed at the new restrictions and they tried to enter the country legally before the visas became compulsory. The tabloid newspapers went wild. 'They're still flooding in', screamed the headline in *London's Evening Standard*. 'In former times', wrote the *Daily Mail*, 'such invasions would have been repelled by armed force.'

For its part the *Sun* demanded that all black immigrants be excluded for all time. 'The axe', it claimed, using a specially vivid metaphor, 'should fall without delay.' Many immigrants were thrown into detention centres like those at Harmondsworth and Ashford; still more were thrown out of the country altogether. Keith Tompson has commented:

> In Britain the incidence of racist attacks has been closely related to the level of government and media-inspired mass resentment against immigration. Of the sixty-four racist murders that took place between 1970 and 1986, no fewer than fifty occurred in the five years – 1976, 1978, 1979, 1980, 1981 – when immigration scares reached fever pitch.
>
> The day after visas were imposed on visitors from Bangladesh, Pakistan and India in 1987 racist thugs attacked an Asian-owned shop in east London and spray-painted the words '3,000 more' all over the proprietor's premises. That was a slogan taken from the previous day's headline in the gutter press. The following day a gang of white youths took out their frustrations on a mosque in Tower Hamlets. Their chant? 'Pakis out', and 'Three thousand too many'.

Activity

In 1989, a Pakistani sociology student at the University of Manchester interviewed fifty Muslim girls at a single-sex comprehensive school. She also interviewed their parents. About half of the parents were in favour of separate Muslim schools to help preserve their religion and culture. Only a quarter of the girls favoured such schools and these were mainly younger girls who disliked the teasing they received in multi-racial schools. The older girls were overwhelmingly against the idea because they did not want to be isolated from other ethnic groups and feared that separation would provoke racism.

Discuss whether the government should fund separate Muslim girls' schools.

GCSE question from Midland Examining Group 1988

(a) Why has the proportion of the population in ethnic minority groups increased since 1945? (4)

(b) Apart from employment problems what other forms of discrimination do ethnic minority groups experience? (4)

(c) Racial prejudice is still a problem in Britain. How do sociologists explain the existence of racial prejudice? (7)

CHAPTER 8

Power and social stratification

A geologist uses the word strata to describe the layers of different rock formations. Sociologists use the term **social stratification** in analysing the power structure of a society. Social stratification refers to the division of society into superior and inferior groups. Such groups may differ from one another in terms of power, wealth, status and respect. People may find that their position in a society depends very much on their race, their religion, their sex and their age.

Most societies contain a number of different types of stratification. Sociologists try to identify these and attempt to pinpoint which one is the most important. Many sociologists claim that social class is the major basis of stratification in capitalist societies. The sections of this chapter look at a number of examples of different types of social stratification.

1 Racial stratification – apartheid in South Africa

When the British set up the state of South Africa in 1910, they handed over power to a government formed by the white minority. This group had a policy of strict racial **segregation**. In 1912 the African National Congress was formed to struggle for the political rights of the black majority and the ANC still leads the fight for a non-racial society in which South Africans of all colours can enjoy equal rights.

In 1948 a government of more extreme segregationists set up a system called **apartheid**, meaning 'separateness'. This excluded blacks from those cinemas, schools, buses and hospitals designated for whites. Even park benches and bathing beaches were labelled 'white-only'. Marriage or sex between whites and non-whites was made illegal.

By the mid-1980s some of these regulations had been relaxed, but the two basic cornerstones of apartheid remained: population classification and allocation to 'group areas'.

The black majority have far less power than the white minority in South Africa.

Population classification

The dominating political power is in the hands of the whites, who form 18 per cent of the population. This group is descended from settlers who came from Holland during the seventeenth and eighteenth centuries and from Britain and other European countries during the nineteenth and twentieth centuries. The non-whites are classified into three groups; in 1982 their proportions of the total population were: African 68 per cent, coloured or mixed race 11 per cent and Asian 3 per cent. Some of the inequalities between these distinct social strata can be seen in these figures.

	Education spending by the government, per pupil in 1983–4	*Infant mortality rate, 1985*
White	1,654 rand	14 deaths per 1,000 live births
Indian	1,088 rand	18 deaths per 1,000 live births
Coloured	569 rand	59 deaths per 1,000 live births
African	234 rand	80 deaths per 1,000 live births

In 1983 there was one doctor for every 330 Whites, 730 Indians, 1,200 coloureds and 12,000 Africans.

(Source: *The Apartheid Handbook* by R. Omond)

Allocation to 'group areas'

The territory of South Africa is strictly segregated with the white 18 per cent of the population allocated 86 per cent of the land and the black 82 per cent getting just 14 per cent of the land. This policy has meant the forcible removal of over 3.5 million Africans from their homes in white areas between 1960 and 1984.

Where do black South Africans generally live?

1   About 40 per cent live in Homelands or Bantustans set up for **separate development**. These poor rural areas were called reserves before 1948. In 1980, in the Bantustan of KwaNdebele almost half the people lived in temporary resettlement camps and 93 per cent of the working population worked outside the Bantustan's boundaries.

2   Others live in townships, such as Soweto on the edge of Johannesburg, and illegal sprawling squatter camps, such as Crossroads outside Cape Town.

3   Migrant workers live in compounds or single-sex hostels, for example at gold mines.

4   Virtually all whites employ black domestic servants some of whom live in servants quarters, usually a room adjoining the garage. It must be a separate building from the white family's house. It is illegal for the servant to have her children with her and if her huband is also employed by the same family he must live in another separate building.

Pass Laws   The 45 per cent of Africans who lived outside the Bantustans had to carry identification passes. The government stored 15 million sets of fingerprints and the copies of 13 million passes in Pretoria in order to ensure 'Influx Control'. The Pass Laws meant that all black workers were treated as foreigners in the land of their birth. They were denied political rights and were often forced to live apart from their husbands or wives and children. Over 12.5 million Africans were arrested or prosecuted under the Pass Laws between 1948 and 1981.

Four examples of how apartheid affects people's lives

1   In 1979, five South African policemen were charged with criminal injury to a white woman. They had beaten her up because they suspected her of sleeping with an Indian South African in her Pretoria flat. The man produced a pass proving he was white. The policemen's defence was that the man had 'acted, talked and looked' like an Indian.

2   In 1984, a twenty-three-year-old black New York dancer, Barry Martin, was on tour with the Hot Gossip dance group when his car crashed. An ambulance picked up his white driver but left him lying on the side of the road. A black passer-by took him to a local white hospital where he was seated on a hard bench and refused treatment while suffering from a fractured spine. A vertebra slipped forward and severed his spinal cord so that his arms and legs are now paralysed. He has since tried to sue the South African authorities for $130 million.

3   In 1984, 795 South Africans were reclassified, including 518 Coloureds who became White; 2 Whites who became Chinese; 1 White who became Indian; 89 Africans who became Coloured; 5 Coloureds who became African.

4   In 1979, Mr Dickson Kohlakala was fined for allowing his wife to stay with him because their baby was very ill. He had been working as a migrant in a white area of Cape Town when his wife brought their sick baby to a hospital there.

Many white South African children have a black nanny who herself sees her own children only once a week, on her day off.

Case study: **Journey to Jo'burg: a South African story**

In this story by Beverley Naidoo, thirteen-year-old Naledi and her nine-year-old brother, Tiro, live with their granny and aunty in a rural Bantustan. The children are very worried because their baby sister, Dineo, is very ill with malnutrition. Their father has died from 'coughing sickness' after working in the gold mines and they only see their mother a few times each year because she works as a maid so that she can pay their school fees.

They decide to walk the 300 km to Johannesburg to tell their mother about Dineo. After a number of adventures, they find their mother who tells her white employer: 'Madam, my little girl is very sick. Can I go home to see her?' The Madam raises her eyebrows and replies: 'Well Joyce, I can't

possibly let you go today. I need you to stay in with Belinda. The Master and I are going to a very important dinner party . . .'

Since it is against the law for Naledi and Tiro to spend the night with their mother in a white area, they stay with strangers in Soweto. These new friends tell them how their brother, Dumi, was one of the older students involved in the Soweto uprising of 1976. Hundreds of pupils were shot and killed by the police. Dumi was imprisoned and beaten up. Now he lives in another country, studying in exile, and he is preparing to return as a freedom fighter.

(To find out how this story ends, you can order it from your library. It is published in the Longman *Knockouts* series.)

2   Feudal and religious stratification – the Indian caste system, medieval England and modern Northern Ireland

Religion and stratification can be connected in two ways. Firstly, religion can be the basis of stratification. This occurs where members of one religion have higher positions in society than members of another religion. Secondly, religion can support a system of stratification by providing a convincing justification for it.

The traditional Indian caste system

In India each individual is traditionally born into a particular **caste** and remains a member of this group for the rest of his or her life. The caste system divides the population of India into five main social groups. In order of importance these are:

1   the Brahmins: priests,
2   Kshatriya: princes and warriors,
3   Vaisya: farmers, traders and craftsmen,
4   Sudras: manual workers and servants,
5   Untouchables: casteless outcasts.

In fact there are as many as 2,500 jatis or sub-castes but surveys have found that in a typical Indian village, with a population of 1,000, the villagers see themselves as belonging to one of between five and twelve basic castes. Surveys have shown that villagers are usually 90 per cent or so in agreement on who in the village belongs to which of these main castes. The Indian Government has tried to abolish the caste system but it still exists.

Castes were rigidly segregated so that marriage was only permitted between members of the same caste (this sort of restriction is called **endogamy**). There was little social contact such as sharing meals between the groups, especially with the Untouchables. Why did the lowest castes and the outcasts put up with this? Some scholars stress the importance of the Hindu idea of **reincarnation**, being born again into another life. If you live a good life you might be reborn into a higher social position.

The English feudal system

In England during the middle ages, the lower groups of the feudal social system, or **estates**, were tenants: villeins (villagers) or cottars (cottagers) and serfs (virtual slaves). They were also socialised into accepting their place at the bottom of the social pyramid by their religion. Christianity taught that a good life would be rewarded in Heaven and that their position was fixed by God. This idea can be seen in one of the original verses of the hymn 'All things bright and beautiful':

> The rich man in his castle, the poor man at his gate,
> God made them high or lowly, and ordered their estate.

Northern Ireland: Protestants and Catholics

The main social division in Northern Ireland, apart from economic class or gender, is religion. Many areas of Northern Ireland are clearly split into Protestant and Catholic communities.

In the 1960s some of the Catholic minority were inspired by the success of the campaign by US blacks for **desegregation**. And so they copied Martin Luther King's tactic of Civil Rights marches to demonstrate peacefully for an end to injustice and discrimination in housing and jobs. In 1976 the British Government passed the Fair Employment (Northern Ireland) Act. This made discrimination on religious or political grounds unlawful and it also set up the Fair Employment Agency to help Catholics get a fair share of jobs.

In the 1981 census 22 per cent of the people of Northern Ireland did not give their religion but it has been estimated that 36 per cent of the adult population is Catholic. If the Catholics had equal employment opportunities, then we could expect them to occupy roughly 36 per cent of the jobs in different occupational categories. We can see whether this is the case by looking at the following findings about the proportions of Catholics in different occupations:

3 per cent of management in the Northern Ireland Electricity Service (1980)

4 per cent of print workers on the Belfast Telegraph (1981)

7 per cent of (non-senior) policemen, firemen and prison officers (1981)

10 per cent of highest grade civil servants, senior principal and above (1985)

14 per cent of managers in marketing, sales and advertising (1981)

16 per cent of scientists and engineers (1981)

(Source: *Research Papers of the Fair Employment Agency of Northern Ireland*)

A republican funeral cortege passes the fortified police station in Anderstown, Northern Ireland.

Case study: youth subculture and ethnic identity amongst Protestants in Northern Ireland

In 1985 Desmond Bell conducted a survey of fourth- and fifth- year pupils in Londonderry schools. Among the Protestant teenagers he found

- less than 20 per cent preferred integrated schooling with Catholics;
- 31 per cent had 'no Catholic friends at all';

- half preferred to live in segregated, all Protestant neighbourhoods;
- increasing numbers were joining the Loyalist marching bands.

(Source: *The British Journal of Sociology*, Volume 38, 1987)

---

3   Gender stratification – women in China, Morocco and Britain

Women in China

Before he led the communist revolution to success, Mao Zedong said that the Chinese people were bound by 'four thick ropes'. He said that a man in China was dominated by three systems of authority: the political, state system; the family, clan system; and the religious, supernatural system. As for women, they were dominated by a fourth authority system: their husbands.

In the early years of the twentieth century Chinese women were still subjected to the traditions of foot-binding and arranged marriages. In 1950 the first article of the new Marriage Law in Communist China abolished the 'compulsory feudal marriage system which is based on the superiority of men over women'. In giving women legal equality, the new communist government was trying to wipe out the centuries-old traditions of gender stratification.

Women in Morocco

By 1971, all but five of the 129 nations in the United Nations allowed women to vote. One of these five was the small state of Liechtenstein and the other four were Arab countries where the Muslim religion gives women an unequal social status.

For many years Morocco was one of the French North African colonies. When it became an independent nation, Morocco's new government passed the Family Laws of 1957 which were based on the Muslim traditions of the seventh century. These laws clearly give Moroccan women an inferior legal status: Article 12 states that a woman cannot give herself in marriage but must be given by a male guardian; Article 29 forbids her from marrying a non-Muslim partner, although a Muslim man may do so. Men are allowed more than one wife (polygamy) and Article 46 allows 'repudiation' which means that a husband can divorce his wife merely by saying 'I repudiate you' three times, in front of a witness.

Women soldiers in China.

While Arab girls may show their faces in Oman, many older women keep their heads carefully veiled.

Moroccan women have, however, to a certain extent been able to join in the modernisation of their society. Thousands have had access to secondary education but only 4 per cent of university graduates are women. In the service sector of the economy, Moroccan women have two main types of jobs. The 1971 census showed 27,700 working for the government (15,200 as teachers) and 100,200 working as maids.

We now consider how far equality of educational opportunity has given women job equality in Britain.

The occupational segregation of the sexes in Britain

There are two types of occupational segregation (or separation):

1   **Vertical segregation** means that men and women are concentrated in different industries. The following chart shows the proportions of women workers in twelve different categories of industry in 1984:

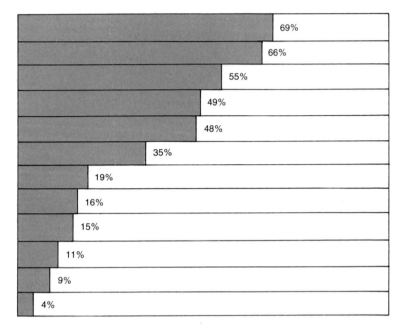

Footwear, clothing and leather manufacturing	69%
Hotels and catering	66%
Retailing (shops)	55%
Banking and finance	49%
Textile manufacturing	48%
Food, drink and tobacco manufacturing	35%
Transport and communications	19%
Agriculture, forestry and fishing	16%
Mechanical engineering	15%
Motor-vehicle manufacturing	11%
Construction	9%
Coal and coke	4%

(Source: *The New Earnings Survey*, 1984)

Unlike the USA we have no female coal miners in this country. Indeed, that type of work is exempt from the Sex Discrimination Act. The women who form 4 per cent of the labour force in the coal and coke industry are probably doing jobs like wages clerk or canteen worker.

2   **Horizontal segregation** means that women tend to be employed in less skilled and less well paid jobs than men, within the same industry. The following figures show the social class composition of people in employment in 1981:

Social class	Occupation	Men %	Women %
I	Professional	6	1
II	Intermediate	16	6
IIIN	Junior non-manual	18	52
IIIM	Skilled manual	38	7
IV	Semi-skilled manual	16	24
V	Unskilled manual	5	8
Armed forces and other categories		2	1

(Source: *1981 Labour Force Survey*)

Jill Barnes, the only woman among 400 engineers at British Telecom's training college.

Julie Young, the first woman in Britain to fly North Sea helicopters.

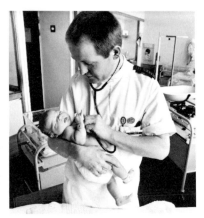

Paul Lewis, the fifth man to qualify as a midwife at London's Whittington Hospital.

The social class categories in the chart on page 111 are explained more fully in the next chapter. The above figures show that women are concentrated into two main areas of work:

1 IIIN Junior non-manual jobs such as shop assistant, typist and hotel receptionist;
2 IV Semi-skilled manual jobs such as production line worker in shoe, sock, cigarette or cake factory.

In 1987 the average weekly earnings of full-time employees were £224 for men and £148 for women.

Data-response exercise: the occupational segregation of the sexes

1 What proportion of workers in the hotel and catering industry in 1984 were female?
2 How much greater was the proportion of male workers than the proportion of female workers in professional occupations in 1981?
3 Women workers outnumber men in a number of junior non-manual occupations. Name three such occupations.
4 Why are opportunities for women in the coal and coke industry different in the USA?
5 What is the difference between vertical and horizontal occupational segregation?

---

4 Age stratification

I was born in Cyprus and lived there for ten years. In common with other Moslem countries the Turkish Cypriots bring their children up to have respect for others especially their elders. I believe Japanese people also have this exaggerated respect custom. As soon as a child is able to walk and talk it has to adopt certain ways of behaving such as the ceremonial kissing of elders' hands when visiting.

(Mike Aziz in *Changing Childhood*, edited by M. Hoyles)

In traditional societies the old are often the most powerful figures. There are no books to refer to, so people consult their elders for knowledge. The elderly are thought to have wisdom and the elders of the tribe or village are asked to settle disputes.

In fast changing modern societies, youth and adaptability are given greater value. The mass media, such as advertising, and fashion equate good looks with youth. Magazines are full of tips on how to stay looking young. And so respect for the old declines. The middle-aged in America feel that they suffer unfair job discrimination: inexperienced workers in their twenties are preferred by employers and this has led to campaigns for laws to combat **ageism**.

Both old and young alike tend to lack the status which comes from financial independence. Children depend on their parents for pocket money and pensioners may be entirely dependent on the government for their income, from the state pension. Housewives without a paid job may similarly depend on their husbands for a weekly allowance. Dependent groups such as these have to be supported from the earnings of the working population.

A gathering of village elders.

One way in which these groups lack power is that they often have no independent means of transport such as ready access to the family car. While they queue at the bus stop with students and the low paid, those who belong to the more powerful groups in society drive past in their own cars. British Rail and coach firms recognise that some groups have lower income by offering concessions such as Railcards which give cheaper fares.

5   Economic stratification – Marx and capitalism

Karl Marx, the founder of **communism**, put forward a view of history that has had a tremendous influence on the way that we think and live in the modern world. Many societies, the communist states such as Russia, China and Cuba, are supposed to be actually based on his ideas. And in non-communist societies there are a number of quite sizeable political parties that follow the teachings of Marx.

Ruling classes and subject classes in history

Karl Marx, 1818 to 1883, spent much of his life studying history. His studies led him to the conclusion that since ancient times all societies have consisted of two main classes whose struggle with each other has led to great social changes. As Marx said, 'All history is the history of class struggles'.

The two main classes are the **ruling class** and the **subject class** and although the nature of these two classes has changed, the basic division between those who have power and those who do not has always existed. According to Marx, in the ancient world the two classes were master and slave, in feudal times they were lord and serf and in modern capitalist society these two classes are **capitalists** and **workers**.

One major event in the calendar of the rich is the Henley Regatta.

Class and economic production

For Marx, class is based on economic position. The ruling class are those who own the **forces of production**, things such as land, tools and machines which are used to produce wealth. The oppressed or subject class is formed from those who possess nothing but their ability to work.

The forces of production have changed in the past which is why classes have changed. In feudal times the forces of production consisted mainly of land, so the two rival classes were formed by those who owned land (the lords) and those who did not (the serfs).

In industrial societies the main forces of production now consist of factories and machines, which are known as **capital**. Marx believed that society would polarise so that everyone would end up on one of two sides:

- Capitalists: the ruling classes who own capital either as bosses and managers or as wealthy holders of shares in big companies – Marx called these the **bourgeoisie**.
- Workers: 'wage slaves' who live by selling their labour to the capitalist employing classes – Marx called these the **proletariat**.

Class conflict and communist revolution

Marx claimed that a ruling class and a subject class would always be in conflict with one another. The reason for this is clear. The ruling class always want more wealth to be produced by the subject class, while the subject class always demand a fairer share of the product of their own labour. This explains why there are strikes and conflict in the workplace: the workers want higher wages while the capitalists or employers want to keep wages as low as possible so that their profits can be as high as possible.

Marx believed that the end to this conflict would only come with the abolition of all classes and the creation of an equal, communist society. He predicted that in the near future the workers would overthrow the capitalist order and construct a communist world. This prediction has not so far proved to be correct.

Conclusion

Apart from nations with communist governments, there have in the past been a number of attempts to set up classless societies. Apart from the kibbutzim described in Chapter 4, examples include communities inspired by the ideas of thinkers such as Kropotkin, Tolstoy, Robert Owen and William Morris. In striving for equality these societies have tried to abolish all types of stratification so that everyone is on the same social level.

Activities

1 What do you see as the main problems that would obstruct an attempt to create a society in which everyone is fully equal?

2 Find out the names of the nations with communist or Marxist governments in
   (a) Eastern Europe,
   (b) Asia,
   (c) Africa,
   (d) Central America.

3 In *Animal Farm* George Orwell described a society composed of different types of animals.
   (a) Find out how that society was stratified. In other words, which animals formed the top social strata and which strata did the other animals belong to?
   (b) What was the basis of the system of stratification in *Animal Farm*?

GCSE question from Midland Examining Group 1988

(a) Describe *three* ways in which women are disadvantaged at work. (6)

(b) Explain the reasons given by sociologists for inequality between men and women at work. (8)

CHAPTER 9 | Social class in modern Britain

Does social class matter?

This chapter looks at how social classes are defined; how they are changing; and at the movement of individuals and occupational groups from one class to another. We also consider whether there is any evidence to support the sort of generalisations made in the following chart.

Case study: stereotyped views of class

The middle classes	*The working classes*
• live in detached or semi-detached houses which they own themselves,	• live in terraced houses or flats rented from the council,
• eat lunch, go to the loo, drink in the saloon or lounge bar,	• eat dinner, go to the toilet, drink in the public bar,
• read *The Times*, *Telegraph*, *Mail*, *Express* and *Guardian*,	• read the *Sun*, *Mirror* and *Star*,
• enjoy tennis, rugger, squash, golf, sailing and bridge,	• enjoy darts, football, boxing, dog racing and bingo,
• breast-feed their babies,	• bottle-feed their babies,
• shop in Sainsburys, Mothercare, Benetton, Habitat and Laura Ashley,	• shop in Tescos, the Co-op, and MFI as well as from catalogues,
• wear pure cotton and pure wool,	• wear polyester and acrylic,
• enjoy drama and documentaries on BBC2 and Channel 4,	• enjoy soap operas and Benny Hill on ITV,
• undress in front of their children and don't lock the bathroom door,	• turn out the light before they undress in front of their wives,
• give their toddlers apple juice and whole-meal biscuits for snacks,	• give their toddlers sweets, crisps and fizzy drinks,
• eat cake with a fork,	• turn their forks over to eat peas,
• volunteer for the PTA.	• keep away from Parents' Evenings.

'Cut-price' furniture and 'distinctive' furniture may appeal to different social classes.

1   The Registrar-General's categories of social class

Who is the Registrar-General?

He is the government official in charge of:

- the registration of all births, deaths and marriages,
- the collection of census statistics when the whole population is surveyed every ten years.

The census has been conducted every ten years since 1801, except for 1941, and since 1911 the population has been categorised into social classes from I to V.

How does he decide which class category to put us into?

The Registrar-General has a list of over 20,000 jobs which are grouped into 223 occupational units. These are then allocated to one of six categories on the basis of the: (a) income, (b) status, (c) skill and (d) educational level of each type of job.

A dustman may earn more than a vicar but the dustman is in class V while a vicar is in class I because the vicar has had a far longer training and is considered to be a more respected member of the community.

Activity

Try to find out the length of training (including years of higher education) required by six of the following jobs:

Registrar-General's category

I	Professional	doctor, lawyer
II	Intermediate	teacher, nurse
IIIN	Skilled non-manual	travel agent, typist
IIIM	Skilled manual	electrician, hairdresser
IV	Semi-skilled manual	sewing machinist, farm worker
V	Unskilled manual	office cleaner, labourer

Working-class housing in Ebbw Vale.

Working-class housing in Kirkby.

Spacious housing in Bishop's Avenue, Hampstead, London.

Why is class III split into two?

This happened in 1970 for two reasons:

1 Class III contained almost half the population,
2 Sociologists were already dividing it to show how our society is split in two like this:

Middle classes	*Working classes*
Classes I, II, IIIN	Classes IIIM, IV, V
Non-manual jobs or jobs mainly involving 'brain' i.e. mental work	**Manual jobs** or jobs mainly involving 'brawn' i.e. physical work
White collar jobs where collar and tie or smart blouse are generally considered appropriate dress	**Blue collar jobs** where denim overalls are often needed since the work involves getting your hands dirty

N.B. The word 'manual' comes from the Latin word *manus* meaning 'hand'.

Blue collar workers.

A white collar worker.

The connection between class and educational qualifications

These figures for men aged twenty to sixty-nine in 1978 should bear some relationship to your results from the exercise above which asks for the length of training required by six different jobs:

Registrar-General's social class:	I	II	IIIN	IIIM	IV	V
Percentage in each class who went beyond A-level to higher education	80	25	24	4	1	2
Percentage with no educational qualifications	2	31	32	53	75	85

(Source: General Household Survey, 1978)

2　Criticisms of the Registrar-General's classification

The Registrar-General's categories of social class have a number of defects. The following problems have been pointed out:

1　IIIN jobs are sometimes described as **routine non-manual** and a worker at the check-out till in a supermarket is IIIN even though this work is far less skilled than the butcher or baker in class IIIM. So jobs higher up the classification are not necessarily more skilled.

2　Bus drivers in class IIIM could well have a high social status in their communities based on positions other than their jobs. They could for example be magistrates, councillors, shop stewards, churchwardens or the treasurers of sports clubs.

3　Section 4 of this chapter describes how occupations have been moved up or down, for example in 1961 postmen were moved from III to IV. Not everyone would agree with these decisions.

4　Pensioners and the unemployed are categorised according to their previous jobs, children by their parents' work and a housewife's class is fixed by her husband's occupation. Classifying housewives in this way has been condemned as sexist.

5　By dividing the whole population into middle class (I, II, IIIN) and working class (IIIM, IV, V), we lose sight of upper-class groups such as the aristocracy and other **elites** which hold great power in society.

6　Marxists argue that the Registrar-General's categories obscure the basic division in society between capitalists and workers.

Some alternatives to the Registrar-General's view of social class are given in the final section of this chapter.

Objective and subjective social class

Using the Registrar-General's classification is an objective way of deciding on someone's class on the basis of his or her job. Another way is to ask people to assign themselves to the class to which they *feel* they belong; this second method gives you their subjective or **self-assigned class** position. For example, some people with manual jobs may identify with the middle class if they have a mortgage or if they have relatives with non-manual jobs.

Activities

Typical occupations in each of the Registrar-General's six social classes:

Class I   accountant, architect, chemist, engineer, optician, scientist, solicitor, surveyor, vet.

Class II   chiropodist, farmer, laboratory technician, journalist, actor, publican.

Class IIIN   cashier, bank clerk, shop assistant, sales representative, estate agent, photographer, police constable, model.

Class IIIM   bus driver, bricklayer, carpenter, cook, plumber, printer, upholsterer, shoemaker, miner (generally crafts traditionally learnt by an apprenticeship of several years).

Class IV   bar tender, bus conductor, hospital orderly, telephonist, gardener, supermarket shelf-filler.

Class V   chimney sweep, railway porter, messenger, kitchen hand, window cleaner.

1 (a) Using these examples above as a guide, look through the 'situations vacant' advertisements in local and national newspapers for jobs which give salary details and list three jobs in each of the Registrar-General's six categories. Next to each job give the weekly income. Annual salary can be converted to weekly income by dividing by 50 – this is easily done by doubling the figure and knocking two noughts off, for example:

£12,000 per year = approx. £240 per week, £7,000 p.a. = £140 p.w.

(b) Plot your results on a chart like this:

Jobs in class

```
I                                           xxx
II                                      xxx
IIIN                               xxx
IIIM                         xxx
IV                     xxx
V                xxx
```
Gross wage
per week
       £50 100 150 200 250 300 350

Do your results form a pattern like the one in the chart above?

2 (a) Select a variety of twelve jobs from the list above and ask several people to rank them in order of social importance from first to twelfth.
(b) Did they disagree very much about the importance of any of the jobs?
(c) Which occupations did they have the most difficulty in ranking?

3 'Snakes and ladders' – social mobility

Within the social class system we can distinguish two types of **social mobility** or movement. People can move up or down in the class system, as individuals or else as part of a group.

Group mobility

The chart on page 122 shows how certain occupational groups have been re-classified in different census years:

Occupational groups which have been moved up.

Year		From	To
1961	University lecturers	II	I
1961	Aircraft pilots, engineers	III	II
1981	Firemen	IIIM	IIIN

Occupational groups which have been moved down

Year		From	To
1931	Clerks	II	III
1961	Draughtsmen	II	III
1961	Postmen, telephone operators	III	IV
1961	Lorrydrivers' mates	IV	V
1981	Investment analysts, company secretaries	I	II
1981	Undertakers, waiters	IIIN	IIIM

Case study: **The Black-Coated Workers**

We have seen how clerks were moved from Class II to III in 1931. David Lockwood's book *The Black-Coated Worker* (1958) gives the following sorts of reasons for the decline in the social position of clerks over the last one hundred years or so:

Clerks in the mid-nineteenth century

High status:

- few offices and few clerical jobs;
- few able to read and write, so only the well-educated middle-class could be clerks;
- usually men, writing copper-plate script with quill pens at high desks which emphasised their importance;
- regarded as a 'good middle-class job'.

Well paid; i.e. a good **market situation**, in the job market.

A work situation allowing a fair degree of power. Often working independently, but in a close relationship with their employers.

Clerks in the mid-twentieth century

Low status:

- many offices and many clerical jobs;
- due to mass education and mass literacy most school-leavers could do simple filing jobs;
- over 75 per cent of clerks are now women, compared to 21 per cent in 1900;
- a good middle-class job now means a university-educated profession.

Clerks in a DHSS office often earn less than they pay out to many claimants each week.

Little power at work. Experiencing proletarianisation – becoming absorbed into the working class; signs may be working conditions or actions, such as joining trade unions and voting Labour.

Activity

Since the 1960s there has been a rapid expansion of trade unions with members in middle-class occupations such as office work and teaching. Name some of these white-collar unions.

Office clerks and postmen are two occupational groups which have been reclassified by the Registrar-General.

Individual mobility

There are a number of different types of individual social mobility:

1 Horizontal mobility For example, a plumber who becomes a carpenter has moved occupations but is still in class IIIM. He or she has moved sideways rather than up or down.

2 Vertical mobility: upward or downward For example, the bricklayer who becomes a property-developer, or a property-developer who becomes a bricklayer.

3 Inter-generational mobility 'Inter' means 'between' and a gardener's daughter who becomes a lawyer is an example of upward social mobility between the two generations.

4 Intra-generational mobility 'Intra' means 'within' and a window-cleaner who becomes a record-producer has been socially mobile within his or her own lifetime.

Avenues of individual upward social mobility

There are a number of ways someone might ascend the social class ladder:

1 Marriage A miner's daughter who marries a stockbroker moves up from the working class to the middle class.

2 Education A dustman's son who qualifies as a doctor has moved up from class V to class I.

3 Promotion An assembly-line worker in a car factory who is promoted to be a foreman and then progresses through middle-management to become a director has risen from manual to non-manual categories.

4 Luck A train driver who wins the pools might use the money to become a restaurant owner.

Opportunities for individual upward mobility have been created by the changing distribution of occupations.

Percentage of occupied men in each social class

	1921 (%)	1981 (%)
I	4	6
II	11	16
IIIN	9	18
Percentage of occupied men in the middle class	24	40
IIIM	40	38
IV	18	16
V	18	5
Percentage of occupied men in the working class	76	60

(Sources: 1921 census and 1981 Labour Forces Survey)

These figures show that the percentage of the workforce in low skilled manual jobs has been shrinking while the percentage employed in non-manual, white-collar jobs has been expanding. This process has created many opportunities for the children of unskilled labourers to find jobs with greater skills and rewards. Indeed, if the son of a ditch-digger wanted the same job as his father he might well find that such work was now done by the drivers of JCB excavators.

As a result of the introduction of new technology, many low-skilled jobs have disappeared. This is partly why unemployment amongst unqualified school leavers is so high. The first report of the Youth Cohort Study, in 1986, found that 40 per cent of those who left school with no examination passes were unemployed a year later. The Youth Opportunities Scheme (YOPS) and Youth Training Scheme (YTS) programmes have been introduced by the government to deal with this type of unemployment.

Societies with differing degrees of social mobility

A closed society	*An open society*
Social status or position is generally ascribed, or fixed, at birth.	It is possible to achieve a higher position in society than one's parents.
Offers little chance for upward mobility.	Offers lots of scope for upward mobility.
e.g. 1 the caste system, 2 apartheid, 3 feudal England, where only a few peasants moved up the social pyramid by joining the army or the church.	e.g. 1 the USA, where the 'log cabin to White House' story is a part of the American Dream, 2 the UK, with self-made men such as Sir John Moores and Alan Sugar. Respectively, they left school at fourteen and fifteen; to be a messenger boy and a barrow boy; they founded Littlewoods Pools and Amstrad computers; their personal fortunes, in 1989, were £1,700 million and £432 million.

How far does the American Dream of an open society match the reality of the modern USA? It is true that blacks (for example Jesse Jackson), women (for example Geraldine Ferraro) and Catholics (for example the Kennedys) have all achieved fame as politicians in the Democrat Party. But it is recognised that you start off in life with a higher ascribed status in the USA if you are a male WASP: white, Anglo-Saxon (rather than of Mediterranean European origin) and Protestant.

4   Social class, life-style and life-chances

Class differences are reflected in nearly every aspect of social life in Britain, from one's accent and style of dress to attitudes and leisure pursuits. **Life-style** refers to the differences between the social groups. These range from possessions such as houses and furniture to social activities such as playing squash and going to dog races. As well as these visible indicators of class position, sociologists often emphasise the way that one's class affects one's **life-chances**, such as one's educational opportunities and one's health prospects.

The British people have enjoyed great improvements in their living conditions compared to previous generations, but an enduring aspect of British society is the extent to which class differences still persist. In other words, class V never catches up with class I and the considerable gap between them remains just as large as ever. Indeed, there is evidence that the gap has been widening: in 1972 the death rate for men aged 25 to 44 in classes IV and V was 90 per cent above their equivalents in classes I and II, but by 1982 the excess had risen to almost 120 per cent, so that they ran well over twice the risk of dying young.

Middle- and working-class leisure activities: whippet racing in Ilkeston, Derbyshire and yachting in the Adriatic Sea.

Case study: social class and health

Class	I	II	IIIN	IIIM	IV	V
Percentage of adult males who smoke cigarettes, 1984	17	29	30	40	45	49
Percentage of adult females who smoke, 1984	15	29	28	37	37	36
Percentage of babies born weighing less than 3,000 grams, 1983	21	21	22	24	28	29
Infant mortality rate, per 1,000, 1981	7.7	7.9	8.5	10.3	12.6	15.8
Percentage of adult males covered by private health insurance, 1982	20	19	11	4	2	4

(Source: Office of Population and Census Surveys)

Accidents in childhood In 1982 Penguin published *Inequalities in Health*, the report of a working party under Sir Douglas Black. This was set up by the Labour Government in 1977 to review differences in health between the social classes. The Black Report found that among child pedestrians the risk of death from being hit by a motor vehicle is about six times greater in class IV compared to class I. For accidental death caused by fires, falls and drowning, the gap between the classes is even larger. The following explanations were suggested for this pattern:

1 Parents in higher occupational classes are more likely to be able to let their children play safely within sight or earshot.
2 The children of semi-skilled and unskilled workers are more likely to be left to their own devices during school holidays and out of school hours.
3 Poorer homes are likely to have less safe furnishings and less safe domestic appliances such as heaters.
4 Poorer mothers lead more stressful lives which leave them less well equipped to provide continuous and vigilant protection for their children.

Data-response exercise: social class and health

1 What percentage of men with skilled manual occupations had private health insurance in 1982?
2 Are men or women more likely to smoke in class II?
3 What evidence is there to support the following statement: 'Babies of unskilled workers are twice as likely to die as those of professional couples'?
4 What evidence is there to support the Health Education Council's claim that 'It is known beyond any doubt that smoking can harm the developing baby, by holding back its growth'?
5 How does the risk of death from road accidents vary between children of different social classes?

5 Alternatives to the Registrar-General's view of class

A modern Marxist analysis of social class

Marx emphasised that the capitalist class consists of those who own capital, the means of production. One recent version of Marxist class analysis emphasises that the capitalist class also consists of those who have three sorts of power. The following chart indicates how different occupations may possess one or more of these sorts of power:

	Has control over the investment decisions of companies; the power to close old factories or open new ones	Has control over the machinery used in production; the power to speed up the production line	Has control over labour; the power to hire, fire and manage workers
Company directors	yes	yes	yes
Senior executives	only partly	yes	yes
Middle managers	no	limited	some
Foremen, supervisors	no	no	limited
Low-level employees, manual and non-manual	no	no	no

We can draw several conclusions from this sort of structure:

1 The division between manual and non-manual workers is not as important as the division between company directors, the capitalist class, and those employees who have no power to control industry.

2 The second, third and fourth groups in the structure have contradictory class locations because they share characteristics with both the most powerful and the least powerful groups.

3 A major aim of socialists and trade unionists may be to alter this uneven distribution of power and control.

Details of these ideas can be found in *Class, Crisis and the State* by E. Wright (1978).

Looking further at the groups in the above table we might ask how far these unequal degrees of control in the workplace are reflected in

- inequalities of ownership of wealth, such as property and shares in companies. (We look at this in Chapter 15 on poverty.)
- inequalities of conditions at work such as provision of pensions, sick pay, holidays, fringe benefits, chances of promotion and a healthy working environment.
- inequalities of life-chances, ranging from health and housing to the educational prospects and opportunities for social mobility of those whose parents belong to the five different groups.

Activity

Find out the contractual conditions of several contrasting jobs, either from job advertisements, employees or employers. How do the jobs differ with regard to pay, hours, breaks during the day, holidays, sick pay, pensions, perks (such as company car or staff discount), and working environment, for example heating, privacy, access to lockers, toilets and canteens? You will get the most detail by preparing a thorough check-list and then interviewing several workers.

Divisions within the working class: embourgeoisement and the underclass

The above analysis stresses the similarities between the class positions of manual and non-manual employees. This view is supported by the idea of **proletarianisation** which describes how non-manual occupations, such as clerks, have become absorbed into the working class. In contrast, the two concepts of an **underclass** and of **embourgeoisement** emphasise the divisions within the working class.

Embourgeoisement   This term was used in the 1950s and 1960s to help explain the **deviant voting** of the third or so of the working class who voted Conservative. Embourgeoisement was used to describe those affluent (well-paid) workers who adopt bourgeois (middle-class) values and life-styles. In Chapter 14 we look at how characteristics of the 'new working class', such as home ownership, may influence voting.

The underclass and the dual labour market   Some manual workers, such as engineering workers in power stations, have obtained a fairly affluent life-style, partly from the strength of their bargaining position in powerful trade unions. On the other hand, the trade union movement has, to some extent, failed to adequately represent the needs of groups such as black workers, female workers and the unemployed: section 4 of Chapter 7 has described how black workers are often given inferior types of employment and section 3 of Chapter 8 has described how women are often concentrated into low paid types of work.

The term 'underclass' has been used to describe those who suffer discrimination in employment and who work in the lowest paid, least secure and most unpleasant jobs. This is similar to Marx's idea of the **lumpen proletariat**. He considered this to be the lowest stratum of capitalist society, consisting of the poor and unorganised members of the working class who have irregular employment or who are unemployable.

The groups who belong to the underclass are also said to belong to the secondary labour market. The idea of a dual labour market divides the market for jobs into two basic categories:

1   The **primary labour market** consists of jobs with high wages and good career structures.
2   The **secondary labour market** consists of unstable, low paid employment where there is little chance to acquire skills.

To a certain extent, these categories fit the idea of a dual economy, with a two-tier workforce of **core** and **periphery** workers, which is discussed in Chapter 16.

Conclusion: How different types of stratification cut across the class structure

Chapter 8 showed how power and social status in a society may depend on whether one is black or white, Brahmin or Sudra, Protestant or Catholic, male or female, young or old. In modern Britain differences of race, religion, sex or age can cut across social class positions based simply on occupation.

Ethnicity or gender may possibly be more significant than whether one has a manual or non-manual job or is unemployed. Different employers in Britain have been shown to discriminate against the elderly, against homosexuals, or against the physically handicapped. Job applicants who are young, black and female may be at a multiple disadvantage with certain prejudiced employers.

The ideas in the last section of this chapter indicate that the patterns of stratification and social class in Britain are far more complicated than the straightforward picture which is offered by the Registrar-General's occupational classification of socio-economic groups.

GCSE question from Midland Examining Group 1988

Percentage of population in each social class

Social class	1931	1971
I	1.8	5.0
II	12.0	18.2
III	47.8	50.5
IV	25.5	18.0
V	12.9	8.4

THE FUTURE OF BABY M

'To be born into the working classes is to

be seriously disadvantaged . . . it means

the certainty of poorer nutrition, poorer housing,

worse health and a shorter life'

(An article caption)

(a) (i) List two ways in which the working classes may be seriously disadvantaged. (2)

(ii) According to the table, which two social classes have declined as a proportion between 1931 and 1971? (2)

(b) Name two groups of people, other than the working class, who are disadvantaged in our society. (2)

(c) Explain three ways in which a person may change his or her social class. (6)

(d) 'Everyone has an equal opportunity to get to the top in Britain today.' To what extent do you agree or disagree with this statement? Give reasons for your answer. (8)

CHAPTER 10 | Education

Case study: the response of the Indians of the Six Nations to a suggestion that they send boys to a college in Pennsylvania, 1744:

But you, who are wise, must know that different nations have different conceptions of things and will therefore not take it amiss, if our ideas of this kind of education happen not to be the same as yours. We have had some experience of it. Several of our young people were formerly brought up at the colleges of the northern provinces: they were instructed well in all your sciences; but, when they came back to us, they were bad runners, ignorant of every means of living in the woods . . . neither were they fit for hunters, warriors, nor councillors, they were totally good for nothing.

We are, however, not the less obliged by your kind offer, though we decline accepting it; and, to show our grateful sense of it, if the gentlemen of Virginia will send us a dozen of their sons we will take care of their education, instruct them in all we know, and make men of them.

Education in the broadest sense means the process of acquiring knowledge and understanding. This occurs throughout our lives as a result of a large variety of influences. We learn from our parents, from our friends, from travel, from observing what goes on around us and we learn from all our experiences of life. All this learning and development of the mind occurs naturally, as an inevitable consequence of living, without any direct teaching. And until comparatively recently, this informal education was considered to be all that the average person needed.

During the nineteenth century, however, leading figures in British society increasingly felt that informal education was no longer adequate and that the government should provide compulsory schooling for all. Today, almost everyone in Britain experiences **formal education** – that is, learning particular subjects from qualified teachers in organised institutions called schools.

In 1989–90 government spending on education was £15,700,000,000. Schooling has become a central part of our way of life. In this chapter we will be looking at our educational arrangements and at their connection with other aspects of society. First we look at the origin of our state schooling system.

A lesson in a Victorian elementary school.

1   Why was schooling made compulsory in 1880?

Compulsory attendance in elementary schools was first introduced in Prussia in 1763. In 1870 a national system of basic schooling for every child was set up in England. By 1880 attendance was compulsory between the ages of five and ten. In 1893 the school-leaving age was raised to eleven and in 1899 it was raised to twelve.

We will now look at the purposes of making this elementary schooling compulsory.

To meet the needs of industry

As the complexity of industry in the 1800s increased, factories needed literate and numerate workers who could read and count. By 1880 Britain was no longer so clearly the world's foremost industrial nation and her position was strongly challenged by Germany and the USA. As William Forster MP said in introducing the 1870 Education Act:

> Upon the speedy provision of education depends our national power ... if we are to hold our position among the nations of the world, we must make up for the smallness of our numbers by increasing the intellectual force of the individual.

To 'mind' children while their parents go out to work

In 1849 T. Beggs complained (in his *Enquiry into the Extent and Causes of Juvenile Depravity*) that, with many working-class mothers out at work: 'Young children are left at home under very inadequate conduct and almost without restraint left to play at will and to expand into every lawless form.' The dual concerns of the authorities were to keep the children off the streets and to enable both parents to go out to work.

To prevent the exploitation of child labour

While the new factory system demanded the labour of both parents, reformers such as Lord Shaftesbury had severely restricted the employment of children with a number of Factory Acts since the early nineteenth century. But they called for schooling to be compulsory in order to stop the continued exploitation of young children who were employed, for example, to climb up inside and sweep chimneys.

To educate for democracy

Worried by the example of the French Revolution of 1789, observers such as Dr J. Kay-Shuttleworth wrote in 1832 that 'The preservation of internal peace ... depends on the education of the working class'. Six years later, he set up the first training college for teachers in Britain. In 1867 most working-class men were allowed to vote for the first time. They now formed the majority of voters which explains why Robert Lowe MP said, 'We must educate our masters'.

To civilise the 'heathen masses'

Lord Shaftesbury spoke in 1843 of girls in mining districts who 'drink, swear, fight, smoke, whistle, sing and care for nobody'. He urged the necessity of education for the children of the 'dangerous classes' whom he called 'a fearful multitude of untutored savages'.

The first schools for the urban poor in the early 1800s had been set up by the Bible Societies. These organisations saw their mission, not only across the Empire but also in Britain itself, to convert non believers, or heathens as they were called, to Christianity and also to instruct them in the manners of civilised, polite society.

To enable individuals to develop fully

Teachers have always tried to help pupils develop their minds and bodies to their full potential. In other words, teachers want pupils to develop strength of character, individuality of personality and a range of hobbies and interests.

Summary: the functions of education

The above outline of the historical reasons for our state schooling system suggests the following functions of education:

1 socialisation: passing on culture and values,
2 preparation for work: teaching basic skills required by industry such as reading, writing and arithmetic and 'sifting and sorting' pupils by exams,
3 personal: developing individual potential,
4 political: preparation for adult citizenship,
5 social control: instilling respectable values into idle youth while their parents go to work.

2 The changing curriculum

The 1988 Education Reform Act

The 1988 Education Reform Act made a number of major changes to the education system, from testing for all seven-year-olds to new systems of financing for polytechnics and universities.

Activity

Read through the summary of the 1988 Education Reform Act below. Try to decide (a) how each of the changes relates to the general functions of education, as listed above, and (b) which of the changes relate to the political ideas of the Conservative Party, such as competition and freedom of choice.

Open enrolment, opting out and control of school budgets

- Parents have the right to send their children to the school of their choice – as long as it is not physically full. Schools now have an incentive to compete for pupils since unpopular schools will decline and close.

- Parents can vote for their childrens' school to opt out from the control of their local education authority (the local council). Such schools will become **grant-maintained** (independent, with funding direct from central government).

- Governors are to control the running of their schools. They are to be free to use resources within their budgets according to their school's particular needs and priorities. Governors will thus be free to decide the numbers of teaching and non-teaching staff.

National Curriculum and testing

- All five- to sixteen-year-olds in England are to take the **core subjects** of English, maths and science. The other compulsory **foundation subjects** are history, geography, technology, music, art and PE and, at secondary level, a modern foreign language.

- The government are to lay down attainment targets, programmes of study and assessment arrangements for these core and foundation subjects. Pupils must be assessed at the ages of 7, 11, 14 and 16.

Religious education

- Religious education is part of the basic, compulsory curriculum but it is not a foundation subject and so does not carry with it requirements for assessment and testing.

- Right wing Conservatives in the House of Lords successfully amended the Act so that schools must have a daily act of collective worship which is 'wholly or mainly of a broadly Christian character'.

Vocational education (providing the skills needed for certain jobs)

- **City technology colleges** are to extend the choice of secondary schools in the inner cities. They are to have extra funds from industrial sponsors and to provide a curriculum with an emphasis on science and technology.

- **City technology colleges of the arts** are to specialise in arts technology, film and video and the range of technical skills that support the arts industry.

- **The Technical and Vocational Education Initiative** (TVEI) provides extra money so that schools and colleges can make lessons more practical and relevant to adult life and work. TVEI is available to pupils aged fourteen and upwards.

- Pupils are to leave secondary schools with **records of achievement** which cover all types of accomplishments, including practical and social skills, as well as more academic successes.

The options at age sixteen

- A and AS levels are the normal route to higher education courses.

- **The Youth Training Scheme** (YTS) is a two-year programme. In 1989 it was fast becoming the normal route into a job for those who left full-time education at sixteen.

- **The Certificate of Pre-Vocational Education** (CPVE) is normally a one-year course. It is for those who have not yet decided on a career. It offers the chance to gain skills and have practical work experience. It may be combined with new or retake GCSE courses.

- Job-related courses can be followed in colleges. Subjects range from engineering and computing to textiles, printing and hairdressing. These courses are mainly offered by the Business and Technical Education Council (BTEC), the City and Guilds of London Institute (CGLI) and the Royal Society of Arts (RSA).

The hidden curriculum

There are many things which pupils learn in school which are not directly taught or are not a part of the timetable of official lessons. The term **hidden curriculum** is used to refer to what pupils learn indirectly (and often unconsciously) from the manner in which the school is organised and from teachers' expectations of pupils.

In most schools this hidden curriculum includes:

1   punctuality: pupils are expected to arrive at lessons, assemblies and registration on time;
2   obedience to authority: pupils are expected to do what they are told without argument;
3   the value of hard work: pupils are constantly reminded throughout their school lives of the importance of working hard and getting on;
4   appropriate dress: pupils are expected to dress suitably and 'respectably', especially when there is a school uniform;
5   co-operation: 'fitting in' and getting on with others is often impressed on pupils in school;
6   honesty: pupils are encouraged not to lie and steal.

These values and others, which make up the hidden curriculum, are communicated to pupils by lectures in assemblies, by remarks from teachers and by punishments and rewards.

Criticisms of the hidden curriculum

Most of us would accept that it is part of the job of schools to socialise the young into the sorts of values listed above. But some critics argue that the hidden curriculum goes much further, that it encourages pupils to become passive, unquestioning mental slaves. They argue that society directs schools to crush individuality because society needs an obedient workforce – workers who will do what they are told to do.

Hargreaves has explained how space and time are part of the hidden curriculum and we can note similarities with factory life. Of space he says:

> It is only teachers who are free to move where they want and when they want. They have free access to what is the closest to being pupil territory, their lavatories. Even territory which is officially shared

What aspects of the hidden curriculum are shown here?

between teachers and pupils, the classroom, is frequently termed 'my room' by the teacher, who has complete control over entry, exits and movements within the room. In a very real sense, then, the pupils have no legitimate territory of their own. Wherever they are, they are subject to surveillance and control. Wherever pupils are in school, they must be ready to be called to account, to explain and justify their location. Thus pupils in corridors must always be 'going somewhere' lest they be accused of 'loitering' with or without intent. In the allocation, use and control of space in school, the teacher's power and authority are constantly represented and reinforced.

Of time he says:

In school, as in the factory, time belongs to those who wield power and authority. And the idea of time conveyed in the school is the same as that conveyed in the factory – the idea that 'time is money'. Just as pupils own no territory, so they have little time they can call their own. Pupils must be ready to give an account of their use of time, for of all pupil sins *wasting* time is one of the most common, and the seriousness of the offence rises if the pupils waste not only their own time but that of the teacher as well. Good children, like good workers, do not waste time. In school, time belongs to the school; in the factory, time belongs to the factory.

(Adapted from *Power and the Paracurriculum* by D. Hargreaves)

Critics, such as I. Illich in *Deschooling Society*, argue that the organisation of the school is designed to produce passive individuals. Thus, for example, pupils are given little choice over the subjects available and little or no choice about learning methods and the structure of the school day.

Case study: a progressive showpiece comprehensive school

The following extract is from a *Sunday Times* story (26 February 1978) which describes the 1,500-pupil Sutton Centre School in Nottinghamshire, claimed to be a bold experiment of progressive ideas put into action:

The school has no uniforms, no bells, no staffrooms and no O-levels. [All pupils did mode III CSE exams designed by the school.] Children can call teachers by their Christian names and detention, lines and the cane have been abolished. There are no set playtimes or playgrounds; children take their breaks in one of the school's 12 coffee bars when they feel like it.

Sutton is the most advanced example in Britain of a 'community school' where children and adults rub shoulders night and day. The school is part of a town centre complex that includes an ice-rink, a bowls centre, a theatre, a sports hall and a day centre for old and handicapped people. Mothers are encouraged to join lessons. The children take the old people shopping, go to the theatre for drama lessons and dance on the ice-rink at lunchtimes. . . .

On most criteria the school is a roaring success. The attendance rate is well over 90 per cent. The head has never had to suspend a child. . . . Most remarkable of all, it has an optional two-hour evening session for children and adults and more than 60 per cent of the pupils attend.

3 The tripartite system and comprehensive schools

In 1900 only one in seventy pupils went to secondary schools. The 1902 Education Act allowed local authorities to provide secondary schools but it was not until 1944 that secondary education was proposed for all pupils. Before 1944 all pupils stayed at school up to the age of fourteen but most were at elementary schools.

The 1944 Education Act

This Act set up the **tripartite system**, so called because it recommended three types of secondary school for all pupils to attend from the age of eleven. The main points of the Act can be summarised by the 'three threes':

1 The three stages of education:
   primary from five to eleven,
   secondary from eleven,
   tertiary, meaning colleges of further education, polytechnics and universities.

2 The three types of secondary school:
   grammar schools for the most able,
   technical schools for training in practical skills,
   secondary modern schools for 70 per cent or so of pupils.

3 The three ways of deciding which type of educational institution a person should attend:
   age,
   aptitude,
   ability.

For example:

- Age: an eleven-year-old would have to take the '11+' examination to be selected for one of the three types of secondary school.
- Aptitude: those who had shown a talent for 'working with their hands' might be selected for secondary technical schools with an emphasis on training workshops.
- Ability: those who failed the 11+ could not go to the grammar schools, unless there were spare places.

The 1944 Act was clearly a major step forward in the development of our education system because, for the first time, free secondary education was provided for all. Also, it genuinely aimed at creating 'equality of opportunity'. In other words, the Act set out to ensure that all pupils had a fair chance to develop their potential. But critics soon argued that selection by the 11+ examination was not fair at all. The 11+ examination, taken in the last year of junior school, usually consisted of an intelligence test based on questions in English, maths and general knowledge. Since those who passed the 11+ were mainly middle class, critics argued that the examination was in fact an obstacle to equality of opportunity.

Criticisms of the 11+ system

1   The whole basis of the 11+ examination has been rejected by those who claim that 'intelligence' cannot be defined and measured.

2   Even its supporters admitted that the 11+ had a 10 per cent margin of error and while late-developers were supposed to be able to transfer to grammar schools at the age of twelve or thirteen, few in fact did so.

3   Middle-class children of the same intelligence as working-class children had an advantage because of their home background. They were often coached for the examination by their parents as well as by the teachers in the primary schools in middle-class areas. 'Cramming' books could be bought which rehearsed typical 11+ questions such as 'What is the name for a family of lions?' (Answer: a pride).

4   The examination reinforced class divisions by providing two distinct types of education: academic grammar schools for mainly middle-class pupils and secondary modern schooling for mainly working-class pupils; very few technical schools were provided.

5   These two types of school were supposed to have **parity of esteem** or equal status but in fact grammar schools often had better teachers and facilities.

6   75 per cent or so were labelled as 11+ failures for the rest of their lives and their education was seen as inferior.

7   Before the introduction of CSE examinations in 1965 and before the school leaving age was raised to sixteen in 1972, most of the 75 per cent at secondary modern schools left with no qualifications at all.

8   Some areas of the country provided a higher proportion of grammar school places than others.

What do you think is meant by the term 'intelligence'?

The growth of the comprehensive schools

The mounting criticisms of selection by the 11+ examination led to a rejection of the whole tripartite system. One of the first councils to experiment with alternatives was Labour-run London which set up eight trial comprehensive schools between 1946 and 1949. These schools aimed to be **comprehensive** by taking all secondary pupils of all levels of ability in their areas.

In 1965 the Labour Government issued its famous circular '10/65' instructing councils to plan for comprehensive schools. This circular said: 'A comprehensive school aims to establish a school community in which pupils over the whole ability range can be encouraged to mix with each other, gaining stimulus from the contacts and learning tolerance and understanding in the process.'

Conservative Governments have since withdrawn this instruction to 'go comprehensive' but any council – such as Solihull in 1985 – which attempted to 'turn the clock back' and re-introduce the tripartite system would be very unpopular with most parents. This is because nobody wants to risk their children going to a secondary modern school for second-best pupils.

By 1984 the state secondary education system in England consisted of

3,300,000 pupils in 3,938 comprehensive schools,
171,470 pupils in 285 secondary modern schools,
117,187 pupils in 175 grammar schools.

Nevertheless, comprehensive schools have remained controversial and they still arouse a lot of opposition.

Three criticisms of comprehensive schools

1 The loss of the 'fine academic' grammar school traditions Grammar schools were said to provide high standards of scholarly learning which met the needs of bright pupils. Critics claim that comprehensive schools fail to provide adequately for the 'gifted child' (although it can be argued that we all have 'gifts' of different kinds). Some parents feel that not enough is demanded of their children, that they are not 'pushed' or 'stretched' in comprehensives which attempt to cater for all abilities, often in mixed-ability teaching groups.

If comprehensives are accused of lowering educational standards, we can consider the following evidence about the qualifications of school-leavers:

	1969 (%)	1987 (%)
Percentage leaving with one or more A-levels	12	19
Percentage leaving with 5 or more O-levels (but no A-levels)	7	11
Percentage leaving with just 1, 2, 3 or 4 O-levels	18	28
Percentage leaving with O-level or A-level passes	37	58
Percentage leaving with no qualifications at all	50	10

These figures show that educational standards were higher in 1987, when less than 4 per cent went to grammar schools, than in 1969, when 21 per cent went to grammar schools. Therefore the abolition of grammar schools has not resulted in an overall decline in examination success.

2 The loss of the upward route for the able lower-class pupil Prime Ministers Harold Wilson, Edward Heath and Margaret Thatcher all rose from lower-middle-class homes via success at their local grammar schools and then at Oxford University. Part of the grammar school tradition was that they enabled upward social mobility for a small proportion of bright working-class pupils. It was for this reason that Harold Wilson once said that grammar schools would only be abolished 'over my dead body', yet it was his government which sent out circular '10/65' asking local authorities to draw up plans to go comprehensive.

Pupils at the Bristol Grammar School in the early 1960s.

Pupils with their form teacher at a London comprehensive school in 1986.

3 The size and anonymity of comprehensive schools The pioneers in London in the 1940s reckoned that a 'real' comprehensive needed three forms of pupils who would have passed the 11+ to produce a viable sixth form. To get these three forms of able bright pupils a school in London would need an intake of thirteen forms. Thirty pupils in each of these thirteen forms would give a year size of almost 400 pupils and 400 pupils in each of the years from first to fifth gives a total of 2,000 pupils plus 200-odd sixth formers.

Schools of this size are said to have **economies of scale** such as being able to offer large libraries and sports halls as well as a wide range of special facilities and courses such as Photography GCSE with several dark-rooms. But many critics believe that individual pupils are 'lost' in such massive schools where they do not know all the 150-odd teachers and where none of the staff can hope to know all the pupils by name. Such anonymity, it is argued, leads to indiscipline and poor results.

4 Home, social class and educational attainment

Educational under-achievement

Comprehensive schools were introduced to create greater equality of educational opportunity. But a large proportion of working-class talent and ability is never fully rewarded with examination success, this is called **under-achievement**. The following figures show part of the picture of working-class educational under-achievement:

	1961		1984	
	Percentage of the male labour force	*Percentage of university students*	*Percentage of the male labour force*	*Percentage of university students*
The middle class	31	74	40	80
The working class	69	26	60	20

In this section of the chapter we will try to identify the aspects of home background which explain under-achievement and in the next section we will look at the aspects of school life which also contribute to this problem.

Case study: homes and schools in Hackney

Paul Harrison's 1985 book *Inside the Inner City* is a detailed look at life in the East London borough of Hackney. When we ask ourselves why it was that Hackney had the lowest examination success in all of London, we might consider the following factors:

- 69 per cent of parents were in classes IV and V (semi-skilled or unskilled manual workers)

- 33 per cent of pupils came from families poor enough to qualify for free school dinners
- 28 per cent came from one-parent families
- 27 per cent came from large families with five or more children
- 18 per cent spoke a first language other than English
- 20 per cent of dwellings in Hackney were 'unfit for human habitation'

Harrison writes that family background affects schooling in two major ways:

> The first is through educational performance. The typical Hackney home . . . offers fewer toys and books; fewer outings and holidays; shortage of personal space for play or study; and shortage of attention from parents because of larger, less widely spaced, families, unsocial working hours or preoccupation with persistent housing and income problems.
>
> The other main impact of family life on schooling is made through pupils' behaviour. The inner-city child is more indisciplined than average. Many children come from homes where arguments, disruption and instability, often involving violence, are everyday occurrences.

Truancy, delinquency and street life all offer counter attractions:

> All these influences are reflected in school in attention-seeking, insolence and inability to concentrate.

Activity

Children who experience the situations described by Harrison are often described as disadvantaged. Explain why a pupil from a working-class home which does not have these disadvantages may be more likely to succeed at school.

This family, in Manchester in 1986, were living on supplementary benefit. The children slept together with their parents, in the living room, to keep warm during the winter.

We now look at aspects of the material and cultural factors indicated in the Hackney case study.

Material disadvantages

1 Poverty One side-effect of financial deprivation is the motivation to leave school at sixteen. In 1974, the National Children's Bureau (Wedge and Essen) surveyed all 9,397 sixteen-year-olds born in the week 3–9 March 1958. This survey found that:

- 19 per cent came from one-parent or large families,
- 12 per cent were in overcrowded or poor housing,
- 13 per cent had free school dinners.

The 3 per cent who had all three of these adversities were categorised as **socially disadvantaged**. Of these, 88 per cent expected to leave school at sixteen, with 45 per cent giving 'family needs the money' as one of their reasons.

2 Poor health Numerous studies have shown that children from classes IV and V have a poorer diet and worse attendance at clinics (for example for immunisation). They also suffer more than the average from poor vision and impaired hearing and have higher rates of chronic illness which can obviously disrupt progress at school. The connection between diet, health and educational success was recognised as early as 1906 and 1907 when school medical inspections for all pupils and school meals for poor children were introduced.

3 Size of family The number of children in a family can clearly be connected with

- less to spend on food per child,
- lack of space and quiet in which to do homework,
- lack of space and quiet in which to get a good night's sleep.

Cultural factors affecting educational attainment

Many of the material factors mentioned above build on each other or overlap; the 1967 Plowden Report on primary education described them as a 'seamless web of circumstance'. This Report also said: 'In a neighbourhood where the jobs people do and the status they hold owe little to their education, it is natural for children as they grow older to regard school as a brief prelude to work rather than as an avenue to future opportunities.' We now turn to the importance of attitudes and way of life in a pupil's home.

1 Parental support and encouragement A parent who hated school may hate parents' evenings at school. A parent who failed at school may be unable to help with homework. A parent who got a job without qualifications may not see any point in getting GCSEs.

2 Preparation for school Compare these two mothers and bear in mind that *either* could be middle class or working class:

Mrs Targett

Treats her toddler to sweets at the supermarket check-out and lets her stay up late now and then.

Never takes the trouble to encourage language development by, for example, recounting the day's events or reading a story each bedtime. She smacks her toddler if she reaches up at the cooker and then just shouts at her.

Emphasises the fun of treats and **instant gratification** or pleasure. The moral of this point is that we may enjoy smoking now or chose to leave school at sixteen for a job to have money in our pockets, but we might regret both decisions later in life.

Mrs Groom

Lays down clear discipline for her toddler with only two sweets from the sweets jar daily and regular bed times.

When reaching up at the cooker her toddler is told about the painful consequences of boiling baked beans falling over one's head: a simple science lesson involving the abstract concepts of gravity, heat and time.

Uses practices like pocket money and a piggy bank to teach **deferred** (or postponed) **gratification**. The years of studying in the evenings and living on a low student grant at university may be endured for an eventual annual income which is three times as large as the early school leaver.

Activities

1　Do you think that Mrs Targett and Mrs Groom are totally unrealistic stereotypes or can you think of anyone who is like either of them?

2　Describe some other ways that parents can help to prepare their children for the demands which are made of them when they start school.

3　A survey using intelligence test results on 400,000 nineteen-year-old male National Service recruits in Holland found that for all social classes there was a gradient in level of ability related to birth order. In other words, first born children tended to be more intelligent than second children, and so on. A British survey of seven-year-olds found that first born children were sixteen months ahead in reading compared to fourth or later born children. The first born seven-year-olds were also taller. What reasons would you give for these findings?

4　Professor Wiseman calculated for the 1967 Plowden Report that home and neighbourhood are 82 per cent responsible for difference in educational success while school itself is 18 per cent responsible. Recently sociologists have emphasised how aspects of school life can affect rates of educational attainment. Which set of factors do you think are more important in determining educational success?

5　The effects of schools on rates of educational success

This section of the chapter concentrates on six aspects of school life and organisation.

Creaming

In order to answer the debate about whether educational standards have fallen with comprehensive schools, a recent study by J. Gray and others surveyed 20,000 teenagers in Scotland (which went comprehensive earlier than most of England did and has far fewer private schools). They compared the results from two categories of schools:

1   **True comprehensives**, meaning schools with sixth forms which take *all* the pupils from a particular area without any bright children being **creamed** away (like the top of the milk) to local grammar or fee-paying schools.

2   Other secondary schools, including 'creamed', or false, comprehensives as well as grammar and secondary modern schools.

The survey found that middle-class children doing A-levels were better off in grammar schools but working-class pupils got better results at sixteen in **true comprehensives** than in selective or creamed schools.

This need for a balanced intake was emphasised in the following case study of twelve South London comprehensive schools investigated by M. Rutter and others in the 1970s. They named their book after the number of hours we spend in school from the ages of five to sixteen.

School atmosphere

Case study: **Fifteen Thousand Hours**

Of the twelve schools studied, the best one had examination results four times better than the worst one. Similarly, after allowing for the different social backgrounds of the pupils, those from the worst school were three times more likely than those at the best to appear at Juvenile Court.

Rutter rejected the following causes put forward to explain the differences between the best and worst schools: single sex not mixed sex; small not big; spacious not cramped; one site not split; year system not house system of pastoral care. Instead he pinpointed the following key factors which made the best schools best:

1   An 'ethos' or atmosphere which is well-organised, encouraging and caring with teachers showing not so much traditional methods of teaching but traditional values of dedication, commitment and preparation.

2   Frequent praise used rather than frequent punishment. (The schools using corporal punishment seemed to *produce* bad behaviour.)

3   A balanced intake: a fair proportion of high ability pupils was shown to improve the performance and behaviour of all pupils of all levels of ability.

Learning often depends on the atmosphere in the classroom.

Zoning

The government circular '10/65' which asked local authorities to plan comprehensive schools urged them 'to ensure, when determining catchment areas, that schools are as socially and intellectually comprehensive as practicable.' A **catchment area** is the local residential **zone** which pupils come from.

Birley High School in Hulme, central Manchester, draws many of its pupils from nearby council flats and some 80 per cent of these are poor enough to qualify for free school dinners. On the other hand parents struggle to get their children into Parrs Wood High School in the South Manchester suburb of Didsbury. Many parents in this second area work at the local university, polytechnic and hospitals and the mainly middle-class pupils at Parrs Wood put the school at the top of the Manchester schools league table for A-level results in 1977. Estate agents claim that parents are eager to move to Didsbury so that they can get their children into the Beaver Road Primary School which 'feeds' Parrs Wood and this demand has helped to push up house prices in the area.

Working-class pupils are less likely to be successful in examinations if they go to mainly working-class inner-city comprehensives. They will usually do better if they go to a middle-class comprehensive in a middle-class area with an intake of mainly middle-class pupils.

Bussing

The USA has experimented with **bussing** black children from the ghetto (or slum) to mainly white schools on the outskirts of cities. This has been done to try to overcome the unfairness of middle-class pupils going to 'good' schools in the suburbs while ghetto children end up in 'bad' inner-city schools.

A version of this occurred in Southall, West of London, when the government imposed a maximum quota of 33 per cent 'immigrant' children in any one school in the early 1960s. By 1967 1,000 pupils, mainly Asian, were being bussed to schools up to ten kilometres away from their homes in order to maintain the quotas while schools in Southall were left with empty places not taken up by white parents.

By 1973, 2,500 black Southall children were being bussed and another 400 were making their way to non-local schools on public transport. This one way traffic had meant that no new schools had been built in Southall itself from 1962 to 1972. Only when local black organisations threatened to prosecute the council for discrimination in 1978, were plans made for two new secondary schools.

'Head Start'

Some people believe that education cannot compensate for society. But after the race riots in many American cities in the early 1960s, President Johnson launched his 'War on Poverty'. This included bussing and programmes of **compensatory education** such as Head Start. The aim of compensatory education is to give help to children from deprived backgrounds so that they can compete on equal terms with other children.

By 1973 Head Start was costing $390,000,000 a year and it was providing, among other things, for deprived ghetto children to attend 'enriched' environments such as summer camps and nursery schools. Another idea was the *Sesame Street* TV series with muppets to help backward toddlers learn their alphabet. It has been claimed though that middle-class mothers made their toddlers watch *Sesame Street* while the deprived toddlers continued watching *Tom and Jerry*. So the ghetto children fell further behind while the middle-class toddlers were given an additional 'head start'.

Peer groups and self-fulfilling prophecy

Pupils may under-achieve at school because they 'run with the pack' and spend their evenings out on the streets with their gang (or peer group) rather than being kept in to do homework. Their lack of educational success is due to their home environment.

On the other hand a peer group can be based on the school environment. Turner has described how 'exam committed' pupils at 'Stone Grove' Comprehensive ended up getting poor results because they were sucked into a group which chose to be known as the 'dossers'. This peer group had an 'anti-school subculture' and obeyed 'work restriction norms'. In other words, they struggled to defeat the school's aim of making them work and promoted their alternative aim of 'messing about', while jeering at the hard-working pupils they called 'swots'.

Such a peer group subculture can be fostered by the way a school labels different categories of pupils so helping to create groups of 'dossers' and 'swots'. Rosenthal and Jacobson conducted a famous experiment concerning this process of labelling which they described in their 1968 study called *Pygmalion in the Classroom: Teacher Expectations and Pupils' Intellectual Development*. They picked certain pupils at random and then lied to their teachers, telling them that the selected pupils were 'late-developers' who were likely to make good progress. As a result, their teachers treated these pupils differently. By the end of the year they had lived up to their teachers' expectations and had indeed scored somewhat better than their class mates in tests. This experiment shows that the expectations of teachers can result in a **self-fulfilling prophecy**, meaning that the teachers' predictions had come to pass.

In England, Lacey and Hargreaves have described how a similar process occurred with streaming in 'Hightown Grammar' and 'Lumley Secondary Modern'. Some comprehensives have compromised between fine streaming and mixed-ability grouping or setting by using broad banding (see below).

1 Fine streaming In a school with a nine-form entry, pupils would be put into nine ability groups and be taught in these for all their lessons.

2 Setting Pupils are put into different ability groups for different subjects. For example, a pupil might be in the top group for maths and the bottom group for French.

3 Mixed ability In many comprehensive schools, pupils with a range of abilities are put into each form or tutor group and then taught in these same mixed ability groups for a number of subjects.

4   Broad banding   In this case the nine forms in each year may be divided up into three broad bands of ability for teaching purposes. In his study of *Beachside Comprehensive* Stephen Ball uses the words of the teachers to show their stereotypes of the pupils in each of the three bands:

The Band One child

> has academic potential . . . likes doing projects . . . knows what the teacher wants . . . is bright, alert and enthusiastic . . . can concentrate . . . produces neat work . . . is interested . . . wants to get on . . . is Grammar school material . . . you can have discussions with . . . friendly . . . rewarding . . . has common sense.

The Band Two child

> is not interested in school work . . . difficult to control . . . rowdy and lazy . . . has little self-control . . . is immature . . . loses and forgets books with monotonous regularity . . . cannot take part in discussions . . . is moody . . . of low standard . . . lacks concentration . . . is poorly behaved . . . not up to much academically.

The Band Three child

> is unfortunate . . . is low in ability . . . maladjusted . . . anti-school . . . lacks a mature view of education . . . mentally retarded . . . emotionally unstable and . . . a waste of time.

If teachers give greater encouragement to higher band pupils and expect higher quality work from them, then such pupils may perform accordingly. In this way the performance of pupils may reflect the expectations of their teachers.

Activities

1   In what ways might teachers show (a) positive, high expectations of pupils, and (b) negative, low expectations of pupils?

2   Why might Rosenthal and Jacobson's experiment be criticised as morally wrong?

Summary

We have seen how school life can affect a pupil's chances of educational success whatever his or her ability or background. Important aspects of school life include:

1   the school's catchment area and the balance of its pupil intake in terms of ability and social class;
2   the attitudes of teachers to different types of pupils and how far pupils are labelled by procedures such as streaming;
3   the atmosphere or ethos of the school in terms of its smooth organisation and the efficient dedication to learning of its teachers.

6 Private, fee-paying, independent schools

Case study: which school?

Which school did seven of the twenty-one ministers in Mrs Thatcher's first, 1979 Cabinet come from? (A Cabinet is the group of senior MPs who run the government.)

In 1981, which school had sixteen of Britain's twenty-six dukes been to? (A duke is one of the top wealthy, land-owning aristocrats; the most senior of the nobility.)

In 1983, which school did the following top people come from?

- the Head of the Home Civil Service and the Head of the Foreign Service,

- the Chief of Defence Staff,
- the editor of *The Times* and the Chairman of the BBC,
- the Governor of the Bank of England and four of its Directors,
- the Chairmen of Barclays Bank, the Royal Bank of Scotland and seven of the sixteen merchant banks in the City,
- the Chairmen of five of the twelve top life insurance companies.

Answer: They all went to Britain's best known public school – Eton.

Definitions

The different names used for the two main types of secondary school can be confusing, but we hope that this makes it clear:

7 per cent of secondary pupils go to independent schools	*93 per cent of secondary pupils go to state schools*
These are all privately run and charge fees apart from some charity schools. In a few cases pupils' fees are paid by scholarships or by the Assisted Places Scheme set up by the Conservative Government in 1979. Many are called 'public schools' because they are open to all the public (who can afford them). Many are boarding schools.	These are run by local education authorities, or councils, and so are part of the 'public sector', meaning government-owned. In 1976, the Labour Government withdrew its funding of 174 direct grant grammar schools and 119 of them became fee-paying, independent grammar schools.

Arguments in favour of fee-paying schools

1 They give parents greater freedom of choice (if they have enough money: full boarding and tuition fees at Harrow School for the Autumn Term in 1988 were £2,475 or £247.50 per week for a ten-week term). It would restrict the liberty of the individual if they were to be abolished. 'Adolf Hitler is the only man in Western Europe ever to have banned private schools' – David Malland, Headmaster of Manchester Grammar School.

2 Many of the private schools have centuries-old traditions behind them and so they are a precious part of our national heritage and culture. They also often have excellent records of academic and sporting achievement.

3 Pupils who are fortunate enough to go to fee-paying schools benefit from establishing social contacts which will help them in later life.

4 Parents who pay fees are in effect paying twice since they are also contributing to the costs of state schools through their taxes and rates.

5 Schools outside the state system have the freedom to use experimental methods of schooling. Examples have included Dartington, Summerhill, Gordonstoun and the Rudolf Steiner schools.

Arguments against fee-paying schools

1 The rich and powerful who govern our country may never be fully concerned about the conditions in the schools attended by 93 per cent of the population as long as their own children join the privileged 7 per cent elite at private schools.

2 The ex-public school students dominate the top jobs of British institutions involving the government, the civil service, the church, the legal system, the armed forces and the financial system in the City. In other words, those who control these institutions come overwhelmingly from a few exclusive schools such as Eton, Harrow, Winchester and Westminster. Those who occupy the top jobs give their own children the unfair advantage of **sponsored mobility** by (a) sending them to these same schools and by (b) choosing new recruits for their top jobs from among those who have been to these schools. This restrictive **elite self-recruitment** is known as the **old school tie network**. The opposite of sponsored mobility is **contest mobility** where those with the most ability can get to the top through open and fair competition in a non-selective education system.

3 Comprehensive schools will not really be comprehensive and non-selective until 100 per cent of pupils attend them. At the moment they are creamed of those pupils with the most influential parents.

4 Fee-paying schools split British society into two and so they are socially divisive. Those who go to such schools are isolated from 'ordinary people'.

5 It is sometimes argued that the bus driver who goes without cigarettes, beer and foreign holidays could afford to send his children to private school. But the cost of sending two sons to such schools from the age of seven to seventeen would be £174,750, which the average bus driver could not possibly afford. This is based on 1988 fees for five years at Hurst Lodge prep school followed by four years at Harrow and does not include the cost of necessary extras such as books, rugby boots and wing collars.

Conclusion

Despite the criticism of private schools, in 1981 a survey by the *Observer* found that 72 per cent of parents would send their children to private schools if money was no problem and if they were unable to get their children into the state school of their choice. In 1982, a *Sunday Times* survey found that a 'significant minority' of the headteachers of comprehensive schools sent their own children to private schools.

Harrow schoolboys.

GCSE question from London and East Anglian Group 1988

Power groups in society from 1980 to 1982

Percentage of posts filled by those with a public school education

	Percentage
Conservative cabinet ministers	87
Judges	76
Conservative MPs	76
Governors of the Bank of England	67
Bishops	66
Top civil servants	59
Directors of leading firms	58
BBC governors	44
Labour cabinet ministers	35
Labour MPs	15

'Only 2.5 per cent of the population can enjoy a public school education but it is from this tiny group that so many powerful positions in society are filled.'

(adapted from *The Public Schools* by Glennester and Pryke)

(a) What percentage of directors of leading firms received a public school education? (1)

(b) (i) Which political party had the larger percentage of public-school educated Cabinet Ministers? (1)

(ii) Using the table, compare the education of Cabinet Ministers and MPs. (3)

(c) Explain how civil servants exercise power in society. (3)

(d) How far is it true that a small group controls our society? (7)

| CHAPTER 11 |

Religion and society

1　The functions of religion

In this chapter we will be attempting to answer a number of questions about the place of religion in society. To begin with we ask what personal and social needs are satisfied by religion. In Section 2 of this chapter we look at two examples of societies in which religion has a strong influence; in Section 3 we will attempt to discover how far the influence of Christianity is declining in modern British society; Section 4 looks at the Islamic faith in Britain and Section 5 considers the ways in which new religious groups differ from the older, more established churches.

What personal needs does religion fulfil?

1　Religion can explain why we are here and what we should do with our lives. Without religion many of us would feel lost in a world and a universe without meaning.

2　Religion can help us to cope with the failures and tragedies that befall us. Most of us experience the death of relatives or friends and all of us face the prospect of death. Religion can provide us with an explanation of such events and help us to come to terms with them by giving them a meaning.

3　Religion can satisfy our need to know what is right and wrong and how we should act in certain situations. By providing a code of behaviour, religion can help us to form judgements about what is good and bad and about what we ought and ought not to do.

So religion can provide for our need to live in a meaningful world, our need to cope with personal disasters and our need for guidance about right and wrong. All the great faiths also recognise that humans are three-fold beings of body, mind and spirit: religion attends to the spiritual aspect of our lives.

What social needs does religion fulfil?

Many sociologists have claimed that religion helps to create unity in society. It does this in a number of ways:

1　All religions provide shared values and standards of behaviour; without a general acceptance of some values between individuals a common way of life would be impossible and society would collapse. An example of a shared value is the Old Testament's Eighth Commandment, 'Thou shalt not steal'.

2   Religion gives further support (sanction) to the rules and laws of society. Thus individuals are fearful of breaking certain rules because they may be punished by God as well as society.

3   All religions have rituals and ceremonies which bring believers together and so strengthen their commitment to a common way of life.

We must be careful however not to exaggerate the unifying function of religion. Sometimes, far from acting as the cement holding the social structure together, religion can be a cause of disunity, as in the case of Northern Ireland. But for Durkheim, one of the founding fathers of sociology, religion has the essential function of binding communities together: religion is a system of beliefs and sacred rituals which unites people into social groups.

Marx saw religion as 'the opium of the people', as a sort of drug which distracted the working class from their exploitation and oppression, and Durkheim similarly wrote that 'religion instructed the humble to be content with their situation'.

Religion is by no means easy to define. One definition sees religion as any set of meaningful answers to the basic dilemmas of human existence such as birth, sickness and death. Another definition is that religion is any system of ideas, practices and rules of conduct that centre on belief in a god or supernatural reality.

Activities

1   If you were to break all of the Ten Commandments, in some cases you would be breaking the laws of the land but in other cases you would not. Which of the Ten Commandments are also part of the law in Britain today?
(You can find the Ten Commandments in Chapter 20 of the second book in the Bible, 'Exodus'.)

2   Name different ceremonies in either the Christian, Muslim or Hindu religions, apart from regular weekly services of worship, which help to bring the members of these religions together.

---

2   Religion in Iran and Poland

The Muslim religion in Iran

On 1 February 1979 the Ayatollah Khomeini returned from exile in Paris to become Iran's new leader after the overthrow of the Shah who had ruled for many years. The new regime was an Islamic dictatorship in which the Ayatollah Khomeini became both the religious and political leader.

The revolution which toppled the Shah of Iran from his throne had a number of causes, such as protest at the way Iran was dominated by American oil companies and disgust at the way that Muslim customs were threatened by modernisation which imposed a Western style of life.

Iran has now returned to strict Islamic practices; its new 1979 constitution enforced numerous **fundamentalist**, or traditional, measures such as:

1   rules for the veiling of women,
2   the abolition of modern divorce laws,

3   executions of homosexuals and adulterers,
4   prohibition of mixed public bathing,
5   a return to strictly Islamic schooling,
6   severe punishments for petty crimes such as theft.

In 1980 a war broke out with Iran's neighbour, Iraq. The Iranian Government of Ayatollah Khomeini has regarded this as a 'Jihad' or Holy War. In other words, the Ayatollah believes that it is the historic mission of the Iranian people to convert other Muslim nations to their 'true' version of the Islamic faith.

The Iranian leader, Ayatollah Khomeini, greeting soldiers at Qom in 1979.

Since the 1979 revolution, the Ayatollah's interpretation of the Islamic faith has been the only one permitted in Iran. Not only have believers in other religions, such as Christians and Baha'is, been severely persecuted but also those who belong to alternative Muslim sects.

Summary   Children in modern Iran are socialised into accepting a view of the world and a code of conduct that conforms to the Ayatollah's Islamic teachings. This socialisation begins in the family and the school. It continues to be reinforced by peer group pressure, daily attendance at the mosque, a government-controlled mass media, compulsory military service and the laws of Iran's new constitution.

There can be no doubt that in today's Iran religion is a central part of socialisation and a powerful means of social control.

The Catholic faith in Poland

While Iran is a society dominated by religion, we now turn to a country which is dominated by the anti-religious system of communism. Yet despite the disapproval of the communist dictatorship, the Catholic Church in Poland plays a very important part in people's everyday lives. The following events illustrate the clash between the communist state and the Catholic Church:

In 1953, Cardinal Wyszynski, the Catholic Archbishop, was imprisoned for his opposition to the communist take-over of the Catholic school system in Poland.

In 1979, the Polish-born Pope, John-Paul II, returned to his native land and he held enormous open-air masses. These were seen by many to be expressions of popular opposition to the communist government. As John Pilger wrote in the *Daily Mirror* at the time: 'The Poles love Pope John Paul II because he is one of them and he has come with two fingers up in the air, metaphorically speaking, at their Russian masters.'

In 1981, the Polish Government of General Jaruzelski imposed martial law and suppressed the free, independent trade union called *Solidarity*. In one year *Solidarity* had attracted ten million members in Poland and its leader Lech Walesa had become world famous. After the crackdown on *Solidarity* all political opposition organisations and public demonstrations were banned. As a result, one of the few ways that *Solidarity* supporters could meet was by attending church services such as the funeral of the Catholic priest, Father Jerzy Popielusko, who was murdered by the Polish Secret Police.

In May 1981, Pope John-Paul II was shot in St Peter's Square in Rome but he survived the assassination attempt. The subsequent trial has revealed that the assassin was recruited by Secret Service agents from communist Bulgaria. Many people believe that the Russians sought to weaken their Catholic opponents in Eastern Europe by eliminating the head of the Catholic Church.

Summary Despite the attempts by the state to impose communist beliefs, 90 per cent or more of Poland's 37 million population are Catholics while less than one in eighteen is a member of the ruling Communist Party. This shows that religion can play an important part in societies ruled by anti-religious governments.

A further conclusion is that the Church can act as a powerful focus for political opposition. Another example of this was the way that the Catholic Archbishop Romero was assassinated in his cathedral in 1980 because of his opposition to the right-wing military dictatorship in the Central American country of El Salvador.

Pope John Paul II receiving an ecstatic welcome on his return home to Poland in 1979.

3   How influential is Christianity in modern Britain?

Many hospitals include a question on their admissions form whieh asks for the religion of the new patient. One purpose of this question is that certain religions have special restrictions about diet. Another reason for the question is to help visiting hospital chaplains to identify members of their church or to help staff to contact priests so that they can administer the Last Rites to dying patients.

It is said that Britain is the least religious of all the nations of Europe, yet surveys have shown that when asked to state our religion very few of us answer 'atheist', 'non-believer' or 'no church' – even though we may not be baptised or may never go to church.

It is difficult to measure how religious people are. For this purpose, two American sociologists, Glock and Stark, have separated five dimensions of religiousness:

1   belief
2   practice
3   experience
4   knowledge
5   consequences.

We will examine four of these, concentrating on the question: 'Is Britain no longer really a Christian society?'

We could reword this question: 'Is Britain now a **secular society**?' Secular means uninfluenced by religion. The process of the erosion and decline of the importance of religious beliefs, institutions and practices is called **secularisation**.

The extent of Christian belief

Here are some of the results of a Marplan survey conducted in 1979 for *NOW!* magazine (21 December 1979):

Percentage of adults agreeing with the statements

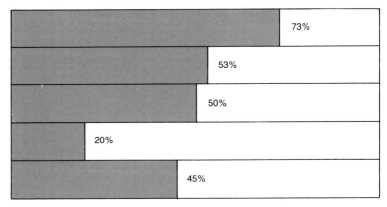

I believe in God	73%
I believe in life after death	53%
Your soul lives on after your body dies	50%
You go to Heaven or Hell for ever	20%
Many of the problems in Britain today come from a lack of religious belief	45%

We might also ask whether the beliefs of Christian church leaders are becoming less religious. In 1984 there was great public controversy when the new Bishop of Durham seemed to argue that it was no longer necessary for modern Christians to believe in the literal truth of the Virgin Birth and that it could be accepted as one of the many myths in the Bible. As liberal church leaders continue to 'water-down' their beliefs to make them more believable in modern society, some sociologists argue that the Church itself has become more secular and less religious. In fact, surveys have shown that 66 per cent of Church of England churchgoers do not believe in the Virgin Birth and so seem to agree with the controversial Bishop of Durham.

Other signs of changing opinions within the Church can be seen in its changing attitudes to birth control and divorce. While the Catholic Church has maintained strict teachings on these subjects, the Lambeth Conference of the Church of England approved of birth control in 1958 and some Anglican priests now remarry divorcees in church.

The extent of Christian practice

Christian church membership numbers in the United Kingdom

	1970	*1985*
Catholic	2,524,000	2,265,000
Anglican (C of E)	2,558,000	2,058,000
Presbyterian	1,890,000	1,483,000
Methodist	673,000	485,000
Baptist	293,000	226,000
Other denominations	561,000	758,000
Total Christian members	8,501,000	7,276,000
Percentage of the adult population	20	16

(Source: *Social Trends*, 1985)

Data-response exercise: Christian church membership in the UK

1 How many people belonged to the Baptist church in 1970?

2 Which Christian church lost the most members between 1970 and 1985?

3 What proportion of adults did not belong to a Christian church in 1985?

4 What was the trend in total membership of Christian churches between 1970 and 1985?

Estimated attendance at Christian churches in England

	1975	1979
Catholic	1,418,000	1,310,000
Anglican (C of E)	1,302,000	1,256,000
Methodist	454,000	447,000
Baptist	193,000	203,000

(Source: *Social Trends*, 1982)

Figures from surveys sponsored by the Bible Society show that while 18 per cent of the adult population of England belonged to a Christian church in 1979, only 11 per cent actually attended church. In terms of church membership and attendance, the Christian churches in Britain are in overall decline. Yet while the majority of British people may not be regular church-goers, large numbers find themselves turning to the Church or to private prayer in times of crisis. An example would be a family seeking comfort from their priest or strength from God when a close relative is dying.

Three major events in our lives are 'hatching, matching and despatching': birth, marriage and death. Many people may never attend church apart from the ceremonies to mark these occasions: known as the **Rites of Passage**, these would be the baptism, wedding and funeral services.

This church, in Winchester, has been converted into offices.

Infant baptisms in the Church of England

1961	*1987*
412,000	188,000

Marriages in Britain

	1971	*1987*
Solemnised with religious ceremony in church	60%	53%
Civil marriages in register offices	40%	47%

(Source: *Social Trends, 1989*)

The extent of Christian knowledge

A 1986 survey of pupils in a London comprehensive school showed that knowledge of the Bible was very limited. Only 18 per cent of pupils knew the authors of the four gospels and only 7 per cent could name the first book of the Bible. There is good reason to believe that Christian religious knowledge has declined in Britain and the following causes have been suggested:

1   the fall in the number of children attending Sunday School and Confirmation classes;
2   the decline in religious teaching in schools and Bible study in the home;
3   the extent to which the mass media have replaced the Church as a focus of activity and interest.

Activity: how well do you know the Bible?

Interview a group of people who say they are Christians. Test their knowledge of the Bible with these questions.

1   What is the first book of the Bible called?
2   What is the difference between the Old and the New Testaments?
3   What are the Psalms?
4   Who wrote the four Gospels?
5   How did God create woman?
6   Who stretched out his hand to part the waters of the Red Sea?
7   Who said 'Esau my brother is a hairy man, and I am a smooth man'?
8   Who did Jesus call 'the salt of the earth' and 'the light of the world'?
9   Who said 'Art thou the King of the Jews?'
10 Who said 'If the dead are not raised, let us eat and drink, for tomorrow we die'?

(Answers at the end of this chapter.)

The religious consequences dimension

This aspect considers how far Christian religion actually affects the daily lives of British people today. We will first list some different viewpoints concerning the general influence of the Christian Church in Britain on our common way of life. We then turn to its influence on individual lives.

Does the Christian Church have any real influence in modern Britain?

Yes	No
1 The Church of England is the state religion, the official church of the government.	1 It is of only incidental interest that Prince Charles was unable to marry a Catholic.
2 Church of England bishops sit in the House of Lords where, for example, they have been able to protect the status of church schools.	2 The thorough 1985 Church report on inner-city problems called *Faith in the City* was scorned as 'Marxist' by members of the Conservative Government, which ignored its proposals.
3 The 1944 Education Act says that secondary schools should have daily collective acts of worship.	3 Only seven out of 296 secondary schools surveyed by the *Times Educational Supplement* (20 December 1985) complied with this law; 30 per cent did not sing hymns in their assemblies.
4 The 1944 Act also makes RE lessons compulsory.	4 Pupils in RE lessons often study world religions and social problems and do not learn much about Christian beliefs.
5 Radio and TV include regular religious programmes, especially on a Sunday evening. (Can you name any of these programmes?)	5 An increasing amount of media output verges on being blasphemous or sacriligious, for example, comedians such as Billy Connolly and Dave Allen.
6 Sunday remains a special day to spend with the family rather than working even if only a small minority actually go to church.	6 Increasingly shift-workers have to work on Sundays and more and more shops are now opening on Sundays.

We can say with some certainty that the general influence of the Church over British social institutions has steadily declined over the centuries. In the middle ages, the Church had considerable political power and in Tudor times Cardinal Wolsey was Lord Chancellor in charge of Henry VIII's Government. In those days the Church controlled entertainment and festivals as well as sponsoring artists. Schools, hospitals and the care of the poor were all aspects of the role of the Medieval Church. Since then many of these functions have been taken over by the welfare state.

The power of the Church to shape society may have declined but we now consider how far people's individual lives are still guided by Christian principles. Some see evidence for a decline in the Christian way of life in trends such as the increase in divorce, birth control, pornography, homosexuality and drug-taking. Yet if we look back in history we might question how 'Christian' English society was in past centuries. For example, the following practices might be considered *unchristian*: public hangings; slavery; cruel animal blood sports; the exploitation of child labour and the grossly unequal treatment of women.

It could be said that in so far as many of the above unchristian practices have ended, we are more Christian in our way of life today than we have ever been. Certainly large numbers of British people would consider that they live good, Christian lives.

Case study: Mary Donnelly

Mary was born in Glasgow in 1968, the year in which the Papal Encyclical *Humanae Vitae* ('Of Human Life') re-emphasised the Catholic prohibition of the use of contraceptives.

She was brought up in a strictly Catholic home where her photo, at the age of seven, in a 'wedding dress' had pride of place on the mantelpiece. This was the dress she wore to her first communion. She had also made her first confession with a priest at the age of seven.

When she was eleven she was 'confirmed' and she also started at the strictly Catholic Notre Dame School. This single sex school was attached to a convent and run by nuns.

She met her fiancé some years ago at the local Catholic Youth Club and she is now attending 'Preparation' for marriage. These classes with her local priest are given great importance by the Catholic Church due to their strict rulings on divorce.

Activities

1 How might Mary's strict Catholic upbringing affect her married life?
2 How might her family life differ from that of a non-religious family?
3 Use this case study to illustrate how the Church can act as a means of social control.
4 Do you think that people need religious faith to lead good lives? Give reasons.

Conclusion

From the evidence which we have looked at it can be seen that no definite answer can be given to the question 'Has Christian influence declined in Britain?' There are two problems with surveys on secularisation:

Firstly, was Britain really religious in the past? Historians have increasingly challenged the view that the middle ages were an Age of Faith and many argue that the religiosity of the Victorians has been exaggerated. A special survey by the Church of England in 1851 showed that in many cities less than a quarter of the working classes regularly went to church. Of the 39 per cent of the general population who did attend church in 1851 it would be interesting, but impossible, to know how many attended for social rather than spiritual reasons.

Secondly, many sociologists have argued that the decline in churchgoing does not necessarily indicate that we are less religious today. It may well be that religion, like family life, has become more home-centred or 'privatised'. For example, members of the House Church movement worship in each other's own homes. A further trend is **TV evangelism** which many predict will spread here from the USA with satellite and cable television.

4   The Islamic faith in Britain

Membership of non-Christian religions in the United Kingdom

	1970	*Projection for 1990*
Muslims	250,000	1,028,000
Sikhs	75,000	218,000
Hindus	50,000	165,000
Jews	113,000	108,000

(Source: *Social Trends*, 1987)

The above figures show that modern Britain is a multi-faith society. A number of non-Christian religions appear to be growing in Britain and a good example is Islam.

The Brick Lane Mosque in the East End of London has been used by different immigrant groups during its history. The building was originally the church of Huguenot refugees, French Protestants who fled from Catholic persecution at the end of the seventeenth century. It then became a Jewish synagogue before being converted, in 1976, into the largest religious centre for Bangladeshi Muslims in Britain, with 1,500 worshippers every Friday. In the same year, the large, new Regents Park Mosque was opened in central London.

There are over a thousand mosques in Britain and the Islamic Foundation claims that there are some two million Muslims living in Britain. They are mainly from the Indian sub-continent but also include Arabs, Turks, Cypriots, Africans, Malaysians and Indonesians.

It is possible to see two contrasting trends in Islam in Britain: a weakening and a strengthening of the faith.

The weakening of Islam in Britain

If Britain is becoming an increasingly secular society with a predominantly secular culture, then this implies that the influence of all religions is declining in Britain. Many of the young people who live in British cities and who have little time for religion may have rural ancestors who, during the eighteenth century, regularly read their Bibles and attended church. In a similar way, many young British Asians have parents or grandparents who have grown up in peasant societies with strict Muslim traditions. Among the new generations brought up in Britain, many find themselves pulled in two directions and some find it difficult to continue with Muslim customs. One example is language. They may use English at school or college, use Arabic for prayers and speak Urdu, Bengali, Punjabi or Gujerati in the home.

Culture conflict   This can take two forms. Firstly, culture conflict can arise because the customs of an ethnic minority differ from those of the majority population. For example, a Muslim may find it difficult to join in social activities with fellow workers because Islam prohibits all kinds of alcoholic drink. In her book, *Finding a Voice: Asian Women in Britain*, Amrit Wilson describes a Muslim student who never looked her cockney landlady in the eye because she had been brought up to consider this to be disrespectful, especially with an older person. The landlady then told her that in British culture if you don't look into somebody's eyes it means that you are telling a lie.

A second kind of culture conflict takes the form of role-conflict. For example, a Muslim teenager may have a foot in both cultures. If a girl is to be a good daughter and a good Muslim, she may feel obliged to accept close parental supervision and rules about modest forms of clothing. But in her role as a teenage school pupil, she may be attracted by her peer group's social world of discos, parties and boyfriends.

A Muslim Imam leading prayers at a mosque in Newport, South Wales.

A strengthening of Islam in Britain

A Muslim's entire life should be transformed into an act of worship by the five pillars of Islamic belief. These are:

1 Shahadah This is the declaration of faith, 'There is only one God and Muhammad is his Prophet'.

2   Salah   Muslims are obliged to pray five times a day. In the winter the times of prayer are at dawn, between noon and 1 p.m., in the afternoon between 2.30 and 3.30 p.m., after-sunset between 4 and 5 p.m., and late in the evening before going to bed.

3   Zakah   Muslims must give $2\frac{1}{2}$ per cent of their wealth each year to the needy and to community projects.

4   Sawm   Muslims should neither eat, drink nor smoke from sunrise to sunset during the sacred month of Ramadam.

5   Hajj   This is the pilgrimage to the holy city of Mecca in Saudi Arabia.

The first two pillars of Islam are daily duties; the second two are annual obligations; Hajj is a once in a lifetime event.

There are perhaps one thousand million Muslims in the world and many Muslim countries have been swept by a tide of Islamic fundamentalism in recent years. This means that many believers have been returning to the fundamental traditions of Islam.

In several parts of Britain Muslim parents have successfully claimed the right of their children to be educated in single-sex schools where girls may keep their arms and legs covered and where ritually slaughtered *halal* meat is served. In 1986 the Borough of Brent offered support to the private Islamia Primary School in North-West London and politicians were considering whether the government should allow state Muslim schools in the same way that it supports Christian 'church-aided' schools for Catholic and Church of England pupils.

The East London Mosque, in Whitechapel Road, opened in 1985 and soon had one thousand daily worshippers, with over two thousand on Fridays. It also has around one thousand six- to twelve-year-olds attending lessons in Islam which are held five days a week, from 5 to 7 p.m.

5   Cults, sects and new fringe religions

In Chapter 3 we discussed youth cults such as skinheads and punks. New **religious cults** similarly seem to suddenly appear as crazes which especially attract young people. Some observers see the growth of such groups as heralding a revival of religion. Examples of religious cults which have been in the news in Britain in recent years are the Moonies, the Hare Krishna movement, the Scientologists, the Children of God and the Bhagwan Rajneesh 'Orange People'. We begin this section by looking at a well-known fringe religion, namely the Moonies.

The Moonies

In 1945 a Korean, Young Myung Moon, claimed to have had a vision in which Jesus bowed down to him and recognised him as the Lord of Creation. Stirred by a number of similar visions, in 1954 Moon set up his own church, the Unification Church. The message of this church includes the following points:

1 The original sin of Adam and Eve has been sexually transmitted throughout history.
2 Christ was sent to earth to marry and have perfect children and so to eliminate the original sin.
3 Christ failed to fulfil this mission because he was murdered on the cross.
4 Now God is making a second attempt and his Messiah this time is the Reverend Moon.
5 Moon is also the leader of the forces of God against the forces of Satan led by the communists.
6 The Bible is obsolete because it is written in a code which only Moon understands. Moon has decoded it into his own Holy Book.

The Moonies have spread from South Korea to most parts of the Western World. By 1980, they claimed to have several million members in over 120 countries including 3,000 in Britain where they had twenty-four Unification Centres and 500 full-time workers.

The Reverend Moon has amassed a large fortune. Some of this comes from his armaments factories in South Korea and some from the donations of his converts. He is reported as saying in *The Times* (5 April 1978): 'When I mobilise 10,000 members it means thirty million dollars a month. Then we can buy Pan American Airlines and the Empire State Building. We shall buy the Ford Motor Company.'

The methods used by the Moonies to attract new converts have brought them much criticism. Reverend Moon claims that evil must be met with evil and that the end justifies the means. He therefore recommends that any methods be used to convert people and raise money. Thus, for example, the Moonies have used 'heavenly deception' to collect funds. That is, they have deceived the public into believing that they are giving to collections for the blind or for handicapped children.

Cults, sects and denominations

Members of Parliament in Britain regularly receive letters from distressed parents whose young adult sons and daughters have been 'kidnapped' by sinister religious cults. After a 100-day court case in 1981, the longest and most expensive libel trial in English legal history, a jury decided that the *Daily Mail* was justified in accusing the Moonies of brainwashing recruits and breaking up families.

A new **religious sect** tends to be a small group which is on the fringe of, or cut off from, the dominant culture in which it exists. Sects are at best indifferent and at worst hostile to society. Other characteristics are that such sects tend to

1 demand total commitment from followers,
2 expel members who do not fully conform, in order to emphasise exclusiveness and purity,
3 exaggerate some aspects of existing religions,
4 regard the established churches as corrupted.

If a sect grows over a number of years, then members may be born into rather than converted to the sect. Religious commitment may become less intense and the sect may evolve into a **denomination** with its recognised interpretation of a religious faith. A denomination is a larger, more established group than a sect and is less at odds with society. A denomination may then evolve into a church and become the official religion of a society.

Christianity itself was once a small cult or sect which the Roman Empire tried to suppress. More recently, Joseph Smith, who founded the Mormon

The Moonies still break up families, says rescued Sonia

They tried to make me believe my sister was Satanic!

By ANDREW McEWEN

FRESH proof emerged yesterday that the Moonies s t i l l break up families — three years after a High Court jury ruled that the Daily Mail was justified in making that accusation.

It comes on the eve of a major conference designed to press the Government to break the power of the destructive cult. Angry parents will meet at the House of Commons today.

Sonia Martin, a 22-year-old travel agent from Falmouth, Cornwall who has just been rescued from the Moonies in America, said: 'They still break up families. They even tried to make me forget my twin sister. They wanted me to b e l i e v e she was Satanic.'

The process of separating Sonia from her past began soon after she was picked up during a visit to San Francisco.

Her aunt who lives there made persistent efforts to contact her at a Moonie indoctrination centre called Camp K. Sonia said: 'Myra Staneki, our leader, got annoyed that my aunt wanted to meet me. She said it was not fair because some members had not seen their families for years.'

When Sonia's twin sister Sara flew over to visit—but refused to accept the teachings of Korean prophet Sun Myung Moon—the Moonies tried to separate her, too, from Sonia.

'Myra said I should forget her. I was to treat her as a Chapter Two case. That's Chapter Two of the Divine Principle, the Moonies' scripture. They did not directly say she was Satanic, but I knew what Chapter Two said and that was what it meant.'

Kidnap dream

When her aunt succeeded in meeting Sonia at a restaurant, an experienced British Moonie woman accompanied her. 'She was my chaperone. She dominated the conversation. They had people outside sitting in cars in case my aunt tried to snatch me.'

By now Sonia was so indoctrinated that she even submitted letters to her mother for approval before posting them. A letter she wrote to her brother she had to re-write three times.

Sonia was strongly warned that her family might hire de-programmers who could beat and rape her to break her faith. When a family friend, Phillip, flew over, and

'When I called my mother they said: Maximum two minutes'

Sonia warned her team, 'one of the team said she had a dream that Phillip was coming with people to kidnap me. They took it as a message from God. I never saw Phillip.'

Sara was allowed to see her three times, but always at Unification Church centres in the presence of Moonies.

When one meeting was set up for a restaurant, 'the team prepared paint bombs in freezer bags and put rocks in socks to pelt the car if she tried to kidnap me. Then they decided it was too risky and the meeting was switched.'

But the cruel separation from Sara was more than Sonia could bear. It led to furtive phone calls. Sara with her aunt and Phillip gradually drew her into a series of meetings — then held her against her will at a motel.

'A woman came past and I screamed "Get the police". We were all taken to the police station. I was handcuffed as my visa was out of date.'

During a five-day stay in prison she received advice from an immigration man and a prostitute. It proved a turning point. By the time the immigration man put her on a plane to London she was having doubts about the Moonies.

Sara and Phillip were on the plane too — but so was Myra, who bitterly attacked them for 'not respecting Sonia's religious freedom'. The British Moonie movement tried to arrange a getaway at Heathrow — but Sonia's family smuggled her away in a wheelchair.

With her consent Sonia was introduced to ex-Moonie Martin Faiers, a publisher's son, who until just over four years ago was public relations officer for the Canadian branch of the Moonies. Now he runs a counselling service to help ex-Moonies. She, Phillip and Sara spent weeks with Martin in Spain and France.

Sonia said that nothing more than persuasion was used to break her faith. Many members of FAIR (Family Action Information and Rescue), the main organisation for cult members' parents, believe that even this softly softly approach is risky.

Damnation

But Sonia has no doubts. 'I would advise parents to do it if they can afford it because I would still be a Moonie if my family had not taken action.'

In leaving the Moonies, Sonia had to cope with intense guilt feelings. 'They say that if you leave you are destined to eternal damnation.'

Mr Faiers's organisation COMA, which represents a vigorous approach to the cult problem, is at B.M. COMA, London, WC1 N3XX. FAIR, which has an information service, is at BCM Box 3535, PO Box 12, London, WC1 N3XX.

A story from the Sunday Mirror, *5 April 1984.*

Church in the 1830s, was persecuted for advocating polygamy and eventually killed by a mob. The Mormon Church has now grown into a respected religious institution in America where it dominates Salt Lake City in Utah and has many members.

In Britain many of the recruits to religious cults are either university students or young immigrants. Some would say that religious cults give lonely, vulnerable, young people a purpose in life and offer them the feeling of belonging to a ready-made community. Do you think that the Moonies are a genuine religion?

Answers to the 'How well do you know the Bible?' quiz:

1 Genesis;
2 BC and AD;
3 The sacred songs of David and Solomon;
4 Matthew, Mark, Luke and John;
5 From a rib taken from Adam;
6 Moses;
7 Jacob;
8 His disciples;
9 Pilate;
10 Saint Paul.

Case study: secular funerals

Unlike weddings, anybody can legally conduct funerals. And an increasing number of atheists are paying for non-religious ceremonies carried out by members of the National Secular Society and the Humanist Association.

Jane Wynne Willson, in the Midlands, prefers a formal atmosphere with poetry and readings from such authors as Pasternak: 'I think the words used should be a little bit flowery ... there's a considerable need for ritual at this time. I try for a familiar kind of pattern that people would have been through with a Christian ceremony.'

In the London area, Barbara Smoker conducts one secular funeral a week on average. She is amazed by the British capacity for double-think. 'Sometimes I spend a long time finding out about the person who died. Then they'll suddenly come out with "Will you just say he is now in a happier place?" and I have to say no, I will not – it would be completely hypocritical.'

(adapted from *The Sunday Times*, 26 February 1989)

GCSE question from Welsh Board 1988

(a) Discuss why societies need to have social control. (4)
(b) Give the meaning, with examples, of the following forms of social control:
    (i) *formal*, and (3)
    (ii) *informal*. (3)
(c) Discuss how religion and religious ideas may affect other areas of social life. (10)

GCSE questions from London and East Anglian Group specimen papers

1 To what extent is organised religion still important in Britain today?
2 What evidence is there to suggest that the influence of religion as an agency of social control has changed over the last 100 years?
3 Consider the parts played by both education and religion in encouraging social conformity.

CHAPTER 12

Deviance, crime and punishment

1 Deviance, crime and social change

The human cost of drug abuse

Which dangerous drug causes the loss of 8 million working days each year in Britain at a cost of more than £600 million? The answer is alcohol. The overall cost of alcohol abuse is difficult to calculate but it has been estimated that:

- 52 per cent of deaths from fire are linked with drinking,
- 50 per cent of murderers were drunk when they killed,
- 30 to 33 per cent of all road accidents, all accidents in the home, all drownings and all cases of child abuse are drink related,
- 25 per cent of all hospital beds are occupied due to alcohol-related illnesses.

Alcohol and tobacco kill about 400 people in Britain *every day*. (A quarter of all smokers kill themselves by smoking.) In contrast, illegal drugs kill about 400 people per year. In 1989, the government gave the Health Education Authority £22 million. Some of this was used to publicise the dangers of alcohol and tobacco. This is only a tiny fraction of the amount which is spent on advertisements to get us to buy cigarettes and alcoholic drinks.

Is it illegal to take a drug such as the tranquilliser called barbiturate? The answer is that it is legal to give yourself the dose prescribed by a doctor, but it is illegal to buy such pills in a club from a 'dealer' or 'pusher' who has stolen them from a hospital pharmacy. We could say that it all depends on whether society has sanctioned the use of a drug. Under certain circumstances the use of an allowed drug may be defined as abuse or misuse – for example, if tobacco is smoked by children.

Conceptions of deviance

Deviance refers to behaviour which deviates from or does not conform to accepted norms. It has been said that 'deviance is in the eye of the beholder'. Whether or not people label behaviour as deviant varies according to three questions: when ? where? and who?

1   When?   Definitions of deviance can change over time. For example, drinking alcohol may have been considered deviant by many Americans during the Prohibition Era (1920 to 1933) when alcoholic drinks were outlawed in the USA.

2   Where?   Strict Muslim states such as Saudi Arabia still maintain a ban on all alcoholic beverages.

3   Who?   Drinking alcohol may be considered appropriate in Britain during an evening out, with a meal, at a wedding reception or at a party, but it would be seen as deviant, or against the norm, for pupils at school or for policemen on duty.

Deviance and crime

A gang of youths might consider it normal to get drunk every Friday night but most people would regard drinking as socially unacceptable when a drinker's condition crosses the divide between 'merry' and 'paralytic'. Drunkenness may be deviant, but is it criminal? This would depend on whether a drunkard becomes disorderly or tries to drive a car.

Not all deviance is criminal, but is all law-breaking deviant? Many people may see it as socially acceptable to break certain laws such as parking briefly on a double yellow line. A large proportion of Americans considered it acceptable to carry on drinking during the Prohibition.

Deviance and social change

Drinking and driving can be illegal, but is it deviant?

Social change has often been inspired by those who have shown a new way of thinking and living but who have also, as a result, been persecuted

It was in the pub that he should have slowed down.

DERBYSHIRE COUNTY COUNCIL
If you're drinking, don't drive.

as deviants. Jesus Christ was a deviant in that he opposed the religious beliefs and practices of his society. And for this he was crucified. But his life and teachings gave birth to the new religion of Christianity which has become the accepted faith in many societies.

The rest of this chapter looks at recent trends in crime and considers some of the causes of such crimes.

2   Patterns of crime

In 1971, the police recorded just over 1.5 million notifiable offences in England and Wales. By 1987, the annual total had risen to just under 3.9 million.

Notifiable, or **indictable**, **offences** are serious crimes, generally those for which an accused person may be sent to prison if found guilty. A defendant may decide to ask for trial by jury with a judge in a Crown Court in such cases.

Non-indictable offences are less serious crimes, such as parking offences, which may be dealt with by a 'ticket' or by a magistrate without a jury in a Magistrates Court. Offenders in such cases often pay fines.

Notifiable offences recorded by the police in England and Wales

	1971	*1987*
Theft and handling stolen goods	1,003,700	2,052,000
Burglary	451,500	900,100
Criminal damage	27,000	589,000
Fraud and forgery	99,800	133,000
Violence against the person	47,000	141,000
Robbery	7,500	32,600
Sexual offences	23,600	25,200
Other offences	5,600	12,000
Total notifiable offences	1,665,700	3,884,900

(Source: *Social Trends*, 1989)

A lot of criminal damage is not reported to the police.

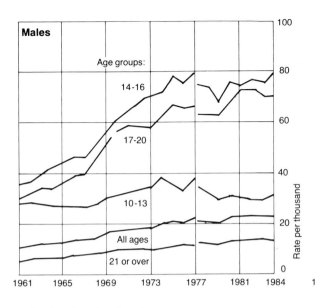

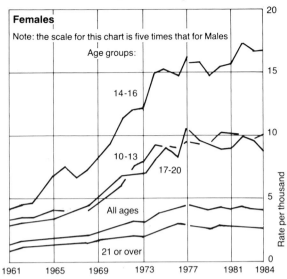

Offenders found guilty of, or cautioned for, indictable offences: by sex and age, in England and Wales (source: Social Trends, 1986).

The graphs above show that teenagers have the highest crime rates (per thousands of their age groups) among the general population. Because of this, many of the theories of crime discussed in section 4 of this chapter focus on **juvenile delinquency**, or offences committed by youths.

Data-response exercise: serious crime rates, by sex and age

1 Which male and female age groups, in the graphs, show the highest crime rates?
2 How do the scales differ between the charts for males and females?
3 Why do the scales differ between the charts for males and females?

4 Among fourteen to sixteen-year-olds, 53,000 boys were sentenced for an indictable offence in 1984 compared to 5,400 girls. List possible reasons for the lower female crime rates.

Crime rates also vary between different parts of the country. The 1986 Islington Crime Survey interviewed a sample of 1,722 households in this inner London borough and found that 31 per cent had been victims of a serious crime in the previous year. Over a quarter of all respondents said that they always avoid going out after dark because of fear of crime, and this rose to over one third in the case of women.

The 1986 Islington Crime Survey also showed how the official total of recorded offences may only be a small proportion of the actual number of offences committed:

	Bicycle thefts	*Sexual offences*
Estimated annual number in Islington	1498	1190
Estimated number reported	1019	255
Number officially recorded	700	110

3   The interpretation of crime figures

The following figures show **crime shrinkage** from an American survey of victims of violence. They demonstrate how 100 violent crimes resulted in an average of one and a half convictions:

- 49 per cent of victims called the police (so 100 crimes were reduced to forty-nine);
- the police responded to 77 per cent of these calls (so forty-nine crimes fell to thirty-seven);
- on arrival the police recognised 75 per cent of the incidents as crimes (so thirty-seven crimes fell to twenty-eight);
- 20 per cent of these crimes resulted in an arrest (so six violent criminals were caught out of the original total of 100);
- 42 per cent of those arrested came to trial (so three of the 100 came to court);
- 52 per cent of the trials resulted in convictions (so 1.5 per cent faced sentences).

This pattern of crime shrinkage can be represented by an iceberg. The often large proportion of unreported crimes, hidden beneath the surface, is known as the **dark figure** (see page 173).

Activities

1   List ten different crimes and say in each case why the victims might decide not to report them to the police.

2   Some crimes are described as 'victimless'. If an underage girl agrees to sex with her boyfriend then he is breaking the law but this may be described as a 'crime of consent'. Can you think of any other victimless crimes?

3   A school pupil caught 'scrumping' apples from an orchard or riding a bike without lights after dark is technically committing a crime but a local police officer might decide just to give a warning so that the crime is left unrecorded. Can you think of any similar examples where the police might use their discretion in this way?

4   The Islington Crime Survey asked the public to say out of seventeen offences which five the police should spend most of their time and energy on. The priorities of the public were:

71 per cent robbery with violence in the street
69 per cent sexual assaults on women
60 per cent use of heroin or hard drugs
58 per cent burglary of people's houses
43 per cent drunken driving
39 per cent racial attacks
27 per cent vandalism
25 per cent bag snatching
23 per cent glue sniffing
22 per cent unruly behaviour at football matches
13 per cent use of cannabis
10 per cent rowdyism in the streets
 9 per cent theft of motor cars
 8 per cent burglary of shops or offices
 7 per cent prostitution
 6 per cent company fraud and embezzlement
 3 per cent shoplifting

The police are often very busy and so they have to use their discretion in deciding which reported crimes to respond to first. List five types of crime to which you think the police would give top priority and give five examples of crimes which might well be regarded as so trivial that they are ignored.

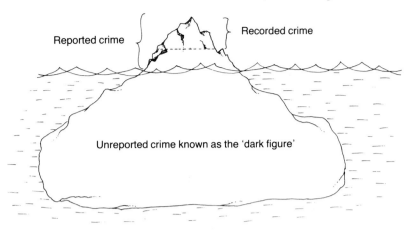

How can we estimate the size of the 'dark figure'?

1   Informed guesses   The most common non-indictable crimes are traffic offences and probably millions of these are committed every day by drivers breaking the speed limits. When the Metropolitan Police introduced the wheel-clamp, they estimated that 3 million cars are parked illegally every day.

As for serious offences, the dark figure is probably largest for sexual offences. For examples, before the 1968 reform of the abortion laws there were reckoned to be about 100,000 illegal abortions per year of which only 250 or so were known to the police. In other words the police only recorded one in 400 cases and so the dark figure was 99.75 per cent.

More recently, Rape Crisis Centres, which offer a 24-hour hot-line and counselling service, have suggested that less than 10 per cent of rapes are reported to the police.

2   Crimes against shops and businesses   It may be impossible to know how much pilfering is done by people at work, but a shop which keeps accurate records of its stock can have a good idea of the extent of shoplifting. It may be difficult to know if the loss of 100 pairs of tights is the result of one theft or 100 thefts, but inside information suggests that about 99 per cent of cases are unreported. This is because store detectives may think that they are doing well if they catch 10 per cent of shoplifters and of these they may hand over only 10 per cent to the police for prosecution.

3   Self-report studies   A famous study called *Our Law-Abiding Law-Breakers* found that 90 per cent of a sample of adult Americans confessed to offences for which they could be gaoled (although one of these offences, 'malicious mischief', included the crime of opening your son or daughter's mail!).

4   Victim studies   The graph on page 174 shows the results of the British Crime Survey which was carried out by interviewing a representative sample of 11,000 members of the population. They were asked about their experiences of crimes over the previous year and their readiness to report them to the police.

Such large scale surveys are very costly. (This one cost about £250,000.) The results depend on the reliability of the victims' memories. They may forget about, or even be unaware of, offences such as criminal damage to their property – which might include the deliberate scratching of the bodywork of a person's car.

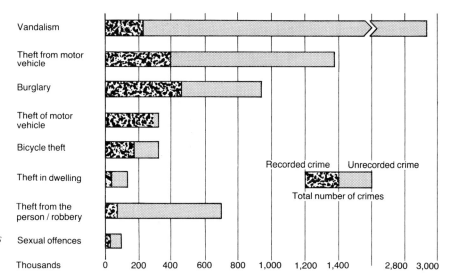

Recorded and unrecorded crime in England and Wales in 1983 (source: Social Trends, 1986).

Activities

1 Why is there very little under-reporting of car thefts?

2 Why might a headteacher decide not to report thefts in school to the police?

3 Why might a store detective hand over to the police only 10 per cent of the shoplifters who have been caught?

4 Describe the problems which you might have if you tried to conduct a self-report study on crimes committed by pupils in your school or college.

5 Constable Alan Nabb was just reading the *Police Review* before going out on the beat. The headline which had caught his eye said *'Women's Committees complain: police accused of inaction over battered wives'*. His duty sergeant called over: 'Mrs Hurd at 92, Hanger Lane says it sounds like her neighbour at number 94 is strangling his wife. Get down there quick, Alan!'

On arrival, PC Nabb found smashed crockery all over the living room and the drunken husband was leaning unsteadily against the wall. His badly bruised wife, with blood on her face, immediately said, 'Please don't arrest him officer. I won't press charges.' What should PC Nabb do?

6 How would it affect the crime figures if the government legalised the possession of cannabis and abolished the laws which restrict Sunday trading by shopkeepers?

Some explanations for the rise in indictable crime between 1960 and 1980

Below are some explanations why indictable crime rose from 700,000 recorded offences in 1960 to 2,500,000 recorded offences in 1980.

1   The number of seventeen- to twenty-year-olds, who commit a quarter of all crime, rose from 1.1 to 1.5 million over those twenty years.

2   90 per cent of all indictable crime involves property and so an increase in property creates more opportunities for crime. A third of all property crime involves cars and the number of cars in Britain rose from 5.5 to 14.5 million between 1960 and 1980.

3   The same two decades saw the number of telephones increase from 2.5 million to 12 million. This made it a lot easier to report crime. Of all crime which is reported, 66 per cent is now reported by telephone.

4   In the same period not only did police numbers grow from 72,000 to 114,000 but improved communications, such as radios and computers, also increased operational efficiency.

The problem for a criminologist is to determine whether the increase in recorded crime is due to

- a real increase in actual crime (so that the iceberg is getting larger), or
- more crime being reported (so that more of the dark figure, below the water's surface, is revealed).

Why a rise in crime might reflect an improvement in society's standards

An increase in divorce may merely be due to a lowering of the water-level over the iceberg of 'empty-shell' marriages. This might be a good thing if it means that fewer people are living miserable lives trapped in unhappy marriages. It could also mean that standards have risen because couples now have higher romantic ideals – so that more may sue for divorce since reality fails to meet their high expectations.

There may have been more unhappy marriages in the past but less divorce and, in a similar way, there may have been far more violence in pubs yet far fewer convictions. Whereas a pub landlord might have expected a brawl at closing time every Friday night in the 1860s, his modern counterpart might be less willing to tolerate such behaviour without calling the police.

4   Causes of crime

Biological theories blaming the individual

In the 1870s an Italian doctor called Lombroso published one of the first scientific theories which attempted to explain why some people commit crime. From his studies of convicts, Lombroso claimed that they had physical features in common, such as a flat nose, a narrow and low forehead and an arm span exceeding their height. Their primitive physiques caused them to lack a properly developed moral sense of right and wrong, thus explaining their criminality.

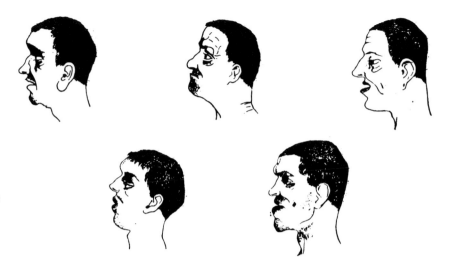

Victorian criminologists tried to identify deviants by their body type. These pictures are from The Criminals *by Havelock Ellis.*

This theory of an inborn criminal nature has been rejected for the following reasons:

- Criminality does not necessarily 'run in families' from one generation to the next.

- The convicts studied by Lombroso were by no means typical of the whole criminal population which includes businessmen who commit frauds, evade taxes and break factory safety laws but are seldom imprisoned.

- Some of the apparent physical similarities between the convicts would have been due to the poor diet they received in prison.

Yet many of us still believe that we know what typical criminals look like and many police probably use certain stereotypes. For example, they may think that the typical football hooligan is a skinhead. A more recent theory which points to innate characteristics is that of the psychologist Hans Eysenck. He claims that certain genetically-based personality traits make some people more likely to commit crimes. He argues, for example, that extroversion makes it difficult for some individuals to learn to accept rules.

Psychological theories blaming the parents

A common idea blames the upbringing of delinquents and says that they are bad because their parents are bad. Parents may be 'bad' because they have little respect for the law themselves or because they fail to control their children. More sociological variations of this idea argue that delinquents are 'depraved' because their backgrounds are 'deprived', for example growing up in broken homes or in poverty caused by unemployment.

One version of this argument highlights the maternal deprivation of children who are deprived of the closeness of their mothers in their early years. In extreme cases such neglect is said to produce psychopaths who, because they have never been shown warm feelings, are unable to feel consideration for others.

Case study: 'Frank' the psychopath

A typical psychopath will appear to have no conscience, no guilt; to feel no shame or remorse and to be coldly lacking in emotion or human feelings. In his study of the *Roots of Psychopathy* Geoffrey Stephenson interviewed twenty young adults who had been sent by the courts to special mental hospitals. Nearly all had similar case-histories to 'Frank' who

> was the illegitimate son of a prostitute who had been shuttled haphazardly between a

children's home and his mother's lodgings during infancy and childhood.

He often ran away and stole.

> He was above average intelligence but never held other than casual labouring jobs. Personal violence and persistent theft led to a short stay in a psychiatric hospital at the age of 18. Here he became violent towards patients and staff, and absconded in a high rage, to be convicted a few days later for armed robbery and rape.

Do you think that all mass murderers must be psychopaths and that they should therefore be sent to secure mental hospitals rather than prisons?

A less severe form of mental illness is that of the kleptomaniac who has a strong impulse to steal but with little obvious motivation. For instance, a teenage girl may secretly fill her bedroom with stolen cosmetics which she never intends to use, give away or sell. This hoard may be seen as compensation for the supply of love which most of us store up in our childhood but which she may never have had. Alternatively, she may be aiming, like many who attempt suicide, to be discovered. And so her actions can be seen as a cry for help.

American sociological theories

1 **The Chicago School**, in the 1920s, produced an **ecological** theory of crime. This focused on the inner-city slums which had the highest official rates of crime. The Chicago sociologists called these areas **zones of transition**. This is because such areas had cheap rooms to let which attracted poor migrants from the countryside and overseas. These new arrivals then struggled to move out to better parts of the city as soon as possible.

Those left behind in the zone of transition showed high rates of

poverty	drugtaking
broken homes	gambling
alcoholism	suicide
debt	crime
illegitimacy	

The rapid turnover of population meant that these areas lacked a stable community to exercise informal social control, for example stopping neighbours from stealing from each other. The zone of transition was thus seen as an area of **social disorganisation**.

2   Anomie   In 1938, Merton used the idea of *anomie* or 'a mismatch between goals and means' to explain crime. He described five different responses to capitalist society's dominant goal of material, financial success:

- *Conformity* = accepting the legitimate means to such a goal, that is hard work (Laurie Taylor has likened this to working hard at playing a fruit machine).

- *Innovation* = using illegal methods to reach the accepted goal (like breaking into the fruit machine).

- *Ritualism* = accepting the means but losing sight of the object of the exercise (like playing the fruit machine mindlessly, forgetting what the aim is).

- *Rebellion* = rejecting society's values in favour of an alternative system, for example turning to communism or religious cults (like trying to build a different sort of amusement arcade).

3   Status frustration   In 1955, Albert Cohen wrote about youths who end up with boring, dead-end work. They are frustrated at their lack of success in the jobs market. To escape from this feeling of failure they create their own alternative set of values: a subculture with norms which give status to those who commit acts of vandalism and violence. (Compare this with Turner's research on page 147.)

4   *Lower Class Culture as a Generating Milieu of Gang Delinquency*   In this 1962 study, Miller, like Cohen, concentrated on delinquent boys. (Females are conspicuously absent from theories of deviancy before the 1970s.) Miller saw much crime as an extension of male lower-class norms. These place high value on concerns such as toughness, getting 'kicks' (excitement) and defying authority.

5   The drift into delinquency   In the 1960s, Matza rejected the idea of a distinct delinquent subculture. He argued that we all have a **subterranean set of values** – for example, we enjoy occasionally abandoning respectable behaviour to 'let our hair down' at parties or carnivals. Adolescents are freer to drift loose from the restraints of conventional conduct. They still accept that crimes are wrong but they justify their delinquency in a number of ways.

Case study: lager louts

More than 2,000 people were arrested in over 250 serious public order disturbances between 1987 and 1988. Many of these events were 'rural riots' in the prosperous towns of the home counties, such as Andover, Witney, Newbury and Guildford. The chief inspector of the Dorking police said, 'Most of those arrested have been aged between eighteen and twenty-five. They seem to have plenty of money to spend and in most cases they have been drinking. There were flashpoints before. In the sixties it was mods and rockers in cafes. Now it's in the pubs.'

Matza has listed some **techniques of neutralisation** which delinquents use as excuses for acts which they know are wrong. We can apply these excuses to the hooligans of the so-called 'lager culture':

- *appealing to higher loyalties* – 'I attacked the copper to save my mate from arrest',
- *denying injury* – 'I didn't do the copper no harm',
- *denying the victim* – 'All coppers are bastards (but I suppose I would ask the police to help if my car got knicked)',
- *denying responsibility* – 'I'm sorry, but I was a bit tanked up like'.

British sociological theories

1 Traditional criminology Large-scale surveys by the Cambridge Institute of Criminology have tended to produce **multifactor explanations** of delinquency. D. J. West (*Are Delinquents Different?*, 1977) judged five factors to have special importance:

- low family income,
- large family,
- comparatively low intelligence,
- parents with a criminal record,
- parents with low standards for bringing up children.

2 The New Criminology In the 1970s sociologists began asking a number of questions from the perspectives of **labelling theory** (developed in America by Becker, Goffman and Cicourel) and **Marxist theory**. Such questions included:

- Do working-class male youths really commit more crimes? Or do the police concentrate more on such groups? (Refer to the examples of moral panics on pages 37–9 and on page 192.)
- Were the crackdowns on 'muggers' or 'social security scroungers', in the 1970s and 1980s, whipped up by the capitalist press in order to justify repressive and intrusive policing (useful for dealing with political and trade union militancy, for example CND activity and strikes)?
- Are the styles of youth subcultures just devices to help young people cope with the stress of finding their own identity during adolescence *or* are such styles part of a resistance to what capitalism has to offer?
- Do the power structures of capitalism mean that law enforcement is not applied with equal vigour to white-collar, business crimes?

Why have feminists concentrated on the role of judges?

Case study: white-collar crime wave

Corporate fraud has become the big stakes crime in Britain with an estimated £5 billion at risk – far outstripping celebrated bank raids and bullion robberies.

By its nature, fraud is difficult to add up. Only those who get caught get counted.

Estimates vary but, according to figures for 1987, the combined company fraud squads of the Metropolitan and City of London police forces had 462 cases of fraud and attempted fraud, involving £1,545 million, on their books at the beginning of the year and took on a further 590 investigations totalling £3,295 million.

This compares with £125 million for theft inquiries, £70 million for burglary and £17 million for robbery, though the actual amounts officially stolen through fraud came to £16.2 million and attempted fraud to £256.7 million.

It is hard to put an accurate figure on the amount involved; many firms, fearful of a loss of client confidence, do not inform the police.

(adapted from the *Guardian*, 4 February 1989)

---

3   Economic and political marginalisation   In 1984, Lea and Young argued that more and more young people were being pushed to the margins of society because of mass youth unemployment. This led to a high degree of **relative deprivation**: large numbers of white and black youth felt poor compared to other groups.

This in turn has led to a contradictory subculture which faces in two directions. On the one hand, the subculture tries to maintain unity and solidarity in the face of adversity and the attack on inner-city communities by military styles of policing.

On the other hand, the subculture faces in the direction of a petty criminality that wears down the community. The subculture has a highly individualistic streak. This stresses survival by predatory crimes such as bag-snatching and stealing car radios.

GCSE question from Southern Examining Group 1988

Item A: The British Crime Survey of 1982

Examples of offences	Percentage of offences reported to the police
Theft from a motor vehicle	29
Burglary in a dwelling	48
Theft from a person	8
Wounding	23
Theft of a motor vehicle	100
Theft of a pedal cycle	60
Sexual offences	26

(adapted from *Social Trends*, 1987)

Item B

The first British Crime Survey, in 1982, looked at the percentage of crimes which were reported to the police in 1981. The results, some of which are given above, were the first evidence in this country of the amount of under-recording of a wide range of offences.

Errors can occur when estimates are put forward to cover the population as a whole. To arrive at its estimates the survey interviewed 11,000 people who were asked about the crimes committed against them over the previous twelve months and whether these crimes had been reported to the police. Some sociologists have termed the difference between the actual number of crimes committed and the number appearing as criminal statistics as the 'dark figure'. A factor which could affect the 'dark figure' may be failure to report crimes, for whatever reasons, to the police.

(a) According to the examples given in Item A, which of the offences is least reported to the police? (1)

(b) (i) Which offence is most reported to the police? (1)
  (ii) Suggest *one* reason why this is the case. (1)

(c) Item B refers to unreported crime. Identify and explain *two* reasons why certain crimes are less likely to be reported to the police. (4)

(d) How would you explain the fact that there are far fewer women than men in our prisons? (5)

(e) A juvenile delinquent is someone under the age of seventeen who breaks the law. What explanations have sociologists given for juvenile delinquency? (8)

CHAPTER 13

The effects of the mass media

Are we manipulated by the mass media?

If I shout across the street to you then I am using my voice as a medium, or method, of communication. Letters and telephone calls are similarly **media**, or methods, of individual communication. On the other hand, any methods which reach a mass audience are part of the **mass media** and so these include: TV, radio, papers, magazines, films, videos, records and comics.

1 Research into audiences

National Readership Surveys

These surveys find out which social groups read different newspapers and magazines. Advertisers need this sort of information before spending millions of pounds on placing advertisements which might, for example, be targeted at rich young men who can be tempted to buy Porsche cars. The Institute of Practitioners in Advertising uses the following social class categories:

A = higher managerial or professional
B = intermediate managerial or professional
C1 = junior managerial or professional and supervisory or clerical
C2 = skilled manual workers
D = Semi- and unskilled manual workers
E = pensioners, casual or lowest grade workers, unemployed

In 1987 the National Readership Surveys found that 74 per cent of class A read a daily newspaper compared to 59 per cent in class E. A number of class and gender differences are shown in the following chart:

Percentage of adult readers in different groups, 1987

	Males	Females	A	B	C1	C2	D	E
Sun	28	23	5	10	20	32	37	27
Daily Telegraph	7	5	28	16	8	3	1	2
News of the World	30	27	9	12	23	36	40	30
The Sunday Times	9	7	35	22	10	3	3	2
Smash Hits	5	6	5	5	5	6	6	3
Exchange and Mart	6	2	3	3	4	5	4	2
Woman's Own	3	18	8	10	12	11	11	9
Good Housekeeping	2	9	15	12	7	4	3	2

(adapted from *Social Trends*, 1989)

In 1987, the most popular daily newspaper was the *Sun*, with 11 million readers, and the most popular weekly magazine was the *TV Times*, with 9 million readers.

Television and radio audiences

The average American sees a million television commercials by the age of forty. Compare your own viewing and listening habits with the following figures:

TV and radio: average viewing and listening per week, by age, 1987

	Age groups			
Hours: mins per week	*4–15*	*16–34*	*35–64*	*65+*
TV viewing	19:14	20:03	27:25	37:41
Radio listening	2:07	11:18	10:16	8:44

(adapted from *Social Trends*, 1989)

Case study: television viewing and gender

The following extracts are from *Family Television* by David Morley, 1986. It describes interviews which were conducted with eighteen families in South London.

Power and control over programme choice
Masculine power is evident in a number of the families as the ultimate determinant on occasions of conflict over viewing choices ... None of the women in any of the families uses the automatic control regularly. A number of them complain that their husbands use the channel control device obsessively, channel flicking across programmes when their wives are trying to watch something else.

Characteristically, the control device is the symbolic possession of the father (or of the son, in the father's absence) which sits 'on the arm of Daddy's chair' and is used almost exclusively by him ... The research done by Peter Collett and Roger Lamb in which they videotaped a number of families watching television over an extended period shows this to comic effect. On at least one occasion the husband carries the control device about the house with him as he moves from the living-room to the kitchen and then engages in a prolonged wrestling match with his wife and son simultaneously so as to prevent them from getting their hands on it.

Styles of viewing

The tapes made by Collett show the families concerned engaging in an almost bizarre variety of different activities: we eat dinner, knit jumpers, argue with each other, listen to music, read books, do homework, kiss, write letters and vacuum-clean the carpet with the television on.

. . . the men state a clear preference for viewing attentively, in silence, without interruption 'in order not to miss anything'.

Moreover, they display puzzlement at the way their wives and daughters watch television. This the women themselves describe as an essentially social activity, involving ongoing conversation, and usually the performance of at least one other domestic activity (ironing, etc.) at the same time. Indeed, many of the women feel that to just watch television without doing anything else at the same time would be an indefensible waste of time, given their sense of their domestic obligations.

Activity

Carry out your own research to check on the above findings about television viewing and gender.

2   Theories of the effects of the media

The uses and gratification theory

The above findings fit in with the **uses and gratifications theory** of Denis McQuail. According to McQuail, we use the mass media for:

- *information* – seeking advice, satisfying curiosity, gaining knowledge;
- *personal identity* – finding models of behaviour and reinforcement for personal values;
- *integration and social interaction* – gaining a sense of belonging, finding a basis for conversations or a substitute for real-life companionship;
- *entertainment* – escaping, relaxing, filling time or getting enjoyment.

This theory sees the audience as consisting of active individuals making conscious choices for themselves rather than passive automatons who are dominated by the power of the media.

The hypodermic needle model

This theory sees the audience as impressionable and open to manipulation. The mass media are seen to directly 'inject' their powerful influences. This theory arose in the 1930s because:

- new media such as radio, cinema and **mass circulation** newspapers were reaching massive new audiences;
- new dictators, such as Hitler and Stalin, were continuously using **propaganda** – distorting information for their own political purposes;
- the breakdown of traditional communities and the decline of the extended family were said to lead to a mass society of rootless, **atomised** (isolated) individuals – who would be more easily open to manipulation;
- **behaviourism**, in early psychology, saw human behaviour as based on conditioned responses to potent stimuli.

The 1936 Olympic Games in Berlin were stage-managed as a vast exercise in Nazi propaganda.

The two-step flow model

Lazarsfeld carried out research on the effects of the media during the 1940 US presidential election. He claimed that the media have only an indirect impact on us. Political attitudes are formed during personal discussions led by influential people within our family or peer group, or among our workmates. These **opinion leaders** filter the influence of the media so that the media's output reaches us in a two-step process.

Three further factors limit the impact of the media:

- **Selective exposure** means that we tend to read newspapers with which we agree. We expose ourselves to a political bias which will reinforce, rather than change, our existing views.
- **Selective perception** means that we reject or reinterpret information which does not fit in with our well-formed attitudes.
- **Selective recall** means that we conveniently forget details which contradict our viewpoints.

Audience dependency theories

These theories argue that voters are increasingly vulnerable to the political influence of the media. This is because there are more and more floating voters who have no strong party allegiance and are quite ready to switch sides. Few voters attend political meetings during election campaigns and few engage in discussions on the doorstep with canvassers from the different parties. This means that voters are mainly dependent on the media when deciding how to vote.

Modern election campaigns are increasingly conducted on television with the emphasis on images, personalities and slick presentation. The popular press is overwhelmingly Conservative (except for the *Daily Mirror*) and has become increasingly partisan (more biased). Millions are spent on advertising and experts advise on how to manipulate the media. Coverage is obtained by staging **photo-opportunities** and offering **sound-bites**. The latter are brief, witty put-downs of the other parties which slot

Open political bias in the newspapers during the 1983 general election campaign.

into the TV news more easily than lengthy speeches with details of proposed policies.

The ideological model

An **ideology** is a set of values and beliefs which have been simplified to support a particular cause. The ideological model sees the media as promoting the ideologies of those with power in society. We are conditioned into accepting a common sense view of the world which supports the existing social structure.

This theory of the media has gained influence since the 1960s. The focus has been on the way that news is manufactured; the way that the ownership of the media is concentrated into a small number of hands; and, the way that stereotyped representations distort rather than merely reflect the world (for example, the media's use of the 'cereal packet norm' of family life, see page 59).

3   The manufacture of news

Gate-keeping

The editors of the news in papers and on radio and television are constantly selecting and rejecting possible material. They may be reluctant to allow foreign news items 'through the gate'. **Gate-keeping**, then, refers to the media's power to refuse to cover certain issues. In typical editions of daily papers you are likely to find the following amount of coverage of overseas events:

Average number of foreign news stories	Type of paper (with examples)
Fewer than ten	Downmarket popular tabloids (*Sun, Star, Mirror*)
Ten to twenty	Upmarket tabloids (*Today, Mail, Express*)
Over thirty	Broadsheet quality 'heavies' (*The Times, Telegraph, Guardian, Independent*)

News values

Editors tend to value events as more newsworthy, more deserving of coverage, if the events are:

1 sudden (for example, murder) rather than slowly evolving (for example, pollution);
2 big, a small event may fail the size threshold;
3 unambiguous, clear in meaning;
4 familiar, relevant, close to home (for example, English-speaking USA may get more coverage than Europe);
5 able to fit our expectations ('most "news" is actually "olds"');
6 rare and surprising (an antidote to 4 and 5 above);
7 already established as news (a running story);
8 providing ingredients for a 'balanced diet' of bad, good and entertaining news;
9 about leading, elite nations;
10 about elite people (for example, presidents), famous personalities (for example, stars);
11 personal (for example, Nelson Mandela has personified the struggle against apartheid);
12 bad, with negative consequences.

The above list, drawn up by media sociologists, can be compared with the *Guardian*'s advice of news priorities (issued to new staff in the 1960s):

1 *Significance*: social, economic, political, human.
2 *Drama*: the excitement, action and entertainment in the event.
3 *Surprise*: the freshness, newness, unpredictability.
4 *Personalities*: royal, political, 'showbiz', others.
5 *Popular ingredients*: sex, scandal, crime.
6 *Numbers*: the scale of the event, numbers of people affected.
7 *Proximity*: on our doorsteps, or 10,000 miles away.

(from *News, Newspapers and Television* by Alistair Hetherington, 1985)

Agenda setting

The media help to determine which issues become the focus of attention. In this way, the media suggest to us which are the most important problems of the day. This power of the media is called agenda-setting.

In the mid-1980s the media highlighted heroin deaths but not fatalities from smoking and drinking; social security swindlers instead of tax evaders; black muggers in preference to racial attacks on black people. Issues like the abolition of the House of Lords or the Monarchy may be kept off the agenda altogether.

Verdict on Demo-Day:

Yes, our police ARE wonderful!

'WELL DONE, LADS.' MR CALLAGHAN CONGRATULATES POLICEMEN IN GROSVENOR SQUARE AFTER THE DEMONSTRATION

By
HARRY LONGMUIR, JAMES LEWTHWAITE, MICHAEL O'FLAHERTY, BERNARD JORDAN and OWEN SUMMERS

THE MAN who won the day in yesterday's big protest demonstration in London was the **ordinary British bobby.**

He kept his head, his humour and his self-control. He kept the peace and sanity as well.

And at the end of a day in which 30,000 demonstrators marched, only eight policemen were injured.

There was only one point on the long march through London when there was an attempt at violence. That was Grosvenor Square

But at five past four, just before the marchers arrived, a senior police officer broadcast a 16-word message to his men: 'Your job is to maintain police lines, according to instructions. There are to be no incidents.'

And the police maintained their lines —magnificently—when, five minutes later, a group of militant followers of Chinese Communist leader Mao Tse-tung led some 3,000 demonstrators away from the main body of 30,000 marchers and into the square. Their target: The U.S. Embassy.

For more than three hours the protesters were forced back by the police.

Persuasion

In spite of rushes from the hard core of 300 Mao-militants, who hacked with poles from their banners and showered the police with fireworks, the police held firm, refusing to be provoked. The police horses stood firm, too, as firecrackers exploded under their hooves.

Home Secretary Mr James Callaghan later went among the police and said: 'Well done, lads. Thank you.'

Behind the triumph for police tactics and behaviour was Deputy Commander John Lawlor.

Commander Lawlor, 62-year-old soft-spoken trouble - shooter of Scotland Yard's riot department, pressed for an outwardly soft approach to the demonstration at a secret conference several weeks ago.

Despite some senior officers' opinions that a harsher line should be taken, his persuasion won through.

It was Commander Lawlor's wish that no tear gas or water cannon should be used and that demonstrators if they wished should be allowed to squat in streets.

Commander Lawlor's plan—and he got backing to the hilt from Mr Callaghan and Metropolitan Police Commissioner Sir John Waldron—was: 'Don't antago-

THE boot goes in. One demonstrator holds PC John Alliston down as another kicks him. PC Alliston, 37, attached to Limehouse Police Station, was pulled out of the cordon and attacked in one of the few outbreaks of real violence. He was rescued from the mob by a police baton charge and taken to hospital. Later he was said to be comfortable.

nise the demonstrators—they've got a right to demonstrate.'

Two thousand hand-picked bobbies were on duty in Grosvenor Square—all men who had attended crowd-control courses at Hendon Police College.

Last night the police were reluctant to discuss their crowd control course. One senior officer commented: 'The methods, which appear to be pretty successful, will be used again. We are learning and improving every time.'

Significantly the use of water, gas or gas masks played no part in the course schedule.

It all ended successfully, with police morale high. An inspector in Grosvenor Square said: 'I'm a proud policeman tonight. The eyes of the world were on us, and we've proved it can be done without the police getting violent.'

And a sergeant joked: 'I think the worst thing about all this is that I'm missing *The Forsyte Saga* on television.'

'The Kick': one demonstrator gave 70,000 a bad name.

Case study: the anti-war demonstration and 'the Kick'

Graham Murdock has studied the press reporting of a massive demonstration which took place in London in 1968. Its purpose was to protest against the American Government's escalation of the war in Vietnam and the British Government's support for the Americans. About 70,000 people marched peacefully along an agreed route to a rally in Hyde Park. A breakaway march of some 3,000 people went to Grosvenor Square where about 250 of them attempted to break through a police cordon to demonstrate outside the American Embassy. This resulted in a number of violent incidents.

Next day the press all concentrated on the events at Grosvenor Square:

'Police win battle of Grosvenor Square as 6,000 are repelled'
(*The Times*)

'Fringe Fanatics Foiled at Big Demonstration – what the bobbies faced'
(*Daily Express*)

'The Day the Police were Wonderful'
(*Daily Mirror*)

All except *The Times* carried a front page picture of 'the Kick'.

Murdock's first point is that the press coverage 'characterised' the demonstration as full of violence and streetfighting. The small print might have mentioned the 70,000 peaceful marchers, but the picture and headlines alone created a false and distorted impression.

Murdock's second point is that by concentrating on the violence the press not only ignored the 'message' of the demonstration but also undermined it. As a result of the papers' reporting of the event, the message or cause of the demonstrators would be associated in the public's mind with violence and lawbreaking. In other words, the press had given the demonstrators and their cause a bad name.

Case study: the Battle of Westminster Bridge

Compare and contrast the coverage of a national demonstration by the National Union of Students in the following four sources:

Source A: from the front page of the *Guardian*, 25 November 1988

Source B: from the front page of *The Times*, 25 November 1988

Clash as 25,000 protest over loans scheme

ADRIAN BROOKS

Some of the thousands of student demonstrators involved in violent clashes near the Houses of Parliament yesterday.

Students battle with police

By Staff Reporters

Mounted police wielding batons yesterday dispersed a student demonstration after thousands of protesters broke away from a march, brought central London to a standstill for hours and confronted police as they tried to reach Parliament.

Missiles of bottles and sticks were thrown by protesters as police officers on horseback fought to clear Westminister Bridge.

Source C: from *the Hornsey and Muswell Hill Journal*, 1 December 1988

Pupils in police charge alarm

FIFTY sixth formers of Fortismere comprehensive school, Muswell Hill, went on the national students' demonstration last Thursday – and a number were horrified when they were unwittingly caught up in the "pitched battles" with police near Westminster Bridge.

The police charged on horseback during the protest against Government plans to bring in loans to replace grants for students gaining college or university places.

Fortismere head Mr Andrew Nixon was disturbed by stories of violent police action which pupils brought back.

"I acceded to a request to take part. This is because they are going to be concerned about grants and loans when they go to university. They also got parents' permission," he said.

"For many it was the first time they had seen what happens when demonstrators and police get into conflict.

"It does seem that some of the police lost their tempers. At one time, police were having to pull colleagues off students. My youngsters got frightened.

"I know of no instances where youngsters from here misbehaved." Some of his pupils might have got the odd bruise (he had been given no details) but none was off sick.

Joanna Simons (17) a Fortismere sixth former said: "They charged at the students on the embankment. They were completely unreasonable."

Source D: from *the Hampstead and Highgate Express*, 2 December 1988

Students 'wanted to kill us'

POLICE from Hampstead station, who helped form a cordon across Westminster Bridge during last Thursday's student demonstration, spoke this week about the "appalling levels of hostility" they encountered.

One sergeant said: "I thought that some of the demonstrators wanted to kill us; it was very frightening."

Two women constables and nine male officers from Hampstead were injured during the demonstration.

WPC Judith Taylor, 21, who has been with the force for 18 months, was rushed to Westminster Hospital by ambulance after being crushed unconscious when people fell on top of her. Another 20-year-old WPC spent two days in hospital, after being bitten in the hand by a protester and punched in the face. She suffered concussion and shock, and is still on sick leave.

A 32-year-old sergeant was brutally kicked in the testicles.

Inspector Keith Walmsley said the officers were accompanying the front of the march when some of the demonstrators decided to turn right towards Westminster Bridge instead of continuing on to the Imperial War Museum.

"We ran along with them to try and stop them and stuck our arms out. But the group, about 3,000 strong, were determined to go on".

At Westminster Bridge the officers from Hampstead met up with horses and vans and helped to form a cordon across the bridge to stop the protesters demonstrating outside Parliament, which is illegal.

"The demonstrators were 60 yards deep from our position on the south side of the bridge. People were pushing and throwing full beer cans and glass bottles and using banners as spears," said Inspector Walmsley. "It was very frightening."

Officers at the front of the cordon lost gloves and ties, had watches ripped off and badges torn from their helmets, he said.

He added that the official NUS stewards on the demonstration had done a "marvellous job".

Data-response exercise: the Battle of Westminster Bridge

Use the four sources on pages 189–91 to answer these questions.

1 What was the demonstration about?
2 Which sources mention the purpose of the demonstration?

3 Sources C and D are both from local newspapers. Both offer local angles on the event. Which local participants are highlighted?
4 How do the descriptions in Sources C and D differ?

4 Stereotyped representations

Gender stereotypes in the media are discussed on pages 19–21 and racial stereotypes are discussed on pages 91–3. According to the ideological model these distorted representations serve to support the ideologies of racism and patriarchy: the beliefs that whites are superior to blacks and that men are superior to women.

Case study: the amplification of drug use

Between 1967 and 1969, Jock Young carried out research on marijuana smokers in London's Notting Hill. The media at that time created sensational stereotypes of hippy drug takers. This moral panic put pressure on the police and courts to take action. A deviancy amplification spiral then developed. The drug users came to feel isolated and persecuted; they began to act in accordance with the stereotypes provided by the media.

Since Young's study of *The Drugtakers* (1971) there have been a number of other case studies of the way the media represents particular groups:

- *Folk Devils and Moral Panics: The Creation of the Mods and Rockers* by Stan Cohen (1972) is discussed on pages 37–9.
- *Bad News* by the Glasgow Media Group (1976) describes the negative portrayal of strikers in television news coverage.
- *Policing the Crisis: Mugging, the State and Law and Order* by Stuart Hall and others (1978) analyses a moral panic about black youth.
- *Images of Welfare: Press and Public Attitudes to Poverty* by Golding and Middleton (1983) discusses the phenomenon of **scroungerphobia**: hatred whipped up against social security claimants (see pages 225 and 226).
- *War and Peace News* by the Glasgow Media Group (1985) claims that there was unfair coverage of the Greenham Common Women's Peace Camp and CND when they campaigned against the siting of American Cruise, nuclear missiles in Britain.
- *Doctoring the Media* by Anne Karpf (1988) claims that the tabloid press promoted homophobic hysteria in its early coverage of AIDS as 'the gay plague'. (**Homophobia** means hatred of homosexuals).

Conclusion: the dominance and pluralist models of media power

Much of the media, from newspapers to satellite television stations, are owned by a small number of men, such as Rupert Murdoch and Robert Maxwell. Does this mean that the daily content of the media is controlled and manipulated by these owners? Two contrasting answers are given by the dominance and pluralist models of media power.

The dominance model sees the media as closely controlled by a ruling elite. The content is decided from above and it offers a selective world view which matches dominant ideologies. The audience is seen as passive. The media are seen to have strong effects in support of the established social order.

The pluralist model denies the existence of a single ruling class and instead sees various political, social and cultural interests competing for influence (see 'the role of pressure groups', page 200). There is a diversity of papers and television and radio stations. Many of them are independent of each other. They compete in the marketplace for audiences and so they must respond to the demands of the audience: they are 'audience-led'. The audience is fragmented and selective. It is active rather than passive. In the pluralist model the effects of the media are seen as 'numerous, without consistency or predictability of direction, but often with "no effect"' (Denis McQuail, *Mass Communication Theory*, 1987).

There is much evidence that we are given only a partial and distorted view by the media. But how far are we influenced by the bias of the media? How important is the media as an agency of social control? In order to measure accurately the influence of the media we would need to isolate its effects from the many other influences to which we are subjected – such as family, friends, class and so on. This, however, is difficult if not impossible to do. It must be remembered that we are not passive automatons, unable to think for ourselves. Many commentators are guilty of implying that only they are capable of critically evaluating the media's output, whilst the rest of us are hapless victims of it.

5 Violence on televison

In 1989 a book by Marie Messenger Davies was published with the provocative title of *Television is Good for Your Kids*. This is provocative because there has been widespread concern about the effects of TV violence on children. There have been a number of sociological studies of this topic, such as *Television and Delinquency* by Himmelweit and others, and *Television Violence and the Adolescent Boy* by Belson. These have tended to deny that TV can be the prime cause of violence. Family background and upbringing are given far greater emphasis.

Apart from the problem of defining what actually constitutes a violent act on TV, the debate has focused on three contrasting effects of screen violence: sensitisation, catharsis and de-sensitisation.

Sensitisation means the process by which people are made more sensitive. In the late 1960s and early 1970s the American people found themselves watching close-up action shots of real killing virtually every night on their TV news bulletins. They were shown the war in Vietnam in a way that no war had previously been seen. Some argue that the Americans became sensitive to the sufferings of the civilians and soldiers involved and that this shock and revulsion helped to fuel the popular protest which led to the American withdrawal. On one of his visits to the troops in Vietnam, Bob Hope told them: 'If your TV ratings don't improve, we'll have to cancel this war.'

Catharsis refers to the process by which we are purged of an emotion. Some people argue that watching screen violence is good for us because it helps to purge or get rid of our violent emotions in a harmless way. We live them out in fantasy when watching, say, Clint Eastwood brutally eliminating his enemies.

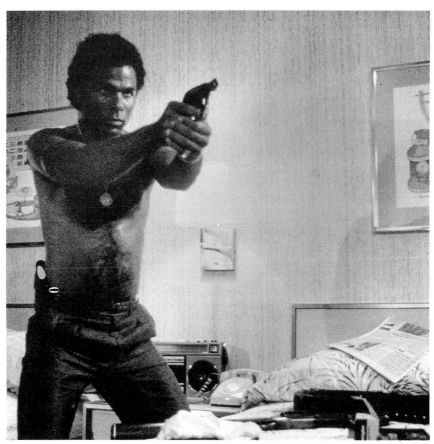

Miami Vice – *catharsis or desensitisation?*

De-sensitisation describes the process by which an experience makes us less sensitive to human suffering. The experience of watching violent programmes may have this effect on us. We may lose our sensitivity to human suffering and come to believe that the use of violence to get what we want is acceptable and normal. The debate on screen violence mostly revolves around this particular effect.

The famous 'Bozo Doll' experiments claimed to prove this effect of de-sensitisation. Young children were shown a film of other children attacking a large blow-up doll with a hammer. They were then observed after being left in the playroom shown on the film. Many were keen to imitate the violence they had just seen on the screen. They sat on the 'Bozo Doll' and hit it with the hammer, just as in the film.

(*The Code of Practice* which lays down the rules governing TV sex and violence may be obtained from the Broadcasting Standards Council, 5–8, The Sanctuary, London SW1P 3JS.)

GCSE question from the Midland Examining Group 1988

By the term 'mass media' we mean ways of communicating with large numbers of people without face-to-face personal contact. They include television, radio, newspapers, magazines, comics, books, films and advertising billboards. The mass media are an important way of getting information and ideas from other people. These can shape people's attitudes and perhaps influence their behaviour. Many sociologists have seen the mass media in modern industrial society as an agent of social control. In particular the media are seen to support the main norms and values of society and the established order.

(a) From the passage, give *two* examples of the mass media. (1)
(b) From the passage, what are *two* of the functions of the mass media? (1)
(c) Explain, using examples, the following terms:
   (i) norm (3)
   (ii) socialisation (3)

(d) Explain how the mass media may influence *either* the attitudes towards women in society; *or* voting behaviour; *or* attitudes towards ethnic minorities. (6)
(e) Explain the ways in which social control takes place in society. (6)

GCSE question from London and East Anglian Group specimen papers

'The mass media have grown rapidly in recent years and have attracted many criticisms, in particular over content and presentation.'

(a) Name *one* function of the mass media. (1)
(b) Describe *two* methods newspapers can use to influence their readers. (2)
(c) Describe *three* possible effects on children of showing violence on television. (6)
(d) Examine the view that the mass media allow for *one-way* communication only. (6)

CHAPTER 14

Politics

Political activity is usually associated with government. Governments take decisions that affect the organisation of a society and in order to do this governments need to exercise **power**. Generally, therefore, politics is concerned with the exercise of power. Governments vary considerably regarding the source of the power that they exercise. **Democracy** and **dictatorship** are terms which primarily refer to different sources of power. Before examining the processes of the political system in Britain, we will look closely at these two important terms.

1 Democracy and dictatorship

Direct democracy in ancient Athens

The word 'democracy' means 'rule by the people' and it was invented by the Ancient Greeks. They not only originated the word democracy but actually practised it. Ancient Greece consisted of a number of independent city-states. For a period of about 200 years, in the fifth and fourth centuries BC, the city-state of Athens was governed directly by regular meetings of the assembly. This assembly numbered potentially 30,000 male citizens. A quorum for important business was 6,000 and all decisions were taken by a majority vote. As well as women, non-citizens such as slaves and foreign residents were excluded. This pure, classical type of democracy, in which the citizens are the government, approximately fits Theodore Parker's famous definition of democracy as 'government of all the people, by all the people, for all the people'.

Representative democracy in modern Britain

In modern Britain citizens do not participate directly in decision making (apart from when a **referendum** is held – a vote by all the people on a single issue), but this does not necessarily mean that British political arrangements are undemocratic. It is true that, unlike the citizens of ancient Athens, British citizens do not actually exercise political power. Rather, the power to make decisions is passed on to an elected group. These representatives meet in the assembly called the House of Commons and they are called Members of Parliament. If the government, formed by the majority of MPs, fails to satisfy the electorate it can be removed at the next general election. So, as in ancient Athens, the source of political power in Britain is the citizen.

The British type of democracy is called **representative** or **parliamentary democracy**. The central part of such a democracy is the process of elections where the voters give their decision-making power to a group of representatives. The largest group of these Members of Parliament then forms the government. It is at elections, therefore, that citizens give their permission or consent to be governed in a particular way by a particular group.

Democratic rights

We have defined democracy as rule by the people and stressed the importance of elections. Yet a democratic society consists of more than this. The democratic way of life in modern Britain also consists of the following rights which give the individual a degree of freedom and security:

1 Equality before the law This right is designed to ensure that, while no one has the right to break the law, all citizens are treated equally by the courts, regardless of race, religion, sex or class; so that no one is 'above the law'.

Inside the House of Commons.

2 Personal freedom In 1215, Magna Carta established the principle that an individual's property or liberty can only be removed by the courts in accordance with the laws of the land. The 1679 Act of Habeus Corpus (which is Latin for 'give me the body') confirmed that an individual cannot be arrested and detained without being charged for an offence.

3 Freedom of speech and writing Section 2 of Chapter 13 listed some of the limitations to this right, but in the main we cannot be punished for expressing our opinions and ideas.

4 Freedom of religion and public worship This right ensures that citizens can practise any religion without fear of harassment and persecution.

5 Freedom of association and assembly This right enables any number of citizens to meet and discuss whatsoever they wish, apart from criminal conspiracies.

6 Free and fair elections Any individual can form his own political party and compete as an election candidate in a secret ballot of all registered electors who wish to vote.

We should note that there is a difference between the theory and practice of rights (for example, Rastafarians would argue that their right to practise their religion is restricted by the law which bans the use of cannabis), but in any discussion of the extent of democracy in Britain we should remember the existence of these rights. The possession of such rights creates notable differences between British society and other societies. In South Africa, for example, the majority of citizens do not enjoy equality before the law, the right to free elections, the right to freedom of assembly, and so on.

Democracy can be seen as a matter of degree. Although the actual exercise of political power by the British people may be small, it is certainly greater than in many countries. The claim that Britain is a democracy therefore is not based on a blindness to the imperfections of British democracy. Rather, the claim is based on the view that the word democracy usefully expresses some of the notable political differences between a society like Britain and one like South Africa, where the majority of the people have no control over who governs them or how they are governed.

Dictatorship

A dictatorship is a type of government which does not rule with the known consent of the people. Dictators often claim the support of the majority but such claims are questionable because the majority are denied the opportunity to show which leader or party they support. Some dictatorships only affect people's lives to a limited extent, to the extent necessary to stay in power. But **totalitarian dictatorships** are not merely content to stay in power, they aim to control every important aspect of people's lives.

A totalitarian dictatorship: the USSR under Stalin, 1928–1953

Under Stalin's dictatorship, the USSR was transformed from an economically backward country into a modern, industrial nation. In the process, the Soviet people paid the terrible price of 20 million deaths. In the early 1930s, Stalin forced 100 million peasants into collective farms. The clash between their resistance and his ruthlessness led to 5 million deaths from grain famines. Another 2 million were killed by machine-gunnings or died from privation after expulsions from their homes. A further 3 million died in labour camps. These gulags, or forced labour camps, were spread across the USSR like an archipelago, or sea full of islands. This **gulag archipelago** killed another 9 million and a further million were shot in prisons before Stalin's dictatorship was over.

Under Stalin, there were no free trade unions. Political parties other than the Communist Party were banned. Stalin tried to control totally every aspect of Soviet life. His secret police had agents spying on the people in factories, offices, the armed forces, schools and apartment buildings. Peasants who refused to help the government take over their farms were sent to labour camps as well as managers and workers who failed to reach industrial production targets.

In Stalin's periodic 'purges' thousands of people who were even remotely suspected of opposing him disappeared and were executed or sent to labour camps. Army officers, Communist Party officials, managers of factories and even leaders of the secret police were 'purged' from time to time.

Mass propaganda in a modern totalitarian dictatorship: portraits of leading Communists are held high during the 1984 May Day parade in Red Square in Moscow.

There was complete censorship. Art, literature, films, entertainment, music, newspapers and broadcasting were all strictly controlled by the state. Much publicity was given to the confessions of innocent leaders at 'show trials'. Such leaders were caught in the purges and then tortured so that they would confess. School children were indoctrinated with Stalin's version of communist beliefs.

The military dictatorship in Chile

Totalitarian dictators such as Mussolini and Hitler were similar to Stalin in having master-plans for completely transforming society. This is not the case with the type of dictatorship which rules present-day Chile. In 1973 this dictatorship overthrew the democratically elected socialist government led by Dr Salvador Allende. The main aim of the leader of the US-backed military coup, General Pinochet, was to eliminate Allende's socialist reforms and any outspoken supporters of those reforms.

The military dictatorship originally rounded up tens of thousands of opponents and held them in the national stadium in Santiago. Despite world-wide condemnation, many were tortured and killed or sent to prison camps. But in the 1980s, officially outlawed political parties have re-emerged and there have been regular, large anti-government demonstrations.

In 1988 General Pinochet lifted the state of emergency. Three hundred exiled opposition leaders were allowed to return and the first legal demonstrations were permitted. A plebiscite was held with Pinochet as the sole presidential candidate. When 55 per cent voted against him, it was announced that presidential elections would be held in December 1989. It is hard to see how such opposition could have occurred in the totalitarian societies of Stalin or Hitler.

2   The role of pressure groups in Britain

Totalitarian dictatorships, such as Communist China, are **monolithic** because politics and society are dominated by the single creed of a single party. Democratic societies, in contrast, are **pluralist**, meaning that they contain many competing centres of power and influence. For example, in Britain, the Hunt Saboteurs' Association and the League against Cruel Sports are opposed by the British Field Sports Society; anti-abortion groups such as LIFE and the Society for the Protection of the Unborn Child are opposed by the Abortion Law Reform Association and the National Abortion Campaign.

Lobbying your Member of Parliament

In a democracy the individual is free to try and influence local and central government in numerous ways. For example, people who feel strongly about an issue can write to their councillors or MPs, write to newspapers, or ask others to sign a petition. Also, we all have the right to directly **lobby** our MPs. There are two ways to gain personal contact. Most MPs hold Saturday morning 'surgeries' where constituents can queue up to see

WHEN WILL POLITICIANS START USING THEIR BRAINS?

UNEMPLOYED
2000 TRAINED DOCTORS.

UNEMPLOYED
8140 TRAINED NURSES.

UNEMPLOYED
38400 TRAINED TEACHERS.

UNEMPLOYED
28900 SKILLED TECHNICIANS.

PUT PEOPLE FIRST.
IF THIS GETS YOUR VOTE MAKE SURE YOU USE IT.

BANG GOES ANOTHER KIDNEY UNIT.

PUT PEOPLE FIRST.
IF THIS GETS YOUR VOTE MAKE SURE YOU USE IT.

VOTE TO SAVE US.
Stop the Tories…
Please, please end our torture.

● Every day dogs, cats, and rabbits are tormented in cosmetic and commercial laboratories.

● Every week, during the hunting season, foxes and deer are condemned to a cruel and horrible death.

● Every year seal pups are clubbed and brutally skinned, sometimes while still alive, to create fashion furs.

Over the past four years, your Conservative government has done virtually nothing to end our pain, even though the vast majority of British people long for our suffering to end.

It's time for a change.

CONSERVATIVE ?

Reg. No. 1556888

 International Fund for Animal Welfare, Tubwell House, New Road, Crowborough, East Sussex TN6 2QH. It is only your donations that make it possible for us to save animals worldwide. Please help.

Three advertisements placed in the press during the 1983 general election campaign.

them. Alternatively, you can visit the central lobby or hallway in the Palace of Westminster and fill in a card requesting to see your MP. Messengers are employed in the Houses of Parliament so that these lobby cards can be swiftly delivered to MPs.

Such individual action is not likely, however, to be as effective as action carried out by an organised group. Organisations which aim to influence the views of the public and the government are called **pressure groups**. These are different from political parties because they do not try to win power by standing in elections.

Sectional and promotional pressure groups

Many observers have divided pressure groups into two categories. **Sectional groups** are concerned with protecting the interests of their members and so their membership is usually restricted to a particular section of the population, such as those in a certain occupation. **Promotional groups** campaign to promote a particular cause and so their membership is usually open to as many supporters as possible.

The *Directory of Pressure Groups and Representative Associations*, by P. Shipley (1979), lists well over 600 organisations. There are also thousands of pressure groups which have no formal structure. These range from a group of parents asking for a school-crossing patrol to the bankers and stockbrokers who constitute 'the City'.

We should note that the two categories often overlap. For example, many trade unions have helped to promote the cause of nuclear disarmament.

A number of pressure groups and charities are listed in section 4 of Chapter 18.

Factors determining the methods used by pressure groups

1   Type of membership   A group which is composed of influential members is likely to be taken seriously by the government. The British Medical Association, for example, has established means of communication between doctors' representatives and the Department of Health and Social Security. While **ministers** have overall responsibility for different government departments, such as the Foreign Office and the Department of Transport, the day to day running of these ministries depends on **civil servants**. When the officials in the Department of Health and Social Security were drafting regulations requiring doctors to retire at the age of sixty-five, they almost certainly consulted the BMA.

2   Financial resources   A rich pressure group can pay MPs for their services or make donations to a political party. In 1972 the Labour MP Brian Walden entered into a five-year contract to act as a paid parliamentary consultant to the National Association of Bookmakers. Another example is the 'Flexilink' consortium of ferry companies and ports which was formed in 1985 and unsuccessfully opposed the proposal to build a fixed link across the Channel. This group spent large sums hiring MPs and professional

Examples of different types of pressure groups

Types of sectional pressure group	Example of organisation	Example of one of their aims
Professional	British Medical Association	Better working conditions for doctors
Trade union	National Union of Miners	No more pit closures
Industry	Solid Smokeless Fuels Federation	Clean air regulations
Commerce	Road Haulage Association	More motorways
Finance	Building Societies Association	Changes in the banking system
Consumers	Automobile Association	Prevent big increases in road or petrol tax

Types of promotional pressure group	Example of organisation	Example of one of their aims
International	Anti-Apartheid Movement	End all investment in South Africa
Political	Campaign for Nuclear Disarmament	Removal of US Nuclear bases from UK
Child welfare	Child Poverty Action Group	Research on how to improve the social security system
Animal rights	Animal Liberation Front	Rescue animals from laboratories and factory farms
Cultural	British Humanist Association	End religious school assemblies
Recreational	Ramblers Association	Extend the number of coastal paths
Environmental	Greenpeace	Close all nuclear power stations
Health	Action on Smoking and Health	Ban tobacco advertisements

lobbyists to organise a public relations campaign and to wine and dine as many MPs as possible.

3 The need for public support In his book on *Pressure Groups and Government in Great Britain*, Geoffrey Alderman has described how the need to mobilise widespread support may lead pressure groups to use a variety of methods. Some of the ways to gain publicity and influence public opinion are listed below:

● Public meetings: the Clean-up TV Campaign was launched by Mary Whitehouse in 1964 with a meeting at Birmingham Town Hall which brought instant nationwide publicity.

- Advertisements: in 1982 the Police Federation advertised in newspapers asking people to return forms if they agreed with the restoration of the death penalty for the murder of police officers.

- Leaflets: in 1981 Action on Smoking and Health sent leaflets to 25,000 family doctors asking them to 'prescribe' the giving up of smoking by their patients.

- Surveys: the Campaign for Lead-Free Air was launched in 1982 with an opinion poll which claimed that nine out of ten people thought lead in petrol was a health hazard.

- Reports: in 1982 the Society of Teachers Opposed to Physical Punishment issued a dossier entitled *Britain's Battered School Children* which catalogued 158 attacks by teachers on pupils.

- Petitions: in 1982 newsagents' and tobacconists' associations arranged for shopkeepers to collect well over a million signatures complaining about an anticipated tax increase on tobacco.

- Demonstrations: the Disablement Income Group gained national recognition in 1967 when disabled people demonstrated in Trafalgar Square.

- Mass lobbies: in 1985 about 20,000 people joined a 'Fight World Poverty' lobby of Parliament. It was organised by the World Development Movement on behalf of the major Third World aid agencies, such as Oxfam, and the churches. Within a month the government announced an addition of £47 million to its aid programme.

- Direct action: in 1981 members of the Sea Shepherd conservation group attracted the attention of the media by spraying seal pups with a blue dye. Since the dye renders the pelts worthless, it saves the pups from being shot or bludgeoned to death for their skins.

- Legal action: in 1977 the National Association for Freedom obtained an injunction from the Court of Appeal against the postal workers' boycott of mail and telecommunications to South Africa.

The role of pressure groups

MPs are not supposed to represent just those who voted for them. (In 1987 the Conservatives won 375 out of 650 seats with only 14 million votes out of 44 million electors.) MPs should try to represent the interests of *all* their constituents. Powerful pressure groups, which only represent particular sections of the population, may make it difficult for MPs to serve the community as a whole.

While those who are poor, badly educated and lacking in organisation might lack an effective voice, influential groups, such as the National Farmers' Union, may routinely help to shape government policy and **deep-pocketed lobbies** may be able to afford expensive campaigns. For example, the tobacco companies can afford to pay over £100,000 per year to FOREST, the Freedom Organisation for the Right to Enjoy Smoking Tobacco.

But without pressure groups, citizens would have to rely on political parties or individual contact with MPs and the media. A democracy should not merely be a tyranny of the majority, it must listen to the voices of all minorities. Pressure groups provide the channels of communication through which governments can be made to change their mind.

Activities

1 In 1986, opinion polls showed that most people supported 'deregulation' of Sunday opening hours and yet groups representing shop-workers and church-goers persuaded enough Conservative MPs to vote with the Opposition to defeat the proposed reforms of the Sunday Trading Bill. Was this outcome a victory for democracy?

2 Give examples of five of the following types of pressure groups and in each case say what their main aims are:
   (a) local, (b) national, (c) successful, (d) unsuccessful, (e) short-lived, (f) permanent, (g) small but rich, (h) poor but with mass support.

3 During the campaign for votes for women, in the early years of this century, public attention turned from the 'suffragists' (National Union of Women's Suffrage Societies led by Millicent Fawcett) to the 'suffragettes' (Women's Social and Political Union led by Emmeline Pankhurst). Compare the moderate methods of the former with the militant methods of the latter.
   or Compare the moderate methods of the RSPCA with the militant methods of the Animal Liberation Front.

4 How would you plan a campaign to attract publicity and supporters in order to (a) prevent the council from building a rubbish incinerator in the field behind your house, or (b) improve the toilet facilities in your school or college?

5 Name four famous personalities who are associated with four different pressure groups.

---

3 The main British political parties

In terms of providing the main means of political recruitment, representation, communication and participation, the established political parties are more important than pressure groups. It is parties which form governments and oppositions. We now look at the main ideas which underlie their differing policies.

The Conservative Party

As their name implies, Conservatives (or Tories) are concerned that any reforms of society should not sweep away historic institutions and traditions. They wish to conserve important parts of the British way of life such as the monarchy, the House of Lords, the Church of England and the public schools. The basis of their policies is expressed by the following comments:

- 'We will all be better off if governments interfere as little as possible in our lives.'

- 'If we rely too much on government, increasing laws and regulations will restrict our freedom.'

- 'If we rely on governments to provide more and more services and facilities, we will be worse off for three reasons:

  1 Higher taxes will be needed and these will reduce incentives to free enterprise.
  2 Lower taxes would be preferable since they would encourage self-reliance. Lower taxes would allow people to keep more of their hard-earned income. They could then decide for themselves how to provide for their families.
  3 Government interference reduces the efficiency of industry; a capitalist economy works best with free markets.'

In 1987 Conservative Party funds received £3,800,000 in company donations. Firms also gave £70,000 to the SDP and the Liberals, but nothing at all to the Labour Party.

Advertisements placed in the press by the Labour and Conservative Parties during the 1983 general election campaign.

The Labour Party

The Labour Party is, to a certain extent, the political arm of the trade union movement. It grew out of the Labour Representation Committee formed by the Trades Union Congress in 1900 and so its purpose is to represent the ordinary worker. Out of a total income of £3,982,000 in 1984, the Labour Party obtained £2,948,000 from the affiliation fees of trade unions, compared to £711,000 from the subscriptions of members in constituency parties. Since 1981 the trade unions have had 40 per cent of the votes in the electoral college arrangement for selecting the party

Leader. Of the 269 Labour MPs elected in 1979, 133 were sponsored by trade unions. In such cases unions may pay most of a candidate's election expenses.

The party's argument against unfair and unjust inequalities of wealth are based on the following ideas:

- 'Whether we are clever or unintelligent, talented or untalented, healthy or disabled, we all share similar needs for education and work, for income and housing, and for a decent standard of living. Wealth should therefore be distributed according to people's needs. Large inequalities of wealth must be reduced because:

  1 they leave an enormous gap between the few very rich and the many very poor;
  2 children either inherit enormous advantages in life or else are severely socially disadvantaged;
  3 the wealth of employers and landlords gives them power over workers and tenants who are left with little power to control their own lives;
  4 inequalities lead to damaging class conflict which could be replaced with the social harmony of a fairer, more classless society.'

- 'The services and goods of more industries, such as transport and medical drugs, should be provided for the need of the people rather than for profits for individual businessmen. The economic system should be less capitalist, with more industries in **public ownership** so that they can be controlled in the interests of the people.'

These ideas have always appealed most to the working class and the class differences between the two main parties are reflected, to some degree, in the social backgrounds of their MPs (elected in 1983):

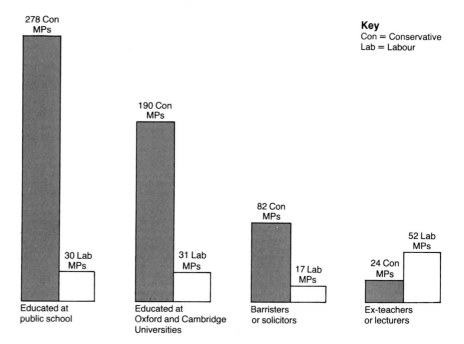

278 Con MPs

190 Con MPs

82 Con MPs

52 Lab MPs

30 Lab MPs

31 Lab MPs

17 Lab MPs

24 Con MPs

Educated at public school

Educated at Oxford and Cambridge Universities

Barristers or solicitors

Ex-teachers or lecturers

Key
Con = Conservative
Lab = Labour

The Liberal Democrat Party

A central concern of the Liberals is to give us all more freedom and this leads to a number of positions, such as:

- 'Many people's freedom is reduced by a lack of power due to poverty, therefore we need a better Welfare State.'
- 'Free enterprise must be restricted because it leads to the growth of really large firms, industrial giants which leave employees and consumers powerless.'
- 'Worker participation or industrial democracy, with workers sitting on the board of directors and each employee owning a share of the firm, would create more productive workplaces with better human relationships.'
- 'Similarly, parent governors should have more control over schools and power should generally be 'devolved' from central to regional and local government.'

In their enthusiasm for breaking down the centres of power and spreading power more evenly throughout society, most Liberals are happy to adopt slogans such as 'Small is Beautiful' and 'Power to the People'. Liberals are usually quick to protect minorities and keen to take up progressive ideas such as legalising abortion and reforming prisons. Such new ideas are often 'stolen' by the bigger parties after a number of years.

In the 1983 election, the Liberals joined in an alliance with the new Social Democratic Party (the SDP) which had been formed by right-wing Labour MPs breaking away from their party in 1981. But our **first-past-the-post** electoral system meant that together they only gained twenty-three of the 650 seats in the House of Commons, although they won 26 per cent of the total votes cast. (The 'first-past-the-post' system means that the candidate with the most votes wins. For example if candidate A wins 8,000 votes while candidates B and C each win 7,000 votes, candidate A is elected although the majority of people voted for the other candidates.) In the local elections of 1985, however, the Alliance succeeded in winning so many council seats all over the country that in twenty-five out of forty-six counties no party had a clear majority of councillors. The two big parties claim that these **hung councils** are ungovernable, but the Alliance prefers to call these county councils 'balanced'.

The Alliance and the middle ground of British politics

The political parties in Britain are like coalitions of pressure groups in so far as they contain wide ranges of opinions, with different internal factions always jockeying for power. In the 1950s and 1960s the Labour Party was dominated by its **right wing** and the Conservative Party by its **left wing**. This meant that they both agreed on many policies, so creating a broad area of agreement, or consensus. But in the 1970s the Conservatives became more right wing. At the same time, the Labour Party shifted to the left and adopted more socialist policies. And so the two main parties drew further apart and left the middle ground of politics vacant for the new Alliance.

More left-wing Labour policies of the 1980s	Con-Lab consensus of the 1950s and 1960s, agreed on:	More right-wing Tory policies of the 1980s
Main aim to reduce unemployment	Need to keep both unemployment and inflation low	Main aim to reduce inflation
Unilateral nuclear disarmament	Need for nuclear weapons	Support new nuclear weapons such as Cruise and Trident
Replace sold council houses by building more	Need for large numbers of council houses to be built	Sell off council houses and create a nation of owner occupiers
Extend nationalisation – for example in the area of banking	Need for a fair sized public sector with basic industries nationalised	Privatise, or sell off, industries such as Telecom, gas and water
Leave the European Economic Community	Need for UK to join EEC	Get tough with the Common Market
Abolish private education	Need for expansion of state education	Support public schools
Abolish House of Lords	Need for Life Peers	Create new hereditary viscounts

Activities

1   Find out the names and policies of some of the left-wing and right-wing groupings within the Conservative and Labour Parties.

2   Find out the meanings of the following terms: *manifesto, mandate, referendum.*

4   The social factors which influence voting

How the pendulum has swung since 1945

Year of general election	Party forming the government
1945	Labour
1950	Labour
1951	Conservative
1955	Conservative
1959	Conservative
1964	Labour
1966	Labour
1970	Conservative
1974 (February)	Labour
1974 (October)	Labour
1979	Conservative
1983	Conservative
1987	Conservative

Canvassing and opinion polls

Just before elections, the supporters of political parties often call at the door and ask people which candidate they support. Voting intentions are then marked against the names on the electoral register, or list of voters. This is called **canvassing** and the results from these canvassing returns help campaign managers to gauge how much support their party is getting.

Newspapers and TV programmes pay for **opinion polls** to predict the results of elections. Pollsters only need to interview a few thousand voters to predict fairly accurately how 31 million will vote because they carefully select samples of different groups in proportions which represent the composition of the whole population. In this final part of the chapter, we will look at how different social groups have voted in recent general elections. Our 1987 figures are taken from the BBC/Gallup Poll quota sample of 4,886 voters. (More details about sampling procedures are given in section 2 of Chapter 17.)

Class and voting

Percentage share of each group's vote in the 1987 general election

	Conservative	Labour
	%	%
Total British vote	42	31
AB (Professional/managerial)	59	14
C1 (Office/clerical)	52	22
C2 (Skilled manual)	43	34
DE (Semi-skilled/unskilled manual)	31	50
Unemployed	32	51

The main social factor to affect how a person votes is his or her class background. This is not surprising in view of the strong class differences between the two main parties. On pages 205 – 9 we have indicated some of these class differences in the areas of the parties' 'three Ps': policies, past histories and personnel (MPs and party members).

The above figures do indeed show a strong preference for the Conservatives among the middle class (categories AB and C1) with Labour's best support from the lower working class (category DE). But the connection between class and voting weakened during the 1970s and 1980s. This process has been called **class dealignment** and can be seen in the following figures:

	Conservative		Labour	
	1974	1987	1974	1987
	%	%	%	%
AB (Professional/managerial)	67	59	10	14
DE (Semi-skilled/unskilled manual)	25	31	54	50

A further point is that more of the skilled working class voted Conservative than Labour in 1987. Ivor Crewe has highlighted the split between the growing 'new working class', which is deserting Labour, and the shrinking 'old working class', which has stayed fairly loyal to Labour:

1987 shares of the vote

New working class	Con %	Lab %	Old working class	Con %	Lab %
Lives in the South	46	28	In Scotland or North	29	57
Owner occupier	44	32	Council tenant	25	57
Non-union member	40	38	Union member	30	48
Private sector worker	38	39	Public sector worker	32	49

Case study: class cleavages and political attitudes

Labour is in trouble not just because its traditional working-class base is in decline but also because this base does not share the more radical views of Labour's middle-class supporters. Heath and Evans have shown that this split is clearest on the 'new agenda' (non-economic) issues, such as women's rights, gays, ethnic minorities and green concerns:

% adopting left-wing position on:	The working-class supporters of		Professional/managerial supporters of	
	Con	Lab	Lab	Con
'Old agenda':				
Inequality of wealth	52	93	88	32
Unemployment v. inflation	61	87	89	47
Trade union power	2	29	37	1
Tax cuts v. social spending	35	61	80	34
Welfare v. self-help	30	60	71	30
'New agenda':				
Nuclear defence	9	38	65	7
Rights to protest	47	70	85	62
Cultural diversity in schools	31	46	69	31
Homosexuality	9	7	43	9
Death penalty	5	15	58	12

(You may find it interesting to work out what a 'left-wing position' would be on each of the above issues – pages 205–9 should help.) Heath and Evans comment that middle- and working-class Conservatives lie quite close together. In contrast, Labour suffers from a clear class split on new agenda issues.

Whereas the Conservative Party is ... a party of conviction, its policies uniting its different class elements, the Labour Party – at present, anyway – is not. Its different class elements have different attitudes ... That they remain in the same party is impressive, but is does not make for an easy life.

(from *British Social Attitudes*, 5th Report, 1988, edited by R. Jowell, S. Witherspoon and L. Brook, Gower Publishing Group)

Ethnicity and voting

The Harris Poll conducted for the *Asian Times* in May 1987 showed the following voting intentions: Asians – Conservatives 23%, Labour 67%; Afro-Caribbeans – Conservatives 6%, Labour 86%. Twenty-eight Asian and Afro-Caribbean candidates stood for the main parties and four were elected as MPs (all Labour):

Dianne Abbott (Hackney North and Stoke Newington)
Paul Boateng (Brent South)
Bernie Grant (Tottenham)
Keith Vaz (Leicester East)

Gender, age and voting

In 1987, the MORI polls found that women and men both split equally
with 43% voting Conservative and 32% voting Labour. But there were
variations according to age (for example, pensioners 47% Conservative
and 31% Labour), particularly among women: Labour's support among
women aged eighteen to twenty-four was 42% as against 27% among
women aged thirty-five to fifty-four.

The neighbourhood effect

Heath, Jowell and Curtice, in *How Britain Votes*, argue that:

> in a predominantly working-class area, both working-class and middle-
> class voters are more likely to vote Labour than in a socially mixed
> area, while in a predominantly middle-class area, voters of both classes
> will be more likely to vote Conservative. In other words, voting may
> be 'contagious'. How you vote may depend on how people around you
> vote.

The decline of old party loyalties and the rise of third parties

An opinion poll in 1970 found that 40 per cent of voters said that they
were staunch, loyal supporters of either Conservative or Labour. A similar
poll in 1979 found that those loyal to the old parties had fallen to 21 per
cent. This was matched by the rise of the 'third parties' such as the Liberals,
the Welsh Nationalists ('Plaid Cymru' in Welsh) and the Scottish Nationalist
Party (SNP). In 1951 the third parties only gained 3 per cent of the vote,
in 1970 they had 10 per cent and in 1974 they had 25 per cent of the
overall UK vote and 40 per cent in Scotland. Although the popularity
of the nationalist parties has fallen, the SDP's alliance with the Liberals
boosted the third-party share of the vote to 26 per cent in 1983 – the
highest since 1923 when it was 29 per cent.

Voters Begin to Choose: the open electorate

While third-party support has risen, in 1974 the Conservative vote fell
to its lowest since 1859 and in 1983 the Labour vote fell to its lowest since
1918. These changes are reflected in the title of Rose and McAllister's
1986 study, *Voters Begin to Choose: From Closed-Class to Open Elections
in Britain*. Their main theme is that

> The electorate today is wide open to change; three-quarters of voters
> are no longer anchored by a stable loyalty determined by family and
> class. More voters float between parties – or are wobbling in their commit-
> ment to one party – than show a lifetime loyalty to a particular party.
> At different times in the 1979–83 Parliament, the Labour, Alliance and
> Conservative parties could each claim the support of nearly half the

electorate in the Gallup Poll; at another point each had the support of less than one-quarter of voters.

Rose and McAllister suggest that aspects of the social structure, such as age, gender and class, now have far less effect on voting than the following four political influences:

1 Political principles Many voters have strong convictions, for example the belief that people should be free to choose on issues such as union membership and private schooling.

2 The current performance of the parties More important than estimation of the party leaders is evaluation of the parties' past record and their proposals for the future.

3 Socialisation The way parents vote remains the single most important early influence on party choice, but the effect of parents is weaker than in the past.

4 Socio-economic interests A school library assistant from a working-class background might belong to the National Union of Public Employees, live in a council flat and vote Labour. The reason he or she votes Labour may not be because of non-manual or middle-class occupation but because of

- opposition to cuts in the library service,
- loyalty to the family's political tradition, or
- the opinion that Labour best represents the interests of council tenants, union members and workers in the public sector.

Activity

Which social characteristics do you think most influence voting in your local constituencies?

GCSE question from the Welsh Board 1988

(a) Outline what is meant by
  (i) *political processes*, and (3)
  (ii) *political movements*. (3)
(b) Describe what is meant by *elite*, and give examples from your home area. (4)
(c) Discuss, with reasons, what you consider to be the *two* most important factors which may influence a person's voting behaviour. (10)

GCSE question from London and East Anglian Group 1988

Describe the differences in policies between any *two* major political parties in Britain. (15)

CHAPTER 15 | Poverty and the welfare state

1 The welfare state

The history of the welfare state

The idea of a welfare state is that the government should provide for the welfare of all citizens from cradle to grave, or 'womb to tomb'. Our social services date back at least to the Elizabethan Poor Law of 1598 which provided for **parish relief** for the destitute. This meant that officials in each village could collect a poor rate from every household and distribute the funds among the needy.

The 1870s saw a number of advances, under both Conservative and Liberal Governments, on the road to our modern welfare state. These included:

- the first national system of elementary schooling;
- the start of slum clearance and council housing;
- Public Health Acts which forced every area to have a Medical Officer of Health and a Sanitary Inspector.

The 1906–1914 Liberal Government made further advances in the provision of welfare, such as:

- old age pensions;
- contributions by employees, employers and government to a national insurance scheme which gave benefits for disability, maternity, sickness and unemployment;
- clinics for children;
- free school meals and medical inspections;
- labour exchanges for the unemployed;
- wages councils which laid down minimum wages for low paid workers in certain industries;
- probation officers.

The 1942 Beveridge Report laid the basis for the next stage in the development of the welfare state. Sir William Beveridge wrote of conquering the 'Five Great Social Evils' and the 1945–51 Labour Government took a number of appropriate measures:

1 Poverty   This was tackled by providing the 'safety net' of **national assistance** which was replaced by **supplementary benefit** in 1966. This is a means-tested benefit payable to people with no other income, or to top up other benefit payments such as **family allowances** (since renamed **child benefit**) which were introduced to help large families.

2 Ignorance   New secondary schools were built providing free secondary education for all in the tripartite system of grammar, secondary modern and secondary technical schools.

3 Disease   The National Health Service was set up to ensure free medical treatment for all.

4 Squalor   One focus for the rehousing of families from slums was provided by the string of New Towns built beyond the 'green belts' around certain cities.

5 Idleness   The 1950s saw successful 'full employment' policies which kept the proportion out of work below 3 per cent.

The welfare state since 1950

There have been many successes since the reforms of the post-war Labour Government. For instance, many new schools, hospitals, universities and old people's homes have been built. But a number of failings have also emerged. The mixture of successes and failures can be shown by looking at the progress made since 1950 in the areas of housing and poverty.

Housing   In 1981 2.1 million dwellings, or 11 per cent of the total housing stock was substandard, with one or more of these characteristics:

- unfit for habitation;
- in need of major repairs;
- lacking basic amenities.

In 1985, 2 per cent of dwellings had no fixed bath or shower but this was a great improvement on the figure of 37 per cent in 1950. Many slums were cleared in the 1950s when 300,000 new houses a year were built. But the house building totals have fallen from a peak in 1968 to the lowest figure since the 1920s in 1985:

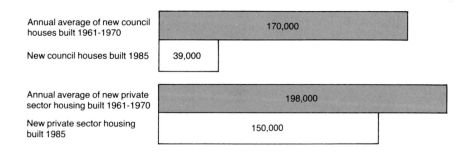

Annual average of new council houses built 1961-1970	170,000
New council houses built 1985	39,000
Annual average of new private sector housing built 1961-1970	198,000
New private sector housing built 1985	150,000

The Conservative Government in 1985 could argue that less council housing was needed since 61 per cent of homes were now owner-occupied but a number of the tower blocks built in the 1960s were now the new slums which councils were demolishing – so adding to the housing shortage.

The government's cuts in 'capital expenditure' on housing affected repairs as well as new building so that, by 1986, there was a new housing crisis with:

- 85 per cent of council houses needing repairs and improvement (a maintenance backlog which would cost £20,000,000,000 to overcome!);
- 1,200,000 people on council waiting lists;
- the DHSS paying £400 million per year to keep 146,000 homeless people living in board and lodgings;
- 40,000 squatters in London and 10 per cent of the population of the London boroughs (600,000 people) homeless or without a secure home according to the report by Professor Greve.

Poverty   The 1970s saw some new social security schemes such as **invalidity benefit** for the long-term sick and disabled and **family income supplement** available for low-wage families according to the number of children. Benefits not only became more widely available in the decades after 1945 but they also increased in value. The state retirement pension paid to a married couple, for example, rose in value between the 1950s and 1978 from a third to almost a half of average earnings.

Rowntree's York surveys found that the proportions of the total population in poverty had fallen from 28 per cent in 1899 to 18 per cent in 1936 and to only 1.5 per cent in 1950. But poverty was 'rediscovered' in the 1960s. The TV drama *Cathy Come Home* highlighted the plight of the homeless and led to a new campaigning group called Shelter. And *The Poor and the Poorest* by Abel-Smith and Townsend estimated that 14 per cent or, 7.5 million people, were in relative poverty in 1960. Their cause was championed by a new pressure group called the Child Poverty Action Group, started in 1965.

2   Definitions of poverty and the extent of poverty

Three definitions of poverty

1   Absolute poverty   Rowntree defined absolute poverty as the condition of those unable to afford 'the minimum provision needed to maintain health and working efficiency'. How did Rowntree decide on his first 'poverty line' in 1899? He consulted the work of a nutritionist called Dr Dunlop who had experimented on the diets of Scottish prisoners. Rowntree estimated that the basic foods needed by parents and three children could be bought for just under 13 shillings per week. He then added amounts to cover the costs of clothing, fuel, rent and 'household sundries'. Any families whose income fell below this poverty line were in absolute poverty.

2   Relative poverty   In 1899 Rowntree decided that the minimum clothing needs of a young woman were: one pair of boots, two aprons, one second-

Angela and Ricky Pulhofer with their children in their bed and breakfast room in a hotel where seventy families share one cooker. In 1986 the Guardian *reported that Hillingdon Council was paying £187 per week for this room.*

Squatters sleeping on the pavement after being evicted.

hand dress, one skirt made from an old dress, a shawl, a jacket, two pairs of stockings, one pair of old boots worn as slippers and a third of the cost of a new hat. What would you regard as the decent minimum nowadays?

Townsend has defined relative poverty as applying to those who cannot afford the amenities and activities which are customary. Cultural norms, or socially approved minimum standards of decency, vary over time and so they are relative. In 1971, 9 per cent of families had no TVs and 31 per cent lacked refrigerators: we could say that, relative to the expectations of the majority at the time, they were deprived of what most considered to be essential.

3   Environmental poverty   Using a broader definition, it has been argued that poverty is not just a matter of money. A family with both parents in full-time jobs might be well above the poverty line, yet they might live in a damp flat in a neglected council block. Their local public services and amenities (such as parks, schools, hospitals and public transport) might be inadequate or 'poor'. Are they living impoverished lives because of their deprived environment?

In his 1968–69 survey, *Poverty in the United Kingdom*, Townsend found that 34 per cent had no safe place for their children to play; 27 per cent suffered from dirty, smelly or smoky air and 22 per cent (or 13 million) lived in defective housing.

A boy begging on the O'Connell Bridge in Dublin in 1979 – a case of absolute poverty?

Case study: the 'Breadline Britain' survey

In 1983, MORI (Mass Opinion Research International) conducted a survey for London Weekend Television's documentary series called *Breadline Britain*. The survey tried to uncover a definition of relative poverty as 'the minimum standard of living laid down by society'. In order to get popular agreement on this, 1,174 interviewees were asked to select which out of thirty-five items they considered to be necessary for all families or adults. The following fourteen indicators of poverty were among those most frequently selected by the interviewees. The figure on the right is the percentage of the sample describing the items as necessary:

Heating to warm living areas	97
Public transport for one's needs	88
A warm waterproof coat	87
3 meals a day for children	82
2 pairs of all-weather shoes	78
Toys for children	71
Celebrations – e.g. at Christmas	69
Roast joint or chops once a week	67
New not second-hand, clothes	64
Hobby or leisure activity	64
Meat or fish every other day	63
Presents for friends or family once a year	63
Holidays away for one week a year	63
Leisure equipment for children – e.g. bicycles	57

Those interviewed were then asked which items they themselves lacked which they wanted but could not afford. From the results to these questions it was estimated that:

> 6 million people cannot afford some essential items of clothing;
> 3.5 million cannot afford carpets, washing machine or fridge;
> 3 million cannot afford to heat the living areas of their homes.

Taking the total in poverty as those unable to afford three or more of the twenty-two 'necessities', *Breadline Britain* calculated that 7.5 million people (or 13 per cent of the population) are in poverty. A simple subjective measure of how many people feel that they are poor was also given in the survey's findings. In 1983, 12 per cent of people said that they were poor all the time (compared to 8 per cent in 1968) and 28 per cent said that they were sometimes poor (18 per cent in 1968). The details of the survey were published in 1985 in *Poor Britain* by J. Mack and S. Lansley.

Children in West Belfast – growing up in a deprived environment.

Data-response exercise: the **Breadline Britain** *survey*

1   What was the size of the sample used in the *Breadline Britain* survey?
2   What was the definition of poverty used in the survey?
3   What proportion of the interviewees did *not* regard meat or fish every other day as necessary for all families?

4   What percentage of the population were estimated, by the survey, to be living in poverty?
5   What is meant by measuring poverty 'subjectively'?

Groups in poverty

Proportion of individuals in low income households, 1985

Economic status of head of household	Percentage with incomes below half the average
Pensioner	7
Full-time worker	3
Sick or disabled	19
Single parents	19
Unemployed	47
All economic types	9 (4.9 million people)

(Source: *Social Trends*, 1989)

- **Children**   In 1988, the Child Poverty Action Group claimed that the number of children living in households on or below the income support benefit level increased by 91 per cent between 1981 and 1985 to 2.25 million.

- **The disabled**   In 1988, the Office of Population Censuses and Surveys published the report of its 1985 survey on disability. Two-thirds of Britain's 6.2 million disabled adults said that they were either 'getting into difficulties' with money or 'just getting by' (on the margins of poverty).

- **The homeless**   In 1988, Shelter's 'Raise the Roof' report claimed that while 370,000 people a year are being accepted as homeless by local authorities, nearly double that number actually approach councils with nowhere to live.

Activities

1   Would you agree that the 22 per cent of households without a telephone in 1984, or the 17 per cent without colour TVs, should be considered 'relatively poor'?
2   In 1899 Rowntree found that the largest groups in poverty were those with large families and low pay. In 1936 he found that the main category was the unemployed and in 1950 pensioners were the largest group among the poor. Which groups do you suppose are the main groups in poverty today?

3 The causes of poverty

'The Poor are to blame': the culture of poverty and the cycle of deprivation

In the nineteenth century it was widely believed that people were poor because of their own inadequacies. Poverty was caused, it was held, by defects of character such as idleness, indiscipline and an inability to plan for the future. A modern sociological variation of this explanation of poverty is the idea of the **culture of poverty**.

This idea was first put forward by Oscar Lewis, in the late 1950s, and it arose from his research among the urban poor of Mexico and Puerto Rico. Briefly, Lewis found that the poor had developed their own subculture in response to the difficult circumstances that they found themselves in. The following four features of this subculture explain why the subculture has the effect of keeping the poor in poverty:

1 a sense of fatalism, feeling that one's destiny cannot be altered;
2 a strong inclination to live for the present and an unwillingness to plan for the future;
3 a feeling of worthlessness and isolation from the rest of society;
4 a lack of interest in joining political parties, trade unions or pressure groups which campaign for social change.

Poverty passes from generation to generation in a cycle of deprivation because the children of the poor are socialised into the subculture of poverty. President Johnson's 'War on Poverty', in the USA in the 1960s, tried to break this cycle by intervening with programmes of compensatory education and help for small businesses starting up in deprived areas. Some would argue that such policies are misconceived since the real cause of poverty is to be found in the way that our society is organised.

'Poverty – it is the fault of the capitalist system'

Marxists claim that poverty is an inevitable feature of the capitalist economic system. A *laisser-faire* or **free market economy** allows capitalists who own businesses to make huge profits while paying low wages to their workers. This argument leads to a number of conclusions:

1 Those who are unable to sell their skills in the market place and those with few skills to sell (such as the disabled, the old and the unemployed) will become 'casualties' of the market economy.

2 Poverty will never be eliminated until a communist system distributes wealth according to need rather than on the basis of skills or inheritance.

3 A Conservative Government, such as Mrs Thatcher's, which represents the interests of big business can be expected to reduce taxation most for the very rich while also dismantling the twenty-six Wage Councils which have set minimum rates of pay for almost 3 million low-paid workers. The unemployed are expected to 'price themselves back into work' by accepting very low rates of pay – because their benefit levels have been reduced.

Case study: income and wealth – the structure of inequality

One reason for the rise in poverty is the increasingly uneven distribution of income and wealth in recent years:

- In 1985 the most wealthy 10 per cent owned 54 per cent of all marketable wealth (compared to 52 per cent in 1980) and the bottom 50 per cent owned 7 per cent (6 per cent in 1980).

- *Percentage of all gross (original) income received by households in*

	the bottom 40%	*the top 20%*
1976	10	44
1986	6	51

(Source: *Social Trends*, 1989)

When we look at net income (income left after tax deductions) it is clear that tax cuts since 1979 have disproportionately helped the rich. The Fair Tax '89 Campaign used official figures to show that the richest 1 per cent gained £26,200 million from tax cuts between 1979 and 1989, while the bottom 10 per cent gained £900 million. The 1988 cuts in income tax, inheritance tax and capital gains tax were worth £400 a week to the top 1 per cent but only 92p a week to the poorest 2.5 million taxpayers.

The life-cycle of the low-paid

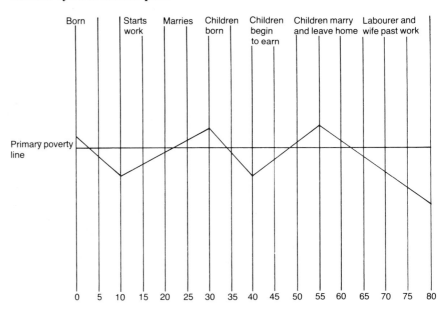

(Source: O'Donnell, 1985, adapted from Rowntree, 1901)

The life-cycle view of poverty

The culture of poverty theory is not only rejected by the Marxists who blame the inequality of the capitalist system, it is also rejected by the view which emphasises the importance of the **life-cycle of the family**. This view stresses that many of the poor are not so very different from the majority of the population.

The idea of the family life-cycle shows that a young married couple or a couple in late middle-age may be fairly well off financially since both partners may be working full-time with no children to support. In contrast, the couple starting a family may struggle financially due to the burden of high mortgage repayments and the loss of the wife's income.

Because the average family has insufficient income to accumulate significant wealth by saving, there is a predictable fall in living standards again when income is reduced by retirement – in the same way that many are vulnerable to any loss of income caused by sickness, unemployment, divorce or widowhood.

This view points out that many of us may, at some stage in our lives, depend on the 'safety net' of the social security system. Much poverty can be seen then as due to the inadequacies of the welfare system or the way that some people 'fall through the net'. The final section of this chapter looks at some of the problems of the benefits system.

Gypsies scraping a living from the Church Marshes rubbish tip in Sittingbourne in 1986.

4   The problems of the social security system

A major problem of the welfare system is its failure to deliver benefits to all those who are entitled to them. Some may choose not to claim benefits because they are too proud or because they find the procedures too humiliating. Many are also bewildered at the size and complexity of the benefits system. (The family credit application form, FC1, is a fifteen-page booklet containing eighty-seven questions in thirteen sections about every aspect of a claimant's domestic and financial affairs.)

In 1988-89 social security spending by the government amounted to £45,900,000,000. This was about the same as the combined state expenditure on education, defence, transport and housing.

Some of the main social security benefits in 1988–89

Benefit	Number of recipients	Expenditure (£000)
Child benefit	12,015,000	4,528,000
Retirement pensions	9,735,000	19,312,000
Income support	4,925,000	8,584,000
Housing benefit	4,465,000	3,874,000
Invalidity benefit	1,040,000	3,211,000
Attendance and invalid care allowances	770,000	1,065,000
Unemployment benefit	755,000	1,481,000
One-parent benefit	665,000	169,000
Mobility allowance	540,000	663,000
Family credit	470,000	409,000
Industrial disablement benefit	205,000	439,000
Sickness benefit	90,000	167,000

(Source: *Social Trends*, 1989)

Improving the benefits system

The late 1980s saw a number of moves to help social security claimants:

- The 1989 budget reduced national insurance contributions for the low paid and so helped them to escape from the **poverty trap**. The (wages/benefits) poverty trap has often meant that wage rises to the low paid leave them little better off. This is because a small pay increase may mean higher income tax deductions and national insurance contributions as well as the loss of benefits such as free school meals.

- Changes in 1988 included introducing loans to the poor from the Social Fund and basing the three main means-tested benefits (income support, housing benefit and family credit) on the same set of rules. One aim was to simplify the system. Another aim was to 'target resources on those most in need'. (The changes also had the effect of cutting benefits by £545 million.)

Claimants waiting outside a DHSS office in Newham, East London, in 1985. The office was closed while staff protested during the visit of a junior government minister, Mr Ray Whitney.

- Family credit is aimed at the families of low paid workers. But by 1989 only 250,000 families were claiming family credit out of an estimated 750,000 eligible families. The government then launched a £7 million 'Due to You' advertising campaign to boost the take-up of family credit.

- The problem of low take-up could be eliminated by the computerisation of all Department of Social Security (DSS) benefits. This, the biggest computerisation programme in Europe, is due for completion in the mid-1990s. It is costing £1,700 million and will reduce DSS staff from 80,000 to 60,000. All benefits and pensions are being put on inter-linked systems. One optimist foresees a quick, error-free service in pleasant surroundings: an end to 'the awfulness of the squalid benefit offices, the interminable queues and the demoralised staff'.

Case study: the Press 'Scroungerphobia' of 1976–77

In *Images of Welfare: Press and Public Attitudes to Poverty*, Golding and Middleton have described how the media created a moral panic about the abuse of the social security system in the late 1970s. The hysteria of the press had a number of effects:

1 Many low-income claimants were made to feel like scroungers, spongers and cheats.

2 Attention was directed away from the extent to which the rich avoid paying tax. In 1980 it was discovered that the wealthy Vestey family, owners of the Dewhurst butcher shops, had exploited a tax loophole so that they only paid £10 tax on £4,100,000 profits in 1978. The response of the press was to agree with Peter Thorneycroft, then Chairman of the Conservative Party, who wished the Vesteys

'good luck'. The Vesteys were portrayed as heroic businessmen and the taxmen as horrible kill-joys.

3   The **post-war welfare consensus** was dismantled. In other words, there was no longer agreement between the parties on levels of welfare spending. The way was prepared for the election, in 1979, of a right-wing government which could claim popular support for cutting benefits and clamping down on abuses of the social security system. By 1987 there were 14,000 prosecutions a year for benefits fraud (estimated at £500 million a year) as against just twenty prosecutions a year for submitting false tax returns. (Tax fraud was reckoned to be running at £5,000 million a year.)

Activities

1   Give examples of

(a) benefits which are universal and available to everyone and
(b) means-tested benefits which depend on the claimant's level of income.

2   List a number of different reasons for the low take-up rate of certain benefits.
3   List some alternative methods for the eradication of poverty.
4   Is poverty inevitable?

GCSE question from Welsh Board 1988

(a)   Explain what is meant by
    (i)   *absolute poverty*, and   (3)
    (ii)   *relative poverty*.   (3)
(b)   Identify where there is still poverty in Britain's society.   (4)
(c)   Discuss the reasons that have been given to explain the causes of poverty.   (10)

GCSE question from Southern Examining Group 1988

(a)   Give *three* reasons why women in the United Kingdom are more likely to be living in poverty than men.   (3)
(b)   Identify and describe briefly any *three* ways that the Welfare State helps people in need.   (6)
(c)   What are the main causes of poverty in the United Kindgom today?   (8)

CHAPTER 16

Work, unions, unemployment and leisure

Collective bargaining?

1 Changing patterns of work and technology

In *The Future of Work*, C. Handy has described some new patterns of work which have clearly emerged in the 1980s:

- Britain no longer seems to be a society which can guarantee full employment, with jobs for all who want to work.
- While many workers (often men) have been made redundant from full-time jobs, many others (often women) have been employed in new part-time jobs.
- Knowledge-based skills, such as data processing, have been replacing manual skills, such as welding.
- Jobs in service industries have been replacing jobs in manufacturing industries.
- The life-time career in one organisation is becoming rarer. An increasingly common pattern is for workers to be occupationally mobile, changing careers as well as employers.

These changes will sweep away many of the patterns of work of previous generations. As Handy says:

> to our grandchildren the massive organisations of this industrial age may look as bizarre as trench warfare does to today's military commanders. The idea of the 100,000 hours, 47 hours per week for 47 weeks per year that everyone used to work, and many still do, may seem as unnatural to them as child labour in the mines does to us.

In facing an uncertain future, Handy reminds us of the following precedents:

1   We have created jobs before. Between 1932 and 1937 we increased the number of jobs by 2.25 million and reduced unemployment by 1.25 million.

2   We have lived with a growing labour force before. In the 100 years from 1860 to 1960 the labour force nearly doubled, but so did employment.

3   We have survived structural change before. Agricultural jobs fell from over 25% of the labour force to under 3% in the same 100 years but were all absorbed into new industries and occupations.

4   We have seen technological change before. Between 1860 and 1960 the capital [machinery] employed per worker doubled, the output trebled. Automobiles replaced horses and society adjusted.

The pace of change in the early 1980s can be seen in the following figures showing the occupational distribution of the UK workforce:

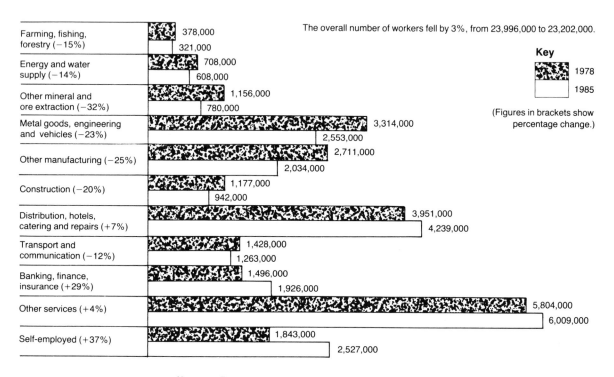

(Source: Department of Employment)

Data-response exercise: the changing occupational structure

1   How many employees were employed in the construction industry in 1978?
2   Which of the categories had the smallest workforce in 1985?
3   Between 1978 and 1985, in which industry did the number of workers
    (a) decline the most?
    (b) increase the most?
4   Between 1950 and 1985 the proportion of UK jobs in the service industries grew from 43 per cent to 65 per cent of the total

workforce and between 1973 and 1983 the proportion of non-manual jobs rose from 43 per cent to 52 per cent of all jobs.
(a) Give three examples of non-manual occupations which have been increasing.
(b) Give three examples of manual jobs which you think are on the decline.
(c) Name three industries that you think are included in 'other services', in the above chart.

Three stages of production technology

1   The division of labour   The specialisation of occupational roles and production tasks is called the division of labour. There has always been a degree of specialisation in human societies. Among Stone Age groups, for example, the young might have gone out hunting while the old kept the home fires burning. In medieval times craftsmen and merchants specialised in different tasks. When textiles were produced by a cottage industry some homes concentrated on spinning or weaving and others on bleaching or dyeing.

But the factory system, which accompanied the Industrial Revolution in the eighteenth century, broke jobs down into simpler, more repetitive tasks. In 1776 Adam Smith noted how, in a pin factory, 'One man draws out the wire, another straightens it, a third cuts it, a fourth points it, a fifth grinds it and prepares the top for receiving the head ... ten persons could make among them upwards of 48,000 pins in a day'.

The historian E. P. Thompson has described how, before the Industrial Revolution, Pennine farmers were also weavers; northern leadminers were also smallholders; servants also joined in with the harvest and Cornish tinners also joined in the pilchard fishing during the peak autumn season. The factory system largely put an end to such irregular labour patterns – where occupations had been mixed and where workers had alternated bouts of intense labour with long periods of leisure.

2   Mass production on assembly lines   In 1911 an American, F. W. Taylor ('Speedy Taylor'), wrote *The Principles of Scientific Management*. He claimed that for any job there was a single best method for organising the work which could be established by careful study of the time and motion involved in each task. Efficiency could be increased by standardising tasks, tools and equipment as well as by offering productivity bonuses.

Ford's assembly line at Halewood in Liverpool.

Specialisation by simplification offered the following advantages:

- inexperienced, unskilled workers could be employed;
- efficiency could be gained by mastery of repetitive routines;
- foremen could monitor work more effectively;
- individual tasks could be better synchronised with one another and with machines, allowing smoother and more intense production.

These ideas were first linked with the use of a continuous assembly line, before the First World War, by Henry Ford. This new method of **mass production** was so successful that by 1921 Ford had 60 per cent of the world car market and every other car on the road was a Model T Ford.

The conveyor belt method was soon applied to other industries. Audrey Swann has described how televisions were assembled at Pye factories in the 1950s:

> The sets came along on runners. We each did our own little bit of wiring, and soldering, and then it went on to the next person, and it was rushed. If you wanted to go to the toilet you had to call a float so that she could take your place, otherwise the sets piled up.
>
> (From *All Our Working Lives* by P. Pagnamenta and R. Overy)

3   Automation

> 'I'm a machine', says the spot-welder. 'I'm caged', says the bank teller and echoes the hotel clerk. 'I'm a mule', says the steel worker. 'A monkey can do what I do', says the receptionist. 'I'm less than a farm implement', says the migrant worker. 'I'm an object', says the high-fashion model. ... Nora Watson may have put it most succinctly: 'I think most of us, like the assembly line worker, have jobs that are too small for our spirit. Jobs are not big enough for people.'
>
> (From *Working* by Studs Terkel)

Several of the soul-destroying jobs mentioned above are now being automated. **Automation** involves machines which work by themselves, automatically, with little human supervision. In recent years robots have replaced many spot-welders and paint-sprayers in car factories and the need for bank clerks has declined because of 'hole-in-the-wall' cash-dispensers.

At some supermarkets the check-out assistant 'wipes' the bar code on goods with a laser pen and the linked computer system (a) gives the customer an itemised bill, (b) automatically re-orders stock from the warehouse and (c) reports to supervisors on the speed and efficiency of the till worker. One can see that the work done by the check-out assistant has become so 'deskilled' that it could well be done by a robot.

Deskilling

The way in which new technology can reduce the traditional craft of a job has been described in an international study of *Microelectronics and Office Jobs: The Impact of the Chip on Women's Employment*, by D. Werneke:

> Some jobs have been made better by the use of new technology. Tedious,

repetitive tasks have been eliminated by machines which have allowed some employees to take on more responsible and satisfying work. However, many more instances have appeared where clerical jobs became poorer as a result of introducing new technology. The traditional skills of the clerical workforce in many cases have been made redundant by machines with the result that many jobs have been deskilled. If, for example, a typist's speed and accuracy are no longer as important when using a word processor, the job has become less skilled unless higher level functions are added to the work. Deskilling not only results in a less satisfying job but it also has a serious impact on career progression as it eliminates traditional paths to promotion.

Keyboarding skills may soon be redundant because voice recognition technology has developed so that advanced word processors can take direct dictation without the need for a human operative with the manual skills of keying in words.

Three examples of how new technology can polarise skills

Low skill	*High skill*
1 Mundane machine minding on an automated assembly line.	Highly skilled maintenance work involving systems control and fault diagnosis.
2 Low level technicians supervising automatic testing or using computer-aided design.	High level technicians undertaking non-routine testing or complex design draughting.
3 'Marginal' word processor operatives with easily replaceable skills – like the 'temp' copy typist in the typing pool.	Personal secretaries with complex multi-function roles which cannot be standardised.

The two-tier workforce

A similar development to the polarising of skills is the emergence of core and periphery workers:

1 Core workers These are **functionally flexible**. They will do a range of tasks, whatever the company demands of them, in return for a secure full-time contract with good conditions, such as company pension scheme and high wages.

2 Periphery workers These are **numerically flexible**. A company can increase the number of these workers and then lay them off again easily, without having to give redundancy payments. They are often on temporary, part-time contracts and are self-employed or employed by sub-contractors. They are less likely than core workers to be protected by trade union membership.

Many organisations, from insurance companies and factories to schools and hospitals, no longer keep canteen, cleaning and caretaking staff on their direct payroll. Instead, these workers are often hired from the cheapest contractor and they are often women and/or from ethnic minorities (see the dual labour market, page 128).

2   Dissatisfaction at work

Symptoms

In 1985, a MORI/*Sunday Times* survey found that 76 per cent of workers were 'very' or 'fairly' satisfied with their jobs. This compared with 83 per cent in 1976. All managers must be concerned with this issue because the dissatisfaction of employees can lead to any of the following symptoms:

- low quality goods with more faults due to poor workmanship;
- high labour turnover with many recruits leaving the job after a short while;
- high absenteeism with large numbers of workers off sick with 'back-ache';
- open industrial conflict such as strikes;
- industrial sabotage with workers 'accidentally' dropping spanners in the works of conveyor belts. The expression comes from the French word *sabot*, meaning wooden clog, because French workers threw these into machines which were taking away jobs. At the same time, 1812–14, the English 'Luddites' were destroying new textile machines for the same reason;
- each of the above can cause low productivity, meaning low output per worker.

Case study: dissatisfaction and domestic labour

The following findings are from Ann Oakley's classic 1974 survey of forty housewives with at least one child under five, *The Sociology of Housework:*

- Hours spent on housework ranged from 48 to 105 per week, with an average of 77.
- 57% reported a high level of dissatisfaction with housework and 84% a medium or low level of dissatisfaction.
- The housewives were more likely to experience monotony, fragmentation, speed and loneliness in their work than the assembly-line workers in Goldthorpe et al's *Affluent Worker* studies.
- 70% of the middle-class housewives disliked housework compared to 30% of the working-class housewives.
- The most favoured tasks (in order) were cooking, shopping, washing, cleaning, washing up and ironing.
- Only 20% of the working-class mothers said that they liked looking after their children 'very much', compared to 70% of the middle-class mothers.

Activities

1 Carry out a survey of a sample of housewives designed to test some of Ann Oakley's findings.
2 Outline some arguments for and against the following development: In 1985 the Post Office employed 8,000 part-timers. They were mainly doing sorting in the evenings and 85 per cent were women. The Post Office aimed to increase the number of part-timers to 20,000 in order to cut the eight hours a week average overtime of postal workers in 1985.

Alienation

To be human is to possess certain needs, such as the need to be creative, to exercise initiative and the need to achieve something worthwhile. When people's work fails to fulfil such needs we describe their working experience as one of **alienation**. Individuals who are alienated at work may feel like alien inhabitants of a world that has little meaning or purpose in relation to their needs. The four classic symptoms of **alienation** at work are:

1 **powerlessness:** no control over the work that you are expected to do,
2 **meaninglessness:** unable to see any point in the product of your labour,
3 **isolation:** cut off from others,
4 **self-estrangement:** prevented from realising your full potential.

We now turn to some of the experiments which have attempted to improve job satisfaction, such as the new Volvo factory at Kalmar in Sweden, opened in 1974. Here they abolished the assembly line and let teams of fifteen to twenty put cars together on trolleys in 'sidings'. This teamwork has given workers more responsibility and variety and has reduced their social isolation at work.

We should, however, bear in mind that a Marxist would argue that the Volvo car workers are still alienated 'wage-slaves' because they are still exploited for profits over which they have no control. For Marxists, alienation is not the same thing as job dissatisfaction. Marxists argue that alienation will only be ended by creating a communist society in which workers no longer lack control over the products of their labours.

A group of workers at a new Volvo factory in Sweden.

Developments in the workplace which may promote greater job satisfaction

1   Teamwork, job rotation and job enlargement   While most car workers do simple, monotonous tasks on an assembly line, the teams of Volvo workers at Kalmar are able to swap jobs around so that they can vary their skills and alter the pace at which they work. At Volvo's old Torslanda plant annual labour turnover was 50 per cent and absenteeism was as high as 30 per cent per day in the late 1960s. In 1976, *New Society* reported that the Kalmar plant's comparable figures were 16 per cent and 12 per cent and in 1978 the *Sunday Mirror* gave figures of 'virtually no turnover of labour' and absenteeism down to 4 per cent.

In 1985, Peugeot cars installed forty-five robots at their Mulhouse factory in northern France. This has meant that the workforce involved in pressing out the shapes of the 205 model from sheet-metal has fallen from 528 to 268 on a production run of 800 vehicles a day. Management, unions and experts from the French Ministry of Research and Technology met to discuss how this development should be introduced. It was agreed to reorganise the workers into 'units' (tightly-knit teams) with 'co-ordinators' (previously supervisors), 'guides' (skilled workers) and 'operatives' (who start with no skills). All three grades do the same work. They are distinguished only by their 'depth of knowledge'.

2   Single status workforce   The traditional **hierarchies** (structures of authority) and divisions of British industry can be seen at the British Aerospace factory in Manchester. Paul Murphy, a supervisor, has described how there are four separate canteens:

> There's a special mess for the directors, there's a mess for middle management. Below them there's another mess for supervision, and ultimately the larger canteen on the shop floor. And yet when things go wrong the directors tell us we're all working for the same company. I can't square that circle.

> (From *All Our Working Lives*)

Many Japanese-managed factories in Britain, such as those in South Wales making TVs and hi-fi's, have insisted that all employees wear the same overalls, eat in the same canteen and work the same hours.

3   Flexible working hours   Many offices now operate a **flexi-time** system. Instead of all cramming on the same bus or tube train in the rush hour and all having to 'clock on' at the same time, staff might be allowed to arrive at any time between 8 and 10 a.m., have up to two hours for lunch, and leave at any time between 3 and 7 p.m. They can work some long days and some short days, some early and some late, as long as they fulfil a total of thirty-four hours per week.

Similar flexible shift systems have been introduced for manual workers by Babcock at Renfrew and Whitbread at Romsey. Under these schemes employees vary their attendance to meet fluctuations in workload. This is perhaps more in the firm's interests than the employees'. In the early 1980s the Associated Society of Locomotive Engineers and Firemen

(ASLEF) train drivers' union went on strike to resist **flexible rostering**. This might mean that a worker gets up early to drive trains for the morning rush hour, has some hours off in the middle of the day and then has to work again in the evening.

Another form of flexibility is **job-sharing** or **job-pairing**. For example, two mothers of young toddlers might return to work by sharing a job. Each alternates between a week at work and a week looking after the other mother's child.

4   Flexible working practices   Demarcation means clearly marking the limits to the work which may be done by those with different trades and job descriptions. In many factories, production line workers are unable to maintain their machines without provoking a **demarcation dispute**. For example, if the engineers find less skilled men poaching their work by carrying out lubrication, cleaning and simple repairs of the machines, then the engineers might go on strike. Examples of new deals allowing greater flexibility are:

● At Shell Chemicals' Carrington plant they aim to create multi-skill workers who can handle 80 per cent of traditional craftsmen's work across all traditional skills (for example, those of an electrician or fitter).

● At Babcock a deal will eventually allow clerical workers in the stores to drive fork-lift trucks.

● An agreement at Caterpillar has reduced the number of job titles from 106 to 24 and the number of grades from 7 to 5.

● In 1981, pilots in British Airways Highlands Division took on extra duties such as supervising refuelling and carrying out their own pre-departure checks and load planning. At the same time, cabin crew began assisting with passenger handling on the ground. The result was that by 1983–84 the division had recorded its first profit in forty years.

5   Quality circles   The Japanese pioneered quality circles in 1962 and now have 10 million workers in a million circles. In 1984 there were estimated to be 1,000 circles in 250 different companies in Britain. The typical circle consists of a dozen workers who voluntarily meet once a week to identify problems and think of solutions.

A mouldmakers' circle at Wedgwood has devised a new process which reduces the number of rejected plates by 10 per cent and a spotwelders' circle at Duracell has designed a new workbench. At Abbey Hosiery a circle secretly removed a roomful of knitwear over five months. They then 'stole' the managing director's Rolls- Royce and gave him a list of seventy-eight suggestions for improving security.

6   Worker participation   In 1979 Volvo ran a series of newspaper advertisements declaring '*When you care about the workers, the workers care about the car*'. The wording beneath said, 'In our paint shops, we stopped using inspectors and reorganised the work so the polishers and grinders were responsible for planning and quality. They became more interested in their jobs and the number of defects was reduced by 30 per cent.' At Jaguar, quality circles can summon any manager from the company chairman downwards.

These innovations give workers a very limited amount of power over decision-making in the workplace but a more thoroughgoing form of industrial democracy was advocated by the Bullock Report in 1977. This recommended that companies' boards should have an equal number of workers' and shareholders' representatives, with all the worker-directors chosen by the union members. This idea is common in West Germany, Holland, Belgium and Scandanavia but one of the few experiments in Britain, when the Post Office recruited seven workers to its board in 1978, was abandoned by 1980.

7   Profit-sharing schemes   While the Liberal Party remain strong advocates of worker-directors, in the 1986 Budget the Conservative Chancellor of the Exchequer declared his enthusiasm for profit-sharing schemes. The idea is that 20–25 per cent of workers' incomes are linked to company profits. This already happens in the John Lewis Partnership where all workers, since the 1920s, have been shareholders or 'partners' in the firm. The advantage to the company is that its wages bill automatically falls if there is a slump in sales causing a drop in profits.

8   Workers' co-operatives   In 1978 the Labour Government set up a Co-operative Development Agency to assist the growth of businesses which are owned and democratically controlled by the workers within them. One source of inspiration has been the Mondragon experiment in the Basque Region of Spain. This began when five young men started a joint venture making paraffin cookers in the early 1950s. By 1970 the Mondragon group of co-operatives had 3,000 members. The 1981 Directory of Co-operative Firms in London listed 118 co-ops providing 954 paid jobs, including the *Spare Rib* collective which produces a monthly feminist magazine, and the 'Last Days of the Raj' Indian restaurant. The fastest growing areas were co-ops in building, wholefoods, printing and publishing.

Case study: the 1985 Nissan single-union agreement

When Nissan set up their new car factory at Washington, Tyne and Wear, in 1985, they made an agreement with the Engineering Workers' Union which has the following features:

1   Only one union will be recognised by the company. (British car plants have always had multi-union bargaining.)

2   There will only be two categories of job description: technical and manufacturing. This flexibility means that production workers can carry out maintenance repairs on their machines and it also means that the introduction of future new technology will not need the re-negotiation of job descriptions.

3   Instead of clocking on, each shift starts with a team meeting and each team is responsible for keeping its own work area clean and tidy.

4   Strikes are to be avoided by negotiation through a works council or **pendulum negotiation** where an arbitrator must decide wholly in favour of one side or the other. This type of negotiation encourages reasonable positions in pay bargaining since both sides know that the most reasonable is likely to be chosen by the arbitrator. In conventional

pay bargaining a firm might offer a 2 per cent rise and the unions claim 14 per cent, with a compromise settlement being 8 per cent.

(In order to get supervisors who are committed to their philosophy of teamwork and quality,

Nissan interviewed 200 out of 3,500 applicants and invited seventy-five to a twenty-four-hour assessment centre in order to fill twenty-five vacancies.)

Intrinsic and extrinsic satisfaction at work

Three main motives for working have been suggested. Firstly, some are influenced by the **Protestant work ethic**, a religious tradition which says that we should lead sober, devout and hard working lives to gain our rewards in the 'next life'. Some people are still influenced by this centuries-old theory in that they believe that it is *right* to work hard and *wrong* not to work, even if they don't need to work.

Secondly, some jobs allow people to express themselves; they offer the **intrinsic satisfactions** of interest and involvement; they are meaningful or sociable. These might include the work of skilled craftsmen, such as stonemasons, or the 'caring professions', such as nursing or teaching.

Thirdly, many people see work as an instrument or a means to an end rather than as an end in itself. The objective is usually to earn as high a wage as possible. This **instrumental orientation** to work might mean that a worker's main satisfactions from work are **extrinsic** to, or outside, the job itself. Such extrinsic factors are the contractual conditions of a job: the pay, the hours, the holidays and the pension scheme.

Many of the suggested cures for dissatisfaction at work aim to give employees more involvement, interest and responsibility – in other words to increase the amount of intrinsic, rather than merely extrinsic, satisfaction.

Activity

Interview six working adults about their jobs. Ask them the following questions:

(a)   What is your occupation?

(b)   How do you usually spend your working day?

(c)   What are the three best aspects of your work?

(d)   What are the three worst aspects of your work?

(e)   How could your job be improved?

(f)   What job would you like to be doing in ten years' time?

(g)   What job do you expect to be doing in ten years' time?

---

3   Trade unions

It was when I got interested in the union, that's when my life took off. It changed my life, it became my life. What excited me? Well, it was the thought of the workers taking part in their lives, workers having a say, the idea that you'd got the right to argue with the gaffer. I felt the blokes weren't going to go back to the old days, they were going to have their say.

(A Coventry car worker who took early retirement at the end of the 1970s, quoted in *Wigan Pier Revisited* by Beatrix Campbell)

Trade unions aim to provide a voice for employees in a number of different ways. Some of the ways in which they represent their members' interests are mentioned below:

The four main benefits of trade union membership

1 Collective bargaining for better pay and working conditions As well as higher wages and safer, cleaner workplaces, unions also press for a shorter working week, longer holidays and better sickness, maternity and pension schemes. In order to press such claims, union members can take a number of forms of **industrial action**. These include the all-out withdrawal of labour, or strike action; the go-slow; the overtime ban; and the work-to-rule (for example teachers refusing to supervise pupils at lunchtimes because it is not ruled in their contract).

Other weapons used by trade unions are:

- The **closed shop**: a workplace where all employees must belong to the union.

- The **picket line**: a group of strikers demonstrating outside a workplace. They might be trying to persuade non-strikers ('strikebreakers' or 'scabs') to join them. Or they might be aiming to get lorry-drivers to 'black' the firm by turning away without making deliveries.

A union can also call on the support of other unions through the Trades Union Congress (TUC). Most unions belong to this organisation which, for example, can channel funds to a union which faces a crisis. (The employers' equivalent institution is the Confederation of British Industry (CBI)).

The strength of a union in a particular factory or office often depends partly on the energy of the worker who is elected by members to be their **shop steward**. This local leader has to recruit members, collect subscriptions, distribute union information, take up grievances with the management and call meetings.

2 Legal and financial assistance Unions originally developed from **friendly societies** which offered payments to members if they were off work due to sickness. The main form of support now is **sustentation** while on strike. Since 1980 the government has cut social security payments to strikers on the assumption that they will get some strike pay from their union. In 1984–85 many miners held out on strike against pit closures for over a year even though (a) the National Union of Miners was unable to afford strike pay and (b) the government still made deductions from their supplementary benefit payments.

3 Courses and training An example of the educational role of the unions can be found during the 1974–79 period when the Labour Government passed a number of laws for which the unions had long campaigned. These included the Sex Discrimination Act, the Health and Safety at Work Act and the Redundancy Payments Act. The unions held numerous conferences and courses, as well as distributing many thousands of booklets, in order to educate their members about their new legal rights.

4 Research and government policy Unions are not only concerned with issues which directly affect their members at work, such as the dangers of asbestos. They also campaign on more general issues such as unemployment, nuclear disarmament and better schools and hospitals. The Labour Party is largely paid for by the unions and the unions have a large share of the votes at Labour Party Conferences. At these conferences, trade union delegates propose many of the resolutions which may become Labour Party policy.

The trade unions in the 1980s

During 1984, 27.1 million working days were lost through work stoppages caused by industrial action in the UK but 22.3 million of these were lost through one dispute alone: the protest at pit closures in the coal industry. Yet strikes account for much less absence from work than sickness. In 1980 5 per cent of full-time employees were absent through sickness in any one week and a total of 359 million working days were lost due to sickness. Between 1974 and 1983 the annual average number of working days lost due to strikes was 9.8 million but in 1983 only 3.8 million were lost. Over the same ten years the annual average number of stoppages was 2,002 but in 1984 there were only 1,206 strikes – the lowest number for any year since 1940.

Case study: the changing face of Britain's trade unionists

Percentage of trade unionists who	1979	1988
are men	75	65
are women	25	35
are middle class (categories ABC1)	29	38
are working class (categories C2DE)	71	62
own shares in companies	6	23
voted Labour in general elections	51	42
	1983	*1988*
live in council housing	28	17
own their own homes	60	75

- Membership of the TUC-affiliated unions fell from 12.2 million in 1979 to 9.1 million in 1988.
- 58% of trade unionists believe that it would be better to have a single-union deal at their workplace.
- 31% believe that single-union agreements should include a no-strike clause.

In 1988, these last two ideas were part of what was called the **New Unionism** or the **New Realism** of the trade unions.

(adapted from *The Sunday Times*, 4 September 1988 © Times Newspaper Ltd/MORI 1988)

Are the trade unions too powerful?

It has often been claimed that the trade unions have too much power in British society. Alternatively, it can be argued that the unions suffer from a number of weaknesses, as can be seen from two famous disputes:

1   The Grunwick dispute   In August 1976, 137 out of 480 mainly Asian women workers at a London film processing laboratory went on strike and joined a union, partly because they were being forced to work overtime at short notice which was disrupting their family lives. They were supported by the whole of the trade union and labour movement with senior ministers from the Labour Government joining in mass pickets, up to 8,000 strong. They were also supported by a report for the government by Lord Scarman which concluded that their employer should not deny them the right to belong to a union. And yet the strikers gave up in defeat after two years of standing on a picket line all day with no wages.

2   The News International dispute   In 1986 Rupert Murdoch (owner of the *Sun*, the *News of the World*, *The Times* and the *Sunday Times*) sacked 5,500 striking print workers. In November 1985 he had demanded that they sign an agreement never to go on strike and never to take any industrial action whatsoever.

Mass picketing at the News International printing plant in Wapping in 1986.

Two points can be made about these disputes. Firstly, an employer in America is compelled to recognise a union which has majority support among the workers and also has to bargain with that union in good faith. Secondly, it is illegal in America to sack workers for going on strike. In Britain, however, an employer can refuse to recognise a union and there is no positive right to strike – the unions only have the limited immunity from prosecution granted by the 1906 Trade Disputes Act. This means that strikers cannot be sued by their employer for compensation for loss of business.

The extent of worker participation or democracy at work is very limited in Britain. Unions are mainly only able to exercise negative power, such as blocking the demands of employers, rather than positive power, such as contributing to company policies. The 1979 TUC Report called *Employment and Technology* contains many positive ideas. It predicts that new technology will mean far fewer jobs and proposes that these be shared out among as many workers as possible by giving priority to:

- a shorter working week,
- longer holidays,
- earlier retirement,
- a reduction in systematic overtime,
- more provision for **sabbatical leave**, such as taking a year off for retraining.

These proposals would give more jobs to more people and would create more leisure for all workers. The rest of this chapter looks at the two related topics of leisure and unemployment.

Activity

Interview six adults about trade union membership. If they belong to a union, ask how much it costs them and what benefits do they get for their subscription. If they do not belong, ask them why not. In all cases ask for their general views about trade unions: 'Do unions have too much power?'

---

4   Work, non-work and unemployment

What is work?

Since 1965, Jimmy Savile, the disc jockey, has worked as a voluntary porter at the Stoke Mandeville Spinal Injuries Unit. In the early 1980s, he raised £10 million from public donations to rebuild the Unit. He has his own room there so that he can work from 10 a.m. to 3 p.m. on the five days he spends there every fortnight.

Most people need to use some portion of their spare time on housework such as washing dishes or ironing shirts. In 1980, British households spent the following amounts on **self-provisioning**, that is on products to be used for work in and around the home:

Home decorating products	£1,035 million
Products for car maintenance	£950 million
Tools and wood products	£890 million
Gardening equipment	£600 million
D-I-Y repairs and improvements products	£325 million

All these sorts of work (voluntary work, housework and self-provisioning) are, however, 'non-work' if we define work as time spent earning a living, time which has been sold to an employer and so is no longer our own to do as we like with.

Rock star Bob Geldof takes a standing nap after Live Aid at Wembley in July 1985. It was the world's biggest ever rock concert, seen by one and half billion people in 160 countries, and raised millions of pounds for famine relief in Africa. Geldof had worked continuously, and voluntarily, for four months to mastermind the project.

Cricket hero Ian Botham walked the length of Britain, from John O'Groats to Land's End, in November 1985. His purpose was to raise a million pounds for leukaemia research.

The psychological meaning of work

In *The Forsaken Families: The Effects of Unemployment on Family Life*, L. Fagin and M. Little have listed the following seven positive aspects of work:

1   Work as a source of identity   When adults meet for the first time at a party, one of the first questions is 'What do you do (for a living)?' A bricklayer or a doctor is defined in many people's eyes by the job that he or she does.

2   Work as a source of relationships outside the nuclear family   One wife in their survey said of her unemployed husband: 'What got me was that him being at home, he didn't see no one, we had nothing to talk about after tea.'

3   Work as a source of obligatory activity   An unemployed person lacks the routine of a worker who is obliged to pursue regular and purposeful activities. Unemployed people lose a framework which regulates how they spend their time.

4   Work as an opportunity to develop skills and creativity   Apart from simple, dead-end jobs, most occupations give workers the chance to learn new skills and to create new ways of carrying out tasks.

5   Work as a factor which structures psychological time   Fagin and Little's study found that unemployed men spent more time in bed but felt more tired than when they were at work.

6   Work as a sense of purpose   Fagin and Little were told: 'I'm surplus to requirements'; 'I'm marginal, a nobody, and nobody gives a bugger'; 'I'm on the scrapheap at fifty-five, with a lot of working life in me yet'.

7   Work as a source of income and control   Many workers only earn poverty wages and so are below the 'breadline', but most people who earn a living find that income from working provides independence and freedom of choice – for example in how to spend leisure time.

There is an old Haitian proverb which says: 'If work were a good thing the rich would have found a way of keeping it to themselves.' It is true that many people have jobs which are boring or stressful, dirty or dangerous. But surveys have found that less than 10 per cent of workers who lose their jobs report an improvement in their mental or physical health. Most suffer a deterioration. The numbers who have suffered from unemployment are shown on the next page.

The rise in unemployment in the UK

In 1985, more than a million or so people, that is 28 per cent of the total unemployed, had been jobless for over two years. In March 1986 unemployment rates varied from 21 per cent in Northern Ireland and 19 per cent in the Northern region to 11 per cent in East Anglia and 10 per cent in the South East.

	Unemployed claimants	*Unemployment rate (jobless as % of the workforce)*
1961	292,000	1.3
1971	751,000	3.3
1976	1,302,000	5.5
1981	2,520,000	10.4
1986 (Jan)	3,407,700	14.1
1989 (Jan)	1,988,000	7.0

The effects of unemployment

Someone who loses their job usually goes through a number of phases: firstly, shock; secondly, refusal to accept the situation and even optimism; thirdly, anxiety and longing for the past; finally, resignation and adjustment. These phases are similar to the process of mourning the death of a close relative or friend.

In his study of *White Collar Unemployment: Impact and Stress*, S. Finneman found that all those he surveyed 'felt a stigma in being unemployed. It was associated with considerable shame, degradation and inferiority'. Those who sought in vain for jobs suffered desperation and despair, chronic self-doubts and anxiety. Some found new jobs but felt unsuited to them, mainly because they had to accept a drop in pay and status. 'Their stress, strain and self-esteem were worse than when they were unemployed.'

The most common consequences of unemployment are poverty and cigarette and alcohol abuse. These in turn contribute to a deterioration in health. M. Harris also found the following patterns from different studies of the unemployed: 'They are up to 19 times more likely to attempt suicide. They are six times more likely to batter their children and twice as likely to get divorced.' Also, '40 per cent of the people appearing before English courts describe themselves as unemployed' (from 'How Unemployment Affects People', *New Society*, 19 January 1984).

5 Patterns of leisure

The separation of work and leisure

In pre-industrial Britain the line between work and leisure was not so sharply drawn as it is today. When work was carried on in the home people had greater freedom to choose when to work and when to relax. Also, work and leisure were more integrated. For example, going to a fair was both an opportunity to trade and a chance to enjoy games and good company. Another example is the use of taverns in pre-industrial times; people went to taverns not only for entertainment but also for business reasons such as making and repaying loans.

Industrialisation not only led to a separation of home and work but also to a separation between work and leisure. Work for many became an activity that took place outside the home in factories, shops and offices. It became an activity over which the ordinary worker had little control. The employers regulated the beginning and end of the working day, the breaks in between and the number of working days per week and year.

Case study: leisure patterns in early retirement

One definition of leisure is that it is **discretionary time**, spare time which can be used at your own discretion for rest, recreation or self-development. Ann McGoldrick has studied 1,800 men who took early retirement and divided them into nine categories according to how they used their spare time:

1   'Rest and relaxers': content to read papers, watch TV and do some gardening and walking.
2   'Home and family men': enjoyed looking after and helping in the home.
3   'Good timers': chose social life, travel and evenings out.
4   'Committee and society men': 24 per cent devoted time to positions such as treasurer of a sports club.
5   'Volunteers': 19 per cent helped charities or friends and neighbours.
6   'Hobbyists': many concentrated on pastimes such as birdwatching, golf, music or fishing.
7   'Further education men': 9 per cent enrolled in courses such as those of the Open University.
8   'Part-time jobbers': 24 per cent got part-time jobs.
9   'New jobbers': one had started a new, 'easy job' – he closed his new business down for each cricket season.

Activities

1   Describe which of the nine options above are available to young people who are unemployed. In what other ways can they usefully spend their time?

2   If you were offered an average yearly income for the rest of your life, on condition that you never took up paid employment, would you accept the offer? Give reasons for your answer.

The effects of work on leisure: opposition and extension patterns

Three contrasting ways that a person's type of job can influence leisure have been described. **Opposition-type leisure** has been found among

A teacher marking books at home: some people's work extends into their leisure time.

workers with dangerous and hard jobs such as steelworkers, miners and trawlermen. Among these male-dominated occupations the worlds of work and leisure are both men's worlds. The loyalties needed for teamwork during the day are carried over into the friendships of the male drinking groups in the evening. And the main leisure activity, drinking in pubs and working men's clubs, is done to relax and forget about the strains of work. Such escapist leisure is in contrast, or opposition, to work.

At the other extreme, professional gardeners may spend their evenings and weekends digging their own gardens and many teachers spend their spare time marking books or organising clubs and outings for pupils. In both of these cases work extends into leisure. Workers in the City of London who are involved in their jobs and get intrinsic satisfaction from their work might spend their spare time reading the *Financial Times*. Their leisure is then an **extension** of their work.

A third possibility is that people such as office workers may be fairly indifferent to their work and their work may have little effect on their leisure. This has been called **neutrality-type leisure**.

How do we spend our leisure hours?

The following figures show that class, age and sex all have a bearing on the way that individuals spend their leisure time:

Participation in selected sporting activities, 1983

	Percentage engaging in each activity in the 4 weeks before interview		
	Professional, employers and managers	*Semi- and unskilled manual*	*Full-time students*
Golf	7	0	3
Swimming indoor	9	4	17
Squash	6	1	8
Darts	6	7	12
Billiards/snooker	9	6	18
Walking (2 miles or more)	24	14	18

(Source: *Social Trends*, 1986)

Time use in a typical week, 1985

Weekly hours spent on	*Full-time employees*		*Housewives*	*Retired people*
	males	*females*		
Employment and travel	45	41	–	–
Essential activities	33	45	77	50
Sleep	56	57	59	60
Free time	33	25	32	58
Free time per weekday	3	2	4	8
Free time per weekend day	10	7	6	9

(Source: *Social Trends*, 1986)

On average, women who work full-time have less free time than men because they spend more time on essential activities such as housework, essential shopping and childcare. (Eating, washing, getting up and going to bed are counted as 'personal care' and are also essential activities rather than free time.)

Activities

1   Ask two adults how many hours they spend each week on major categories of activity such as eating, travelling, active and passive leisure (for example participating or spectating). Compare their figures with an analysis of your own typical week.

2   Select four of the following possible trends and in each case explain why you would, or would not, welcome them:
   - an increase in the proportion of people who change careers during the course of their working lives;
   - an increase in the proportion of mothers returning to full-time work while their children are still toddlers;
   - increasing automation of production processes; for example, in bakeries and biscuit factories;
   - increasing automation of service industries such as banking and petrol retailing;
   - a polarisation of the workforce into core or periphery workers;
   - more widespread shiftwork;
   - more widespread flexi-time working;
   - more widespread home-working;
   - more widespread non-strike agreements between trade unions and management;
   - a shorter working week and a shorter working life.

3   **Discussion:** how far do the findings shown in the graph below contradict the ideas of deskilling on pages 230 and 231?

The impact of advanced technical change on jobs (percentages)

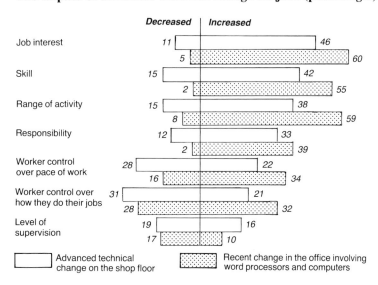

(Source: *Workplace Industrial Relations and Technical Change* by W. W. Daniel, PSI Bulletin, 1988)

CHAPTER 17

Research methods

Participant observers may not find it easy to fit in.

1 Doing scientific research

A typical piece of scientific research involves six stages. Let us take as an example two botanists who are interested in the effects of light on plant growth:

1 Observation   The botanists notice that beans which germinate in a cupboard, with very little light, grow into tall, pale and weak plants.

2 Hypothesis   Our scientists then put forward a proposition to be tested. Their theory is that extra light can improve plant growth.

3 Selection of methods   Two groups of bean plants are grown in similar conditions, with the same amounts of water, except that one group is left on a windowsill with sun-lamps above them which are turned on at night. The other group is a **control group**, growing on a similar windowsill but without any sun-lamps.

4 Collecting data   The growth of the plants is systematically observed. Measurements are taken daily.

5 Analysing and interpreting data   From the information which they have recorded, our botanists try to establish how far the **dependent variable** (sturdy growth) is influenced by the **independent variable** which has been altered (extra light under the lamps).

6 Making conclusions   In the report of their experiment, they might claim to have proved that too much light is harmful to young bean plants.

The problem of objectivity

In conducting research, scientists try to follow two general rules:

1   Researchers should use standard scales of measurement and should describe their methods fully. This allows others to test their findings by repeating their research.

2   Researchers should remain unbiased and objective. Being objective involves not taking sides and not making judgements as to whether what one has observed is good or bad. It also involves not allowing personal values and preferences to influence the conclusions of one's research.

If sociologists were alien beings it would be relatively easy for them to remain **objective** while studying human society. But sociologists are, of course, very much part of the social world that they are studying. This makes it difficult for them to maintain an objective, neutral stance. Like everyone else, sociologists have their own particular beliefs, moral preferences and political opinions which can all too easily affect their research.

   Total objectivity is an impossibility and it cannot be obtained by any discipline. But a high degree of objectivity can be achieved if certain habits of mind are adopted:

1   Patience is needed so that the sociologist will take the time to consider all of the evidence.
2   Open-mindedness is needed so that the sociologist is receptive to different viewpoints and interpretations.
3   The sociologist needs to be reasonable and only prepared to offer explanations that are based on the evidence.

2   Conducting a survey

The **survey** is a method that sociologists frequently use to collect evidence. It plays a similar part in sociology to the part played by the laboratory experiment in the natural sciences. A survey about pupils and smoking is a typical piece of research which might be carried out by some sociology students. Like researchers in the natural sciences, such as biology or physics, the social science students would follow the same six stages of research:

1   **Observation**   They notice that fewer fourteen- and fifteen-year-old girls take part in sports than boys. It also seems that more female pupils take up the habit of smoking in the fourth and fifth year at secondary school.

2   **Hypothesis**   Our researchers may test the proposition that active teenage sports enthusiasts are more likely to be non-smokers and male.

3   **Selection of methods**   It might be decided to interview some fourth- and fifth-year pupils.

4   **Collecting data**   A sample of pupils are interviewed using a standard schedule of questions.

5   Analysing and interpreting data   The answers show whether there is a correlation, or connection, between smoking and gender. There may be a significant difference between the proportions of males and females who smoke.

6   Making conclusions   It might be clear that fewer girls take part in sports and that these same girls are more likely to smoke.

Choosing a sample

It is important that the sample of fourth- and fifth-year pupils chosen for the survey is a **representative cross-section** of *all* fourth- and fifth-year pupils. If general conclusions about a group under study are drawn from findings about an unrepresentative sample, then we cannot be sure that these generalisations are accurate.

How can we try to make sure that those selected for the sample are typical? Firstly, the **survey population** must be defined and, secondly, a **sampling frame**, or list of the survey population, must be drawn up. In our case, the survey population is all fourth- and fifth-year pupils in our school and a suitable sampling frame could be compiled using up-to-date form registers. We can now choose between three sampling procedures:

1   A systematic, or quasi-random, sample   If we want to select a 20 per cent sample, then all we have to do is take every fifth name on the list of all fourth- and fifth-year pupils.

2   A random sample   In a truly random sample everyone listed on the sampling frame has an equal chance of selection. We can ensure this by picking the names out of a hat or by numbering the list and then getting a computer to select numbers at random. If there are 200 pupils in the fourth year and 200 in the fifth year, then we take the first eighty random numbers in order to get a 20 per cent sample.

3   A stratified random sample   We are interested in comparing boys and girls and we might also want to ensure equal numbers of fourth- and fifth-year pupils. In this case we would stratify, or layer, the survey population into four separate sampling frames: for example 100 fourth-year girls, 100 fifth-year girls, 100 fourth-year boys and 100 fifth-year boys. We then select twenty names at random from each group to get our 20 per cent overall sample.

Having selected a sample of fourth- and fifth-year pupils, information can be collected from each pupil using a number of different methods. Each method has its weaknesses as well as its strengths.

Collecting information by using interviews

Structured interviews   In a structured interview all those who are interviewed, the **respondents**, are asked the same questions in the same order. The main advantage of this method is that the interviews can easily be repeated by others in order to verify the results. This is because the inter-

*Pupils conducting
interviews.*

views are standardised and the role of the interviewer is kept to a minimum.

The chief disadvantage of structured interviews is that they can only yield limited, superficial information. The respondent has little opportunity to give information that may be useful but is not prompted by the questions.

Unstructured interviews   An unstructured interview is more like an informal, relaxed discussion. Rather than use a list of fixed questions, the interviewer might hope to raise a number of topics, in any order, during a fairly natural conversation. Since the questions are not imposed on the respondent, the interview may reveal what he or she actually thinks. This type of interview therefore allows the interviewer to probe beneath the surface and acquire deeper knowledge than can be gained in a formal, structured interview.

The main problem with this type of interview is that because it is unstructured and personal, the information gained from it cannot be easily checked by others. That is, the interview cannot be precisely duplicated.

Interviewer bias   A major problem with both types of interview is that of interviewer bias. This occurs if the interviewer influences the answers of respondents. The age, sex, class, race or other aspects of the accent or appearance of the interviewer may influence respondents so that they give answers which are not genuine.

The problem of interviewer bias can be minimised by the use of trained and skilled interviewers. But interviews remain artificial situations. If the respondent does not act 'typically' then the findings of the interview may be unreliable.

Collecting information by using self-completion questionnaires

This method asks respondents to fill in their answers to printed lists of questions. The questions may be 'closed' or 'open-ended':

Closed questions   A closed question allows only a limited response. For example, the question 'Do you like to take part in sporting activities?' might only allow respondents to answer 'yes', 'no' or 'don't know'. An example of a pre-coded question is: 'How many cigarettes do you usually smoke each week? (Please tick a, b, c, d, or e.)

(a) none   (b) less than 20   (c) 20 to 40   (d) 41 to 60
(e) more than 60'

The answers to such questions may be easily analysed by computers.

Open questions   A wide-ranging discussion may be invited by an open-ended question such as 'Why did you take up smoking?' If the response to this type of question is likely to be a ten-minute-long answer, then a tape-recorder may be used. Unstructured interviews generally employ open questions.

Self-completion questionnaires are likely to be cheaper and faster than using interviewers. Postal questionnaires allow coverage of a wide geographical area. And the information from questionnaires with closed questions may easily be quantifiable so that it can be presented in figures and percentages.

The problem of response rates   A major problem with self-completion questionnaires is that a large number of respondents may not fill them in and return them. If there is a **low response rate** then those who have completed the questionnaire may not be truly representative of the sample as a whole.

Loaded questions   Questions should not contain any bias. For example, the following question was asked in an opinion poll of black South Africans in 1986: 'President Botha is totally opposed to the imposition of economic sanctions by other countries. Are you in favour of such sanctions?' The majority answered 'no'. Many were probably influenced by the wording of the question.

Pilot surveys   Another problem in composing a questionnaire is that of ensuring that the questions are clear and likely to elicit the information required. Investigators often try to overcome this problem by conducting a small-scale pilot, or test, survey. Weak and ambiguous questions may then be altered before the main survey is conducted. A further measure, which is used by the census survey, is to collect self-completion questionnaires and check them through on the doorstep so that any misunderstood questions can be explained.

Overall problems of using surveys

While it may be possible, using sampling techniques, to ensure that a survey is representative, there are two main problems which all surveys face:

1 Validity The validity of any research depends on whether it actually measures what it sets out to measure. A careful study might accurately measure how often people pray or go to church. The answers might be reliable, meaning that they would be the same if the survey was repeated, but the survey may still fail to succeed in its original purpose.

If the aim of the survey is to measure the degree of secularisation in society, the decline in religious influence, then it might be argued that the information about the proportions of the population who pray and attend church is not a valid indicator of secularisation. In this case the whole survey would be reliable but invalid.

2 Qualitative rather than quantitative research Quantitative research, such as self-completion questionnaires, may have the advantage of yielding large quantities of data, but one alleged problem of surveys is that they impose the sociologists' views of what is important on the world of those being surveyed and thereby fail to understand people's lives.

For example, a questionnaire or structured interview investigating football hooliganism might concentrate on questions about the amount of alcohol which fans drink ignoring the role of the police or the point of view of the fans themselves. Unstructured interviews and participant observation, such as Peter Marsh's research at Oxford United, have revealed that the behaviour of fans is informally organised by a complexity of rules and roles.

Aggression among football fans may be seen as a ritual which allows young men to gain status which compensates for their failure at school and the way that they are denied dignity in employment. Those who establish reputations as violent leaders may be grateful that the traditions of the ritualised confrontations, and the control exercised by other fans, usually restrains them from inflicting or incurring injury. This delicately balanced control, which is exercised by the crowd, may be quickly undermined if the police over-react to the threatening displays of rival fans.

The informal rules which govern such ritual behaviour may be invisible to outsiders so that they can only be uncovered by careful participant observation. This method, which gives the 'feel' of complex social situations, may be called qualitative research. It is discussed in section four of this chapter.

3   Some examples of different types of surveys

An in-depth survey

The book entitled *From Here To Maternity: Becoming A Mother*, by Ann Oakley, describes a research project conducted between 1974 and 1976. Oakley first spent six months as an observer in a London hospital. She then selected a sample of sixty-six women who were expecting their first babies and attending the hospital. Fifty-four of these were interviewed on four occasions: twenty-six weeks and six weeks before delivery as well as five and twenty weeks afterwards. All interviews were tape-recorded and they lasted an average of 2.36 hours each. Oakley also observed six of the births.

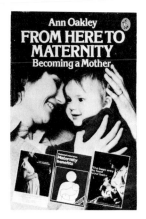

The front cover of Ann Oakley's book about first time mothers.

Case study: the sample used by the 'Breadline Britain' survey

The fieldwork was carried out in February 1983 with a quota sample of 1,174 people from throughout Britain . . . The sample was designed, first, to enable a view representative of the population as a whole to be gained and, second, to ensure that a sub-group of the poor was large enough to enable their living standards to be examined. The first of these aims has been achieved. The checkbacks made on the weighted sample as a whole – whether on, for example, age of the respondents or housing tenure – show that the sample is in line with Britain's population profile. The survey's findings that refer to the sample as a whole can be taken to be representative of the adult population of Britain.

The second aim was more difficult to achieve within the cost constraints of the survey . . . the analysis of the living standards of the poor is based on a sub-group of about 200 households . . .

It was decided to use the ACORN sampling method to produce a sample of some 200 poor households. ACORN (A Classification Of Residential Neighbourhoods) is an analysis of the social characteristics of small areas throughout Great Britain . . . For the purposes of the Breadline Britain survey, the oversampling was confined to three ACORN groups: urban areas with local authority housing, areas with most overcrowding, and low-income areas with immigrants . . . Although ACORN sampling does have various disadvantages, it controls fieldwork tightly – unlike conventional quota sampling, which allows a fair amount of interviewer choice – and can be used for sampling purposes.

(Source: *Poor Britain* by Joanna Mack and Stewart Lansley)

Data response exercise: the 'Breadline Britain' sample

1 (a) How many people were surveyed in the overall quota sample?
   (b) How large was the sub-group of poor households?
2 Why was it difficult to examine thoroughly the living standards of the poor?
3 How was the overall quota sample checked to ensure that it was representative of the total population?
4 Why is ACORN sampling better than conventional quota sampling?
5 Which three types of residential neighbourhoods provided the areas for the extra sub-sample of poor households?

Market research: a quota sample

If a brewery wants to find out whether a 'special offer' of free cigars might help sell more beer, then they might hire a **market research** company. Interviewers might be sent out to twenty different shopping centres around the country to ask people which beer they drink and whether they enjoy cigars. Each interviewer might be told to use his or her judgement in select-ing fifty men in their twenties, fifty in their thirties, fifty in their forties or fifties and fifty aged sixty or over. If the interviewers do not find fifty elderly men who agree to reply, then they will have failed to 'fill' their quotas.

Two longitudinal age-cohort studies

In 1982 the Channel Four series *Citizen 2000* started filming a number of babies born into a variety of British homes. The series has continued to show how their lives have varied as they have grown up and they will be filmed regularly until they become adult citizens in the year 2000. Because they were all born in the same year they all belong to the same **age-cohort** and this sort of follow-up research is called a **longitudinal study**.

In *How Voters Decide*, Himmelweit and others describe how they first interviewed a cross-section of over 600 London boys aged between thirteen and fourteen in 1951. Since there was an election that year, they asked the boys how they would have voted if they had been old enough. In 1962, 450 of the original sample were followed-up and interviewed again. Further questionnaires were sent the day after each of the following general elections:

Year	Numbers sent	Numbers returned	Response rate
1964	450	371	82%
1966	371	325	88%
1970	325	246	76%
1974	246	178	72%

The 178 of the original sample who were successfully contacted in 1974 were now aged about thirty-seven. Notice how the non-response rate in the different survey years eroded the number of respondents.

Primary and secondary data

The information researchers gain from their own surveys is called **primary data. Secondary data** refers to information which has been collected by others. The study of male voters conducted by Himmelweit and others over a period of twenty-three years led them to construct a 'model' or general explanation of how voters decide to cast their votes. In order to test this theory they analysed the results of some secondary data. In other words they compared their hypothesis, based on their own observations, with the findings of other people's surveys. In fact, they examined six separate British election surveys carried out between 1970 and 1983 which had involved over 15,000 voters.

Government statistics

As well as the ten-year census which surveys the whole population, the government carries out a number of continuous surveys. Examples are the General Household Survey and the Family Expenditure Survey. These involve between 10,000 and 15,000 households in a series of detailed interviews. The data from these surveys can be found in a number of Central Statistical Office (CSO) publications such as the annual editions of *Social Trends* and the *Annual Abstract of Statistics*. They are published by Her Majesty's Stationery Office (HMSO) and are available in the reference sections of large libraries.

The secondary data from these government surveys can be very useful but official statistics are by no means 100 per cent reliable. Previous chapters have looked at the problems of interpreting divorce and crime figures. We now consider the debate about the accuracy of the unemployment figures.

In July 1986 the Labour opposition's spokesman on employment, John Prescott, said that the latest unemployment figures were 'little better than fraudulent propaganda'. This was because, for the first time, the government had included Britain's 2,600,000 self-employed in the working population. This had the effect of reducing the percentage unemployed from 13.1 per cent to 11.7 per cent.

Prescott also claimed that the government had 'carried out 18 fiddles' with the unemployment figures in order to keep them lower than the real number who were jobless. Officials at the Department of Employment then admitted that the basis on which the figures have been calculated has been changed seven times since Mrs Thatcher came to power in 1979. For example, students on vacation and men over sixty may no longer register when unemployed.

Some critics of the official unemployment figures say that they should be up to 1.5 million higher, mainly because of those who are unemployed but unregistered as well as those who are on special schemes such as the Youth Training and Community Programme schemes. Other critics, however, argue that 1.5 million should be subtracted from the official total because of groups included in the figures such as claimants who are not really looking for jobs, 'unemployables' who are mentally or physically incapable, 'job changers' who are out of work for less than a month and **black economy** workers who are illegally claiming unemployment benefit.

1   Give five possible reasons for the following
occurrence: the answers from a carefully
selected national sample lead an opinion
poll in a newspaper to confidently predict
that 40 per cent will vote for Labour; but,
in a general election a week later, Labour
candidates only attract 30 per cent of the
votes cast.

2   Give reasons for each of the following
surveys having a poor response rate:
(a) a postal questionnaire to teachers
asking for their views concerning a new
syllabus;

(b) a truancy survey of school pupils;
(c) a questionnaire to be conducted with
drug users.

3   Why might there be a problem of
representativeness with:
(a) a postal questionnaire which has a low
response rate?
(b) a self-selected sample, such as the
25,000 women who replied to the 1986
Women's Own survey on rape? (12 per cent
of them said that they had been raped and
of these 76 per cent had not reported it to
the police.)

Conclusion: a case study using mixed methods

A **case study** is a piece of research which focuses on a single good example.
It is somewhat artificial to argue whether one research method is better
than another because many case studies which focus on a particular community or group, such as a religious cult, in fact use a mixture of methods.
Well-known case studies which have analysed documentary evidence, such
as media coverage, as well as using interviews and observation, include
Tunstall's study of the trawlermen of Hull and Cohen's study of mods
and rockers in the 1960s.

In *Beachside Comprehensive: A Case-Study of Secondary Schooling*,
Stephen Ball describes how he used the following methods during his three-
year study of one school:

1   He interviewed pupils and teachers.
2   He carried out several small-scale questionnaire studies.
3   He worked through and analysed school records and registers.
4   He also used **participant observation** to find out about the school.

4   Participant observation

Participant observation means that the researcher actually joins the social
world of those whom he or she wishes to study. In his case study of Beachside
Comprehensive, Ball observed many different lessons and he also partici-
pated in the daily life of the school in a number of ways. He taught three
or four periods per week for two years and he also did some supply teaching.
He joined forms on school visits, went on one school trip, invigilated examinations, took registers for absent teachers, played in the staff against pupils
cricket match, and so on.

Why use participant observation?

In a study entitled *Hooligans Abroad*, Williams and others joined English
football fans travelling to three matches in Europe during 1982. This is

their explanation for using participant observation:

> A standard survey methodology using questionnaires and/or interviews is, of course, a means of gaining information about the social composition of a crowd. It is also a useful way of obtaining quantitative data about the attitudes and opinions of its members. But, in the context of crowd research, questionnaires are difficult to administer and, in some respects, unreliable. Moreover, the survey method cannot tell one anything in a direct sense about the dynamics of disorderly incidents. For that, direct observation is required. In particular, the presence at such gatherings of a trained participant observer is a useful way of providing information of a richer and more reliable kind than that to which we have been accustomed hitherto. Here, too, of course, one encounters problems. How, for example, can one be sure that one's observations are accurate and would not be disputed by another participant observer or by the 'ordinary' participant in the event?

West Ham supporters confront rival supporters. What might be the problems of carrying out a participant observation study of a gang of football hooligans?

Some problems of participant observation

Laurie Taylor's study *In the Underworld* describes how he used an ex-convict, John McVicar, as a **key informant** who helped him to gain access to professional criminals in secret drinking and gambling clubs:

> He usually introduced me as 'Laurie', accompanied by a single nod of the head, which I took to mean 'not one of us, but all right'. Not that there was ever any chance of me being confused with the usual clientele. Wherever we went, I stood out... My greatest embarrassment was always reserved for the moments when I attempted to buy a round of drinks... I would keep fiddling with single pound notes in order to assem-

ble the heavy cost of the round – sometimes £10 or more could disappear with one order – while everyone else seemed to deal exclusively in twenties and fifties.

On one occasion McVicar took Taylor to interview two con-men who were busy practising the signatures needed to cash a wad of stolen travellers' cheques. Did Taylor, a Professor of Criminology, aid and abet the con-men by his presence? Taylor answers:

> Look, they'd have committed the crime anyway. Whether I'd been there or not. They completely ignored me. Looked through me. I couldn't have stopped them if I'd wanted to. And if I had reported the matter to the police, it wouldn't have led to their detention. I had no idea where they were going or whose cheques they were carrying. By the time they were found, they'd have been clean. What's more, any such call to the police would have meant the end of the project. Absolutely no more introductions by John and so no chance to discover anything of interest about the tactics and style of a group of criminals about whom we know so little.

Some criticisms of participant observation

1   Participant observation is usually carried out on small groups. This limits the method's usefulness because sociologists often want to make general statements about large sections of the population. Such statements may be better supported by surveys of large, representative samples.

2   Those who use participant observation often face moral difficulties. If they are observing covertly, without revealing their true intentions, then it may be difficult to record data with note-books or tape recorders. They will also be involved in deception: lying to and cheating those they observe. They may also find themselves getting involved in dangerous and illegal activities.

3   It can be an expensive and time-consuming method of collecting information. If participant observation is to be done properly the researcher may need to spend two or three years with the group under study.

4   It is a very personal and subjective method of research. The findings of participant observation depend to a great extent on the researcher's powers of observation and interpretation. But how do we know whether such findings are accurate and true? It is not easy to repeat a participant observation study.

5   Experiments

Experiments in the carefully controlled environments of science laboratories have the great advantage that they can be re-tested by other scientists who wish to repeat the same procedures. Psychologists use the artificial environment of the laboratory to test how individuals may be influenced by small groups, for example in obedience tests. Other psychologists experiment on animals. In a famous experiment conducted by Harlow in the

1950s, baby monkeys were taken from their mothers and observed in cages with artificial mothers made from wire or terry towelling. Such experiments probably tell us more about the cruelty of some psychologists than they do about maternal deprivation in human beings.

The sociologist's laboratory is the real world and the sociologist can seldom be justified in altering people's lives just to see what might happen.

An experiment on wife-batterers

In recent years organisations like the National Women's Aid Federation have pressed for the police to take tougher action against husbands who beat their wives. But many sociologists might argue that the police have been correct in their traditional 'softly, softly' approach which tries to patch up any domestic affray. Sociologists might be concerned that 'labelling' violent husbands by pressing charges may damage marriages irrevocably by **criminalising** the husbands and **amplifying deviance**.

Two American sociologists, Sherman and Berk, tested these ideas with an experiment which depended on the co-operation of the Minneapolis police department. Officers agreed to deal with domestic assault in one of three ways, on a strict rota basis, without reference to their own judgement. The three options were: arrest; asking the suspect to leave for eight hours; and trying to patch things up between the partners. Between March 1981 and August 1982, Sherman and Berk followed up 314 cases by monitoring whether the police intervened during the subsequent six months and then interviewing the victims. Their conclusions support the feminist argument for a tougher line because domestic assaults were more likely to be repeated where partners were merely separated and were less likely to recur when husbands were arrested. Prompt arrest proved to be a strong deterrent against re-offending.

Conclusion

A sociologist's choice of research methods is dictated by the amounts of time and money which are available. For example, Hannah Gavron's study of *The Captive Wife: Conflicts of Housebound Mothers* (Penguin, 1966) was carried out while she was a postgraduate student, working as a single researcher without large funds or a supporting organisation. These practical limitations meant that she was only able to conduct a small-scale survey of forty-eight working-class wives and forty-eight middle-class wives, all living in North London. She acknowledged that large-scale generalisations could not be made from such a sample.

A student doing research for a GCSE project should also be aware that time and resources are limited. It is advisable therefore to plan a project which is not too broad in scope. This point is discussed further in the next chapter which takes up the issue of project work for the GCSE examination.

Case study: the sociology of religion as a science

The following extract is from *Religion in Sociological Perspective* by Bryan Wilson (Oxford University Press, 1982):

Mixing with a religious group, a sociologist may feel deeply drawn to them and their activities, and this may be necessary for the fullest understanding of them. But he must also remember that his brief is to interpret religion sociologically; his values lie in scientific discipline, and in consequence he must always maintain an appropriate distance. It is sometimes objected by religious people that properly to understand a religion one must belong to it. Scholars in any of the disciplines that make religion their object of study cannot accept that. One does not need to be a medieval man to study medieval society . . .

The sociologist will never understand as much as does a believer of equal intelligence. . . . At another level, however, since he sees from the outside, he may acquire a much sharper perspective of its adherents than is possible for those who are committed and who can see only from the inside. Thus, at best, the sociologist should be able to add a whole dimension to the understanding of a religious movement which believers themselves could not obtain from their own perspective. In certain ways he will know less than they do; in other ways he will know more. Part of his way of knowing 'more' will of course come not only from his objectivity and detachment, but also from the fact that he has access, or should have access, to a wider body of information about other comparable religious movements. Comparison is a fundamental requirement of sociological method.

Data-response exercise: the sociology of religion as a science

1 Would the author agree with the claim that you can only properly understand, say, a gang of delinquents by joining in with their activities?

2 Explain why it is that 'in certain ways' a sociologist studying a religious movement will never know as much about it as a believer.

3 Suppose that a sociologist has been privately educated; she now votes Conservative and sends her son to a fee-paying school. Would she be able to compare state schools and fee-paying schools in an objective and unbiased way?

GCSE question from Welsh Board 1988

Read the passage and then answer the questions.

In general, the larger the *sample* taken the more representative of the *population* it will be – provided that *bias and sampling errors* are avoided as far as possible.

State what sociologists mean by
(i)   population,   (2)
(ii) sample,   (2)
(iii) bias and sampling errors.   (3)

CHAPTER 18

Project work

BUT COULD I
JUST ASK YOU
A FEW........

1   The requirements of the GCSE examination groups

All of the GCSE examination groups set examinations in GCSE Sociology and in each case they require a project of some kind to be undertaken. Their requirements are as follows:

The London and East Anglian Group (LEAG) requires a *sociological enquiry* which carries 25 per cent of the final marks. (75 per cent of the final marks are based on two written papers.)

The Northern Examining Association (NEA) requires a piece of *coursework* which carries 20 per cent of the final marks. This coursework must consist of one *investigation*. (80 per cent of the final marks are based on two written papers.)

The Southern Examining Group (SEG) requires a *project* which carries 30 per cent of the final marks and must be undertaken in the twelve months preceding the written examination. (70 per cent of the final marks are based on two written papers.)

The Midland Examining Group (MEG) allocates 40 per cent of the final marks to *coursework* which must consist of one *enquiry* and six *assignments*. (60 per cent of the final marks are based on two written papers.)

The Welsh Joint Education Committee allocates 20 per cent of the final marks to a folio of coursework comprising three *assignments*. (80 per cent of the final marks are based on two written papers.)

2 The aims of project work

Although the mark allocations and the terms used differ, all the examination groups require some form of *project, investigation* or *enquiry* on a topic which is related to the syllabus. Marks may be allocated under headings like these:

1 Aim/Hypothesis You should explain your choice of topic and clearly list any questions to which you hope to find the answers, any theories which you hope to test.

2 Methodology and sources You must use a variety of sources and investigative techniques from the following list:

- direct or participant observation,
- experiments,
- interviews (unstructured and structured),
- questionnaires (open, closed and coded questions),
- surveys (comparative and longitudinal),
- case studies/diaries,
- secondary data such as official statistics, mass media reports and published studies.

You must give convincing reasons for your choice of methods as well as a clear description of how you collected data. In other words, you should show a well planned procedure of enquiry with sources and methods justified by relating them to your original questions or hypotheses.

A teacher offers advice about project work.

3 Presentation This should include all the following features:

- a table of contents,
- clear separation of chapters,
- good layout,
- clear language,
- use of appropriate diagrams and illustrations (any graphs, tables, charts, photos, recorded tapes or cassettes must be clearly labelled),
- a detailed bibliography.

4   Content   NEA expects that the report of an investigation will not need to be more than 3,000 words in length. SEG recommends a length of 2,000 to 4,000 words and says that credit will be given for clear and concise work. LEAG requires between 2,500 and 4,000 words and says that the enquiry should be written up accurately and succinctly. LEAG also warns that 'mere copying in large amounts from secondary sources will be inadequate; the emphasis must always be on synthesis and evaluation'. The Welsh Examination Board requires three assignments, each within the range of 700 to 1,200 words.

5   Evaluation   You should draw together your own conclusions, in your own words, from a variety of sources. Conclusions, like the content, should be relevant. In other words, conclusions must be consistently related to the questions or hypotheses posed.

Your conclusions should evaluate your methods as well as your theories. So you should make some observations about the strengths and weaknesses of the methods used in your study. You should indicate how far your interpretations are supported by the data collected and you should identify any deficiencies, such as gaps, inconsistencies and bias, which reduce the value of your data as evidence.

One good idea is to keep a **log** recording the progress of your project on different days. A summary of this, on just a page or two, could be included as an **appendix** – a supplement added to the end of the project. A description of any difficulties, 'blind-alleys' or unexpected findings which you encountered, will show that you have used a thoughtful approach.

6   Personal contribution   You can expect to be awarded marks for the degree of initiative you display in seeking out and using primary and secondary sources as well as for your personal involvement in the content of the project.

Primary sources are first-hand evidence such as an autobiography, a diary or an original piece of research undertaken by yourself. Secondary sources are second-hand evidence such as a biography based on diaries or a textbook.

SEG allows candidates to collaborate in the early stages of planning and collecting data but the analysis and writing up must be the work of each individual candidate. MEG allows group enquiries 'provided that each candidate has a clearly recognisable aspect of the enquiry so that the work of the individual may be clearly distinguished'.

3   Some ideas for a project

You might have a strong interest in an area of the syllabus such as religion. But instead of amassing vast quantities of information about all the different faiths in Britain, it would be far better to narrow this down to a survey of religious beliefs and activities among fellow pupils.

Even a fairly specific part of a general topic, such as the deviant and criminal pursuits of drug-takers, can be a potentially vast area of research. Using an original questionnaire is infinitely preferable to just amassing a hoard of second-hand information about tobacco, alcohol, cannabis, cocaine and heroin.

With a large subject such as leisure, you could focus on particular aspects by using case studies of the members of a few families. You could, for example, examine their different patterns of leisure in order to try to trace the influence of social factors like age, gender and class.

A group project may be a possibility.

Some further ideas for a project

The study	*Possible sources of data*
1 The relationships within three or four generations of a family.	1 First-hand interviews with some members of the family.
2 The activities of a local pressure group, a local trade union branch, a religious group, a political party, or a youth group.	2 First-hand interviews with members and second-hand reports collected from newspapers.
3 How a specific issue is presented by the media or how a week's news coverage varies between different papers and/or TV/radio.	3 Analysis of content of a sample of the mass media.
4 Experiences at work concentrating on working conditions and job satisfaction.	4 A case study based on a student's personal experience compared with interviews of others.
5 Sexism in the workplace.	5 Participant observation during weekend, evening or holiday job.
6 Sexism in the classroom.	6 Quantitative data (e.g. how often girls are asked questions by teachers compared to boys) collected by direct observation.
7 How different groups of pupils come to opt for different courses at school.	7 Analysis of options figures and interviews with pupils, teachers and parents.
8 Social norms, such as illegal parking and dropping litter.	8 Observation at a busy shopping centre.

One promising alternative might be to consider the methods, examine the findings and assess the conclusions of an existing, published research study. This could involve:

1 describing the aims, methods and main findings of a well-known study;
2 testing the study's findings by repeating part of it in a simplified form or by using different sources;
3 concluding by an evaluation of the reliability and validity of the study's original findings.

4   Some useful addresses

These addresses are included in order to show the range of organisations which might be useful. When writing to such organisations for information always send a large self-addressed envelope and always give a clear description of the aims of your project.

Age Concern (National Old People's Welfare Council),
Bernard Sunley House, Mitcham, Surrey CR4 3LL.

Animal Aid Campaigns Against Vivisection,
7, Castle Street, Tonbridge, Kent.

ASH (Action on Smoking and Health),
5–11, Mortimer Street, London W1N 7RH.

Asian Women's Resource Centre,
134, Minet Avenue, London NW10.

Campaign for Homosexual Equality,
69, Corporation Street, Manchester 4.

Campaign for Nuclear Disarmament,
22–24, Underwood Street, London N1 7JQ.

Campaign for Press and Broadcasting Freedom,
9, Poland Street, London W1.

Child Poverty Action Group,
1, Macklin Street, London WC2.

Equal Opportunities Commission,
Overseas House, Quay Street, Manchester M3 3HN.

Fair Employment Agency for Northern Ireland,
Andras House, 60, Great Victoria Street, Belfast BT2 7BB.

Friends of the Earth,
377, City Road, London EC1V 1NA.

Help the Aged,
St James's Walk, London EC1B 1BD.

The Institute of Alcohol Studies,
12, Caxton Street, London SW1.

Low Pay Unit,
9, Upper Berkeley Street, London W1H 8BY.

MENCAP (Royal Society for Mentally Handicapped Children and Adults),
123, Golden Lane, London EC1.

MIND (National Association for Mental Health),
22, Harley Street, London W1.

National Campaign Against Solvent Abuse,
245a, Unit S, 13, Coldharbour Lane, London SW9.

National Council for One Parent Families,
21, Tabard Street, London SE1.

National Society for the Prevention of Cruelty to Children,
67, Saffron Hill, London EC1.

Prison Reform Trust,
Nuffield Lodge, Regents Park, London NW1 4RS.

Radical Alternatives to Prison,
BCM Box 4842, London WC1.

SHELTER (National Campaign for the Homeless),
157, Waterloo Road, London SE1.

Spastics Society,
12, Park Crescent, London W1.

Trades Union Congress,
Great Russell Street, London WC1B 3LS.

Women's Aid Federation,
374, Grays Inn Road, London WC1.

Youthaid,
9, Poland Street, London W1.

CHAPTER 19

Answering data-response questions

Data-response questions and the GCSE examination

One of the objectives of GCSE Sociology examinations is to assess a candidate's ability to analyse, interpret and evaluate evidence. The evidence given in a question may be a prose extract from a book or a picture such as a photo, a cartoon or a newspaper cutting. Candidates also need to be prepared for questions which include simple statistical data. Questions using these types of stimulus material are called **data-response** or **stimulus questions**.

Stepped questions

Data-response questions are usually structured with sub-sections. The first few parts of the question are often straightforward comprehension questions which test whether candidates can understand the data. Further parts of the question may award increasing numbers of marks and may present candidates with an **incline of difficulty** as they proceed through the stepped or tiered series of questions.

How to approach data-response questions

Useful tips

1   Read through the stimulus material and *all* the questions before putting pen to paper. Sup-

pose that part (b) asked you to describe the trends of the birth rate in Britain since 1900 (for 6 marks), while part (c) asked for explanations of these trends (for 12 marks). If you answered part (b) before reading the question of part (c), you might end up discussing how the downward trend was reversed in the 1950s and linking this with the factors which explain the post-war baby boom. If, however, you had read all the questions through first, then you would have known that explanations of the birth rate trends were needed in part (c) rather than part (b).

2   Be guided by the allocation of marks which is given in brackets after each part or sub-section of the question. Parts (a) and (b) often require figures to be extracted from the data for only a few marks. In such cases it is best simply to write down just the figures. It is a waste of valuable time to give such answers in a full sentence.

3   Sectionalised questions need sectionalised answers. In other words, you must answer each sub-section of the question in the required format, clearly labelling which part of the question you are answering.

4   Always check the titles and scales of tables and graphs. Check whether figures for births in Britain are given in thousands or millions; whether they are annual figures or totals for each decade. The figures might be for the birth rate, in which case they are expressed in numbers of live births per thousand of the population per year.

Example 1

B13 Study the data below and then answer the questions which follow.

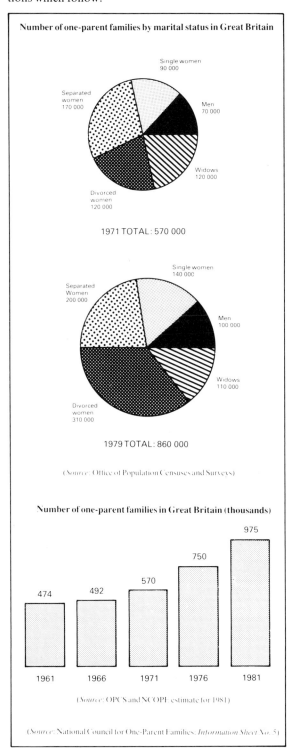

Number of one-parent families by marital status in Great Britain

Single women
90 000

Separated women
170 000

Men
70 000

Widows
120 000

Divorced women
120 000

1971 TOTAL: 570 000

Single women
140 000

Separated Women
200 000

Men
100 000

Widows
110 000

Divorced women
310 000

1979 TOTAL: 860 000

(*Source*: Office of Population Censuses and Surveys)

Number of one-parent families in Great Britain (thousands)

| 975 |
| 750 |
| 570 |
| 492 |
| 474 |

| 1961 | 1966 | 1971 | 1976 | 1981 |

(*Source*: OPCS and NCOPF estimate for 1981)

(*Source*: National Council for One-Parent Families, *Information Sheet No. 5*)

Questions

(a) How many one-parent families were there in 1981? (1 mark)

(b) What type of person was most commonly found as head of a single parent family (i) in 1971, and (ii) in 1979? (2 marks)

(c) How might a Sociologist explain the change in the type of person most commonly found as head of a single parent family in 1971 and 1979? (2 marks)

(d) Give **three** reasons which might explain why the number of single parent families has increased. (3 marks)

(e) Some people believe that the increase in single parent families causes problems for British society. What reasons might they give, and what arguments and evidence could be produced to oppose their view? (7 marks)

The rubric It is very important to read the rubric, or instructions, carefully at the start of each part of an examination paper. Example 1 is taken from Part B of Paper I of the Northern Examining Association's GCSE Sociology specimen examination papers. In this case the rubric tells us that the question is compulsory. It is worth a total of fifteen marks and the mark allocations are shown after each question. Candidates are advised to spend half an hour on the question.

Section (a) We must first spot that the figures which we need, for 1981, are in the bar chart rather than the pie-charts (which refer to 1971 and 1979). It is now advisable to check the title above the bar chart. This tells us that the number of one-parent families is given in thousands. Therefore the figure of 975 for 1981 means 975,000 families.

Because this is a stepped question, we can see that most marks (almost half of the total) are allocated to section (e). Of the half hour which we spend answering this question, we want to spend as much time as possible in answering part (e) in the fullest way. The more points we can make, the more likely we are to pick up the maximum available marks. We should therefore avoid wasting time while answering (a). Our answer to (a) does not need to be written in a full sentence. All that is needed is the figure of 975,000.

Section (b)   The slice with the bigger black dots appears to be the largest of the slices in the 1971 pie chart and the white-dotted slice seems biggest in 1979. We can check this by comparing the numbers given next to each slice. Our answers need only say: (b)(i) Separated women, and (b)(ii) Divorced women.

In answering sections (c), (d) and (e), candidates are expected to go beyond the data and demonstrate their knowledge of changes in the patterns of modern family life in Britain.

Example 2

QUESTIONS SHEET
ANSWER ALL THE QUESTIONS; THEY MAY BE ATTEMPTED IN ANY ORDER. THE MARKS SHOWN SHOULD BE TAKEN AS GUIDES TO THE LENGTHS OF ANSWERS EXPECTED.

1 State four ways in which 'we are socialised into falling in love.' (2 marks)
2 (a) What was the average age of marriage in 1911 for females? (Source C) (1 mark)
   (b) What has been the trend, for each sex, of the 'Average age at first marriage' during this century? (Source C) (1 mark)
3 What does Source E show about divorce? (3 marks)
4 Does the concept of 'romantic love' apply to marriages in all societies? Explain your answer with reference to Sources A and B. (4 marks)
5 Some sociologists argue that there is now greater equality in marriage. To what extent does Source F support or oppose this view? (4 marks)
6 What can be learned from the Sources about the ways in which marriage in Britain has changed during this century? (6 marks)
7 Source B deals with an example of a society very different from our own. Why are sociologists concerned to look at such examples? (9 marks)

SOURCE MATERIAL

SOURCE A

Love is now considered important to marriage in most parts of the world. But only in societies like ours is the ideal of romantic love all powerful. From early childhood we are socialised into falling in love – not just by parents and friends but by popular songs, films, TV programmes, magazines and the other mass media. This influence is so strong that young people may be led to expect too much from marriage, and be bitterly disappointed when the passion of courtship is cooled by the daily routines of married life.

R J Cootes, *The Family*,
published by Longman Group Ltd (1974)

SOURCE B

Margaret Mead spent a lot of time with Manus people in New Guinea in the 1920s before the impact of modernized societies like America and Australia had much influence on their way of life. In Manus societies marriages were arranged and the relatives lived together in extended family groups.

'The relationship between husband and wife is usually strained and cold. The blood-ties with their parents are stronger than their relationship to each other, and there are more factors to pull them apart than to draw them together.

The bridegroom has no attitude of tenderness or affection for the girl whom he has never seen before the wedding. She fears her first sex experience as all the women of her people have feared and hated it. No foundation is laid for happiness on the wedding night, only one for shame and hostility. The next day the bride goes about the village with her mother-in-law to fetch wood, and water. She has not yet said one word to her husband.

This sense that husband and wife belong to different groups persists throughout the marriage, weakening after the marriage has endured for many years, never vanishing entirely.'

J L Thompson, *Examining Sociology*,
published by Hutchinson, London (1980)

SOURCE C

Average age at first marriage: UK 1911-71

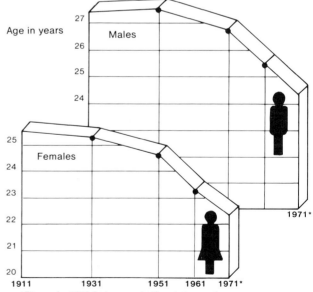

*Figures for 1972-6 show no significant change, thus suggesting that the downward trend has stopped.

R J Cootes, *The Family*,
published by Longman Group Ltd (1974)

SOURCE D

Percentage of women who had lived with their husbands before their marriage

Great Britain	*Percentage*	
	Year of Marriage	
	1971–73	*1977–79*
First marriage for both partners:		
age of woman at marriage		
Under 20	4	16
20–24	8	17
25 and over	10	34
All ages (percentages)	7	19
Second or subsequent marriage for one or both partners:		
All women (percentages)	43	59

Adapted from *Social Trends 12*, published by HMSO (1982)

SOURCE E

Divorce

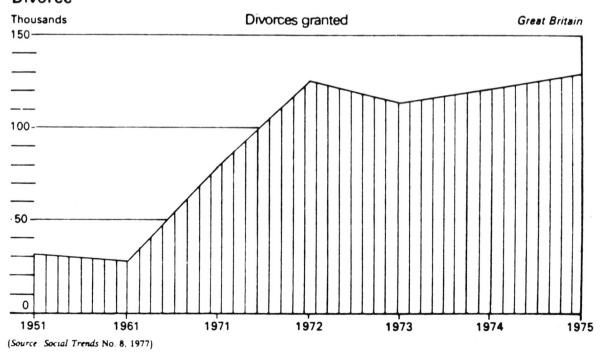

(*Source: Social Trends* No. 8, 1977)

Reproduced from R Whitburn, *Investigating Society – Talking to People,*
published by Macmillan, London and Basingstoke (1979)

SOURCE F

Though the 1980s couple go into marriage on technically equal footing, true equality within marriage
is still something of an ideal. The idea of the 'house-
husband' is still fairly rare, as Ann Oakley found
when she looked at the domestic division of labour
in 'The Sociology of Housework' (1974). She asked
20 working class and 20 middle class housewives
how far their husbands helped out with the housework and looking after the children. Fewer than
a quarter of the husbands gave the kind of help that
could be described as doing an equal share of the
work – and these tended to be middle class.

'Society Today', 13 Nov. 1980,
published in *New Society*

The rubric   Example 2 is from the London and
East Anglian Group's GCSE Sociology specimen
examination papers. The rubric instructs candidates to answer all the questions on this examination paper. One hour and ten minutes is allowed.

The LEAG syllabus states that a variety of
types of stimulus material will be used in this
paper – literary, graphical, photographic, statistical and pictorial. The paper provides candidates
with several pieces of material concerned with
one or more themes. The rubric advises candidates to spend ten minutes reading through the
whole paper and planning their answers.

Question 6   This question asks about changes
in marriage in Britain during this century. We
might wish to write about the way that increased
life expectancy means that growing numbers of
partners enjoy golden wedding anniversaries.
But the question asks us to use the evidence given
in the stimulus material. Because Sources C, D,
and E gives us figures for two or more different
years, we can make comparisons and discern the
following trends:

- Source C indicates that between 1911 and 1971
  the average age at first marriage fell for both
  brides and grooms.
- Source D shows that during the 1970s an
  increasing proportion of partners lived
  together before their marriages.
- Source E tells us that from 1961 to 1972 there
  was a steep rise in the numbers of divorces
  granted.

- Source E also demonstrates how easily a graph
  can be deceptive. An apparently continuous
  scale of years in fact jumps in its spacing from
  decades (1951, 1961, 1971) to single years
  (1971, 1972, 1973, 1974, 1975).

Question 3   In answering this question we must
be guided by the allocation of marks. A fuller
answer is needed than just saying that Source
E shows us that divorce has risen steeply. In order
to be sure of getting all three of the available
marks, either we need to describe fluctuations
in the trend (there was a slight fall in divorces
between 1951 and 1961 as well as from 1972 to
1973), or we could give figures and years to support our claim that Source E shows a steep
increase in divorce.

We could write: 'Divorces granted in Great
Britain rose from around 30,000 in 1961 to over
120,000 in 1972. In other words, the figures rose
by some 400 per cent, or quadrupled.'

Example 3

The following diagrams show the birth rates and death
rates in three societies over a period of time.

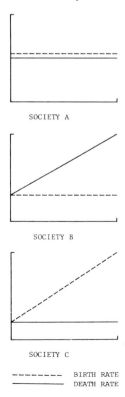

SOCIETY A

SOCIETY B

SOCIETY C

- - - - - - - -   BIRTH RATE
———————   DEATH RATE

(a) From the above diagrams:
  (i) what is happening to the population size in society B; (1 mark)
  (ii) what is happening to the population size in society C; (1 mark)
  (iii) what is happening to the population size in society A? (1 mark)
(b) Name **two** factors other than birth rate and death rate which affect population size. (2 marks)
(c) Define the term birth rate. (2 marks)
(d) Define the term infant mortality rate. (2 marks)
(e) Suggest **three** measures which might reduce the high death rate in society B. (3 marks)
(f) Identify and explain **two** reasons why the infant mortality rate is higher in social class 5 (unskilled manual workers) than in social class 1 (e.g. top managers). (4 marks)
(g) Draw a diagram which shows the relationship between the birth rate and death rate in a society with an ageing population. Give **three** social consequences of an ageing population. (4 marks)

Example 3 is taken from the Southern Examining Group's GCSE Sociology specimen examination papers. The example is an optional question from Paper 1 where candidates have to answer three out of five questions in one and a half hours.

The diagrams   Like all graphs, bar charts or tables with columns of numbers, these diagrams show the relationship between two sets of variables. The horizontal axis measures time while the scale along the vertical axis measures birth and death rates. Although no actual numbers are given, we should bear in mind that rates are always expressed 'per' something. The death rate tells us the number of deaths per thousand of the population in a given time period.

Section (a)   In Society B the death rate is rising while the birth rate is stable and so the population will be falling. In Society C the situation is exactly the reverse. But in Society A both the birth and the death rates are stable. This does not however mean that the population in Society A will stay the same from year to year. If the birth rate remains steadily above the death rate this could mean that, for example, there are fifteen births and twelve deaths per thousand of the population each year. Such a pattern, where births are regularly slightly more numerous than deaths, would result in a steady increase in the population.

Example 4

Social stratification and power

Read carefully the article below.

What do the British mean by 'poverty'? When Peter Townsend's interviewers asked people all over Britain what poverty meant, most of those who replied spoke either of starvation and subsistence needs, or of particular groups such as pensioners and the disabled who are likely to be poor. A few spoke more disapprovingly of people who spend too much on drink and the like (poor people themselves were more inclined than most to say such things). But hardly anyone gave poverty the relative meaning which Townsend himself uses: 'It's when you can't have the things everyone else has.' The table summarises replies.

Replies to the question: What is poverty?

	Percentage
subsistence	31
starvation	7
minority groups (e.g. pensioners, low-paid)	29
mismanagement	8
compared with past	5
compared with others	2
no definition given	8
other answers	10
total	100
Number in sample	1,964

Source: Peter Townsend, *Poverty in the United Kingdom*, Survey Date 1968

(a) (i) What do you understand by the term 'subsistence' used in the passage? (1 mark)
   (ii) Explain what is meant by the word 'relative' in the statement: 'but hardly anyone gave poverty the **RELATIVE** meaning which Townsend himself uses.' (2 marks)
(b) Why might 'poor people' be more likely than those who are better off to think that poverty is caused by 'too much drink and the like'? (2 marks)
(c) (i) Using the information in the passage, explain why people find it hard to agree about the definition of poverty. (4 marks)
   (ii) How is poverty officially defined in modern Britain by the Department of Health and Social Security. (3 marks)
(d) According to sociologists, what are the most important causes of poverty in modern industrial countries? (8 marks)

This question is taken from Paper 2 of the Midland Examining Group's specimen question papers.

Example 5

B14 Look carefully at the two tables below and then answer the questions which follow.

Table 1: Percentage of people registered unemployed, by ethnic group and sex

The following figures show the percentage of people registered as unemployed for various ethnic and gender groups. The data are the result of a survey of 5001 black people and 2263 white people. It was a national survey.

	Men			Women		
	White	*West Indian*	*Asian*	*White*	*West Indian*	*Asian*
Percentage of whole adult population who are registered unemployed	10	21	17	4	11	8
Percentage of population aged under 25 who are registered unemployed	20	33	19	13	21	19

(Source: adapted from *Black and White Britain: The Third PSI Survey* by Colin Brown, Gower 1985)

Table 2: Intentions on leaving school, by ethnic group and sex (shown as percentages)

The following figures show the percentages of school students who intended following different paths after 16. The data are the result of interviews of 394 school students in Bradford.

	Get a Job	*Higher Education*	*Further Education*
All	54.9	13.2	25.6
White	66.7	9.5	18.7
Pakistani	33.3	27.8	31.5
Bangladeshi	33.3	8.3	50.0
Indian	26.2	19.0	45.2
West Indian	40.0	10.0	40.0
Male	69.3	13.6	14.5
Female	43.8	10.8	35.1

(Source: adapted from *Ethnicity and Educational Achievement in British Schools* by G. K. Verma and B. Ashworth, Macmillan 1986)

Questions

(a) In Table 1 which ethnic group shows the highest rate of registered unemployment? (1 mark)
(b) In Table 2 which ethnic group most wants to continue in education after the age of 16? (1 mark)
(c) In Table 1 why are the figures for women registered unemployed generally lower than the figures for men registered unemployed? (2 marks)
(d) Why is it difficult to compare the figures for registered unemployment (Table 1) with the figures for intentions on leaving school (Table 2)? (2 marks)
(e) Why are young people more likely to be registered unemployed than adults? (4 marks)
(f) How could you explain the relationship between ethnic grouping and life chances? (5 marks)

This question is taken from Part B of Paper I of the Northern Examining Group's specimen examination papers.

Example 6

Study the following table and answer the questions which follow:

Population changes and projections – United Kingdom

Period	Population at start of period – MILLIONS	Average annual change – THOUSANDS		
		Live births	Deaths	Natural increase
1974–75	55.9	721	671	+50
1975–76	55.9	689	681	+8
1976–77	55.9	655	660	−5
1977–78	55.9	664	665	−1
PROJECTIONS (FORECASTS)				
1978–81	55.9	671	689	−18
1981–91	55.7	854	715	+139
1991–2001	56.7	840	717	+123

Adapted from *Social Trends* (1979)

(a) Give the number in the population for the period 1975–1976. (1 mark)
(b) Give the forecast average number of deaths for the period 1991–2001. (1 mark)
(c) Give the natural change in population for the period 1977–1978. (1 mark)
(d) State the period with the highest forecast natural increase. (1 mark)
(e) Under what circumstances, according to the figures, does a natural decrease occur? (1 mark)

(f) Population changes and projections of this kind are used by Government departments for future planning. Describe *two* ways in which numbers of births forecast might affect planning in the area of education. ($2 \times 1\frac{1}{2}$ marks)

This question is taken from Section B of Paper 1 of the Welsh Joint Education Committee's specimen question papers.

Example 7

ITEM A

ITEM B

Jonathan Steinberg

The candidate flushed. I had clearly embarrassed her but how? All I had asked was how she intended to spend the time between the end of her work with a well-known engineering company and starting university the following October. It's the sort of dull question that all interviewers ask when they cannot think up anything brighter. She took a while to answer and this is what she said:

'Well, my mum thinks, after all this engineering, that I ought to do some normal things . . . you know, cooking and sewing . . .'

There was an awful silence. Both of us were embarrassed now. We had touched the delicate issue of the "female engineer"; the collision of two opposing role models could be seen in my poor candidate's red face. Other female engineering candidates had told me similar stories, of mothers who allow bumbling dads to make messes of their toasters but won't allow daughters to change a plug.

ITEM C
(Source, *New Society*, March 1983)

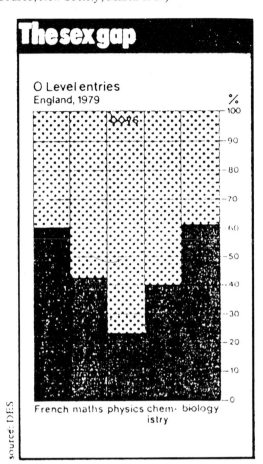

source: DES

boys
girls

(a) Look at the cartoon (Item A). What does the wife do which embarrasses her husband? (1 mark)
(b) A sociologist might call the husband's reaction an attempt to conform to social pressure. Briefly explain the meaning of the term 'social pressure'. (2 marks)
(c) What is meant by 'role conflict'? Give an example. (3 marks)
(d) Explain why the mothers of the female engineering candidates find it difficult to accept the career choice made by their daughters (Item B). (6 marks)
(e) Examine the table (Item C). Which 'O' level subjects had a mainly male entry? Discuss the extent to which schools are responsible for continuing this pattern of entry. (8 marks)

Example 8

The Number of Certain Crimes in Birmingham in 1978 and 1981

	Birmingham	
	1978	1981
Population	1,041,000	1,020,300
Murder	45	35
Rape	93	83
Robbery	1,060	1,543
Burglary	40,633	57,702

(Source: *Police Review*)

(a) According to the above information, how many cases of rape were there in Birmingham in 1978? (1 mark)
(b) From the above information, give **one** example of a crime which has increased between 1978 and 1981. (1 mark)
(c) What is the difference between legal and illegal deviancy? Give an example of each. (4 marks)
(d) Identify and explain **three** reasons why crime statistics do not necessarily show the true extent of crime in society. (6 marks)
(e) What explanations have sociologists put forward to explain juvenile crime? (8 marks)

Example 9

Parliamentary by-elections

	May 1979 –June 1983	Previous* General Election May 1979
Number of by-elections	20	
Votes recorded by party (*percentages*)		
Conservative	23.8	33.7
Labour	25.7	35.2
Liberal	9.0	8.0
Social Democratic Party	14.2	
Plaid Cymru	0.5	0.4
Scottish National Party	1.7	1.4
Other	25.1	21.2
Total votes recorded (=100%) (thousands)	715	852

* Votes recorded in the same seats in the previous General Election.

(Adapted from: *Social Trends*, 1985)

(a) How many by-elections were held in the United Kingdom between May 1979 and June 1983? (1 mark)

(b) How many votes were recorded in these constituencies in the General Election May 1979? (1 mark)

(c) What change took place in the percentage of votes recorded for:
  (i) the Labour Party; (1 mark)
  (ii) the Liberal Party; (1 mark)
in- the by-elections compared with the General Election May 1979?

(d) Name the Nationalist parties mentioned in the chart. (2 marks)

(e) (i) Explain why no votes were recorded for the Social Democratic Party in the General Election May 1979. (1 mark)

(ii) With which party is the Social Democratic Party now in alliance? (1 mark)

(f) Name **two** different types of pressure group. Give an example of each. (4 marks)

(g) Give **four** methods used by pressure groups by which they hope to influence government policy and/or public opinion. (4 marks)

(h) Identify and explain **two** reasons why the result of a poll on voting intentions taken one month before an election may not accurately reflect the actual result of the election. (4 marks)

Examples Seven, Eight and Nine are all taken from the Specimen Papers of the Southern Examining Group.

CHAPTER 20

GCSE examination questions

GCSE question from Welsh Board Specimen paper

Study the following carefully. For each definition in Column A find the most appropriate term in Column B. Then record your answer by writing the number from Column B before its appropriate definition in Column A. (10 × ½)

Column A

(a) An established practice and usage which governs the relationships between individuals and groups.
(b) The system of social stratification which operates in Britain.
(c) A relationship which has indirect, contractual and impersonal contact.
(d) A traditional practice in society.
(e) The process of learning the ways of a society so as to be able to function within it.
(f) Any means used by a group to discourage deviant or non-conformist behaviour.
(g) Power that is accepted as proper and legal by most members of a group or society.
(h) A status position one is born into.
(i) That which refers to people's behaviour in groups.
(j) Biased and oversimplified ideas about the characteristics of the members of a particular social group.

Column B

1 ascription
2 organisation
3 elite
4 authority
5 sanctions
6 socialisation
7 function
8 stereotype
9 socialism
10 secondary
11 institution
12 gender
13 belief
14 perception
15 class
16 custom
17 exchange
18 interaction

GCSE question from Welsh Board 1988

Study the following. For each definition in Column A find the best term in Column B. Record your answer by writing the number from Column B before its appropriate definition in Column A. (3)

Column A

(a) When two or more people take account of each other and change their behaviour.
(b) Social differences between male and female.
(c) People with a common nationality, or racial background, who share a common culture.
(d) A person's position within a social situation.
(e) Standards, usually accepted by a group, which are used to judge behaviour.
(f) The way in which people are ranked within a society.

Column B

1 Values
2 Status
3 Beliefs
4 Stratification
5 Organisation
6 Exchange
7 Power
8 Gender
9 Role
10 Ethnicity
11 Mobility
12 Interaction

GCSE question from Northern Examining Group 1988

Study the extracts on page 280 and answer the questions below.

(a) The extracts identify some of the different demands made
    upon women. Name *two* of these demands which may conflict.   (2)
(b) What proportion of people who are responsible for the care of
    dependent adult relatives are men? (*Use Extract* C)   (1)
(c) In what ways may members of a family be dependent on each
    other at different stages of their lives? (*Use Extract A and your
    own knowledge and experience.*)   (4)
(d) Using the extracts give *one* example of each of the following
    with reasons for your choices:
    (i)   evidence
    (ii) value judgement
    (iii) bias   (6)
(e) The policy of 'community care' or 'family care' may have a
    different impact on different social classes.
    (i) What effects may it have on the wealthy?   (2)
    (ii) What effects may it have on the poor?   (2)
(f) (i) In which social class would you expect to find the greatest
        incidence of disability and disease?   (1)
    (ii) Explain the causes of your answer in f(i) above.   (6)
(g) Explain how the socialisation of boys may make men less able
    or willing to offer care to relatives.   (6)

GCSE question from London and East Anglian Group 1988

Number of Social Security claims

Type of payment	Year			
	1961	*1971*	*1981*	*1986*
Retirement pensions	5793	7677	8680	9525
One-parent allowances	78	217	370	615
Unemployment benefits	227	485	550	935
Child benefits	3731	4464	13330	12035

(All figures in thousands)

(*Social Trends*, No. 17, 1987)

(a) How many one-parent allowances were claimed in 1971?   (1)
(b) Give *two* reasons why people entitled to benefits do not
    claim them.   (4)
(c) Explain the difference between relative and absolute poverty.   (4)
(d) What evidence is there for the view that poverty continues
    in spite of the Welfare State?   (6)

THE FAMILY
Unreal expectations

Current policy in the UK is for community care. This means that elderly and disabled people live with relatives who are responsible for looking after their needs. It can be argued that it is much more pleasant for an elderly or disabled person to live in the community. On the other hand, it can be argued that this is merely an excuse to close nursing homes and hospitals and reduce public spending.

It can also be said that "community care" is the wrong name for what actually happens. Perhaps it should really be called "family care", or even "care by female relatives". Men hardly ever take on the responsibility of caring for relatives, apart from their wives.

Since the mid-1970s government policies have included the aim of strengthening the family. Yet, just because people **do** look after their relatives does not mean that they feel they **ought** to do so. It may be that there are no other alternatives, that people provide care though they feel they should **not** have to do so.

Policy makers have no idea what would happen if people found the responsibility of caring for relatives too much to cope with. Relationships between adult relatives tend to consist of a carefully balanced give and take, and we can only guess at the effect on these relationships of giving compulsory care.

Feminists have pointed out the contradiction of governments claiming to encourage women to take a full role in society as citizens and workers, while at the same time producing policies that rely on women's unpaid labour to care for dependent people. One reply is to say that government should develop policies to encourage men to take an equal share in these responsibilities. There does not appear to be any sign of this happening yet.

The other group whose views should be considered is the elderly and infirm. They might not choose to be forced to depend upon relatives only because there are no other alternatives available.

Extract A

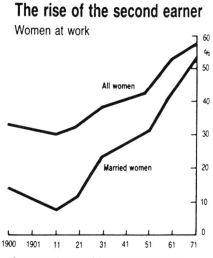

The rise of the second earner
Women at work

Source: H. Joshi, R. Layard and S. Owen: why are more women working in Britain? Centre for Labour Economics, LSE, June 1983

The increasing number of women at work gives the lie to the assumption that women are at home and therefore available to provide care.

Extract B

The value of family care

● There are at least 1.3 million people caring for a dependent relative or friend.

● Three quarters of them are women — one woman in eight. Two thirds of these women are over 40.

● The "value" of informal care — if carers were paid — is estimated at between £5 billion and £7 billion a year.

● If ten per cent of those now cared for, free, at home had instead to be looked after in residential institutions, more than £1 billion a year would be added to public spending.

Source: Family Policy Studies Centre.

Extract C

GCSE question from Midland Examining group 1988

Culture, socialisation and the individual

Education in inner cities

This question is based upon several pieces of source material. They are about educational under-achievement in inner city schools. Educational achievement is usually measured by public examination pass rates and pupil behaviour. A pupil under-achieves when examination pass rate or behaviour is worse than expected. Read all the sources carefully before answering the questions which follow.

Source A

Schooling Problems of the Inner City

Inner cities have some of the worst records when it comes to education. They have low rates in exams and the highest rates of pupils missing school for illness and truancy ... In one inner city area a survey estimated that almost 40% of pupils didn't turn up for school on some days.

But that's not all. Bad behaviour, lack of respect for teachers and even violence are common. Poor standards are the norm! This is a very sad situation which the schools and teachers have allowed to develop. They must all take a large share of the blame!
(from: Newspaper report, June 1986)

Source B

15000 HOURS – Secondary schools and effects on children

Michael Rutter studied twelve secondary schools in Inner London. He looked at several hundred children of the same age as they went through school. Data was gathered using questionnaires, interviews and observation with pupils, teachers and parents. Official statistics were also used. Rutter was trying to answer two questions, 'Do schools affect a child's educational achievement?' and 'What makes a good school that helps children to be successful?' In his conclusion he says that:

> 'Secondary schools in inner London differ a lot in the behaviour and attainment shown by their pupils: for example, in their attendance, the numbers staying on after 16 in the sixth form, in public examinations and delinquency rates.

These differences between schools can be explained by the quality of the school as well as the type of children who go to the school. For example schools where teachers work hard and which make an example of success, use rewards and praise and give pupils a chance to take responsibility tend to get better examination results and well behaved pupils.'
(adapted from M. Rutter, *15000 Hours*, 1979)

Source C

A Science lesson in an inner city comprehensive school

Source D

I studied an inner city part of the east of London. I believe that family background affects schooling in this type of area. It gives children fewer toys and books; fewer outings and holidays; little space for play and study; less attention from parents because of larger, very young families, unsocial working hours and problems with housing and income that take parents' time. In these areas many children are not given the experiences and help they need to develop and do well in school.

Family life also affects schooling through the pupils' behaviour. The inner city child is less self-controlled and more badly behaved than average. Many children see arguments, the break-up of 'relationships' and sometimes violence in family life as everyday happenings. They bring this type of behaviour into their school, which can cause disruption of learning in class.

(adapted from P. Harrison, *Inside the Inner City*, 1985)

Source E

In Hackney, a borough in the east of London's inner city:
  (i)   69% of parents are in social class IV and V (semi-skilled or unskilled manual workers).
 (ii)   33% of pupils come from families poor enough to get free school dinners.
(iii)   28% come from one-parent families.
 (iv)   27% come from large families with five or more children.
  (v)   18% speak a first language other than English.
 (vi)   20% of housing in Hackney is 'unfit for human habitation'.
(adapted from C. Townroe and G. Yates, *Sociology for GCSE*, 1987)

Source F

Percentage of children with attainment of	Father's occupation	
	Non-manual	Manual
5+ GCEs	34	11
1–4 GCEs	34	32
No GCEs or CSE Grade 1s	32	57

(From HMSO, *Social Trends*, 1985)

Look at Sources A and B (page 281)

These sources suggest that schools and teachers may be one of the causes of educational under-achievement in inner city areas.

(a) According to Source A, what are *two* of the problems of inner city schools? (2)

(b) 'The newspaper report in Source A is biased.' Choose a sentence from the source which could be used as evidence to support this statement. Briefly explain your choice. (3)

(c) 'Source A is biased, so it is of no use to a sociologist studying under-achievement in inner city schools.' Do you agree or disagree with this statement? Give reasons. (5)

(d) Source A concludes that *all* schools and teachers must share the blame for inner city educational under-achievement. Does the evidence in Source B support this conclusion? Explain your answer carefully. (5)

(e) 'Source B is more reliable than Source A.' Do you agree or disagree with this statement. Give reasons. (7)

Look at Source C (page 282)

(f) From the evidence in the photograph what can you tell about teacher-pupil relationships in this classroom? (7)

(g) How useful is Source C as evidence of teacher-pupil relationships in the whole school? (7)

Look at Sources D, E and F (pages 282 and 283)

'The family background of pupils is the main cause of educational under-achievement in inner city schools.'

(h) Use the evidence in Sources D, E and F to write an argument supporting this statement. (7)

(i) Is the evidence in Sources D, E and F enough to reach this conclusion? Explain your answer carefully. (7)

GCSE question from Midland Examining Group 1988

Source A

This Land of Ours

The Moaning Minnies and Whining Willies – The Trendies and the Commies should shut up or GET OUT.

Now is the time to stand up and tell the Wets just how lucky they are to live in this GREAT DEMOCRACY OF BRITAIN – where everyone can decide their own future: where you can say what you like, when you like and vote for who you like. Rule is by and for the majority – no Army Colonel is going to walk into Buckingham Palace and take over the country.

This is the LAND of the FREE where press and television report all views fairly and without fear – you cannot buy votes in Britain!

Here is the LAND of OPPORTUNITY where effort is rewarded and all have a straight chance to get to the top ...

Source B

Votes cast in the General Election of 1987 (GREAT BRITAIN)

Party	Votes cast	Number of MPs
Conservative	13,763,134	375 (Conservative Government elected)
Labour	10,033,633	229
Liberal/SDP Alliance	7,339,912	22
Scottish Nationalist and Plaid Cymru	540,462	4

General Election		Labour	Conservative	Liberal	RESULT
1951	Votes	13,949,105	13,718,069	730,552	Conservative
	Seats	296	320	6	Government
1974	Votes	11,661,488	11,928,677	6,056,713	Labour
(Feb)	Seats	301	296	14	Government

Source C *British national newspapers 1986: circulation and ownership*

DAILY PAPERS

Conservative papers [a]

Daily Express
The Daily Telegraph
Daily Mail
The Sun
The Times
The Star

The Electoral Impact of the Partisan Press

Although television must give 'balanced' political coverage, newspapers are free to follow a partisan line — and most do support only one of the political parties. During general elections the press might be expected to become even more partisan than usual, but in May and June 1987 the behaviour of certain newspapers was seen by some people as reaching new depths of bias, lies and distortion.

Labour papers [a]

Daily Mirror
The Guardian

Alliance papers [a]

Today

Non-partisan papers [a]

The Independent

Title [a]	Owner	Circulation, Sept. 1986	% of market
Daily Express	United Newspapers	1,806,247	12.2
Daily Mail	Associated Newspapers	1,790,228	12.1
Daily Mirror	Robert Maxwell (Pergamon)	3,260,516	22.1
Sun	News International	4,151,478	28.1
Daily Telegraph	Daily Telegraph (C Black)	1,131,004	7.7
Daily Star	United Newspapers	1,347,759	9.1
Financial Times	Pearson Longman	258,312	1.7
Guardian	Guardian	527,194	3.6
Times	News International	488,681	3.3
Total		14,761,419	99.9

Note: (a) Today is not included as its circulation figures have not been checked by the Audit Bureau of Circulation. 'The Independent' began publication in October 1986. Its current circulation is around 300,000 copies.

**Share of circulation by top
three ownership groups
74.8%**

BRITISH NATIONAL NEWSPAPERS 1986: CIRCULATION AND OWNERSHIP

[Adapted from: *SOCIAL STUDIES REVIEW* (1987)]

Source D

The social background of Cabinet Ministers (1868–1970)

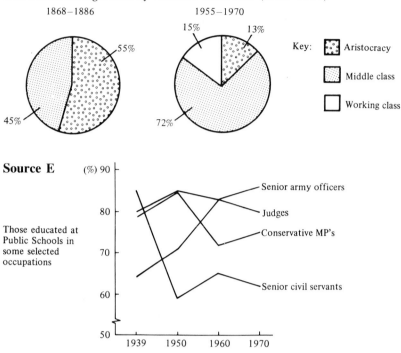

1868–1886   1955–1970

55%

45%   72%   15%   13%

Key: Aristocracy

Middle class

Working class

Source E

Those educated at
Public Schools in
some selected
occupations

(%) 90

80

70

60

50

Senior army officers

Judges

Conservative MP's

Senior civil servants

1939   1950   1960   1970

Public Schools are private, fee-paying secondary schools. Going to a public school is sometimes thought to give a person a privileged position in society.

In terms of examination results, many state schools achieve standards as high as, or higher than, those of many Public Schools. In 1981 there were 4,992,000 children in secondary education in the UK and, of these, some 5 per cent might be described as attending 'Public Schools'.

> ... in 1982 the chairman of the BBC, the editor of *The Times*, the Foreign Secretary, the heads of both foreign and civil services and half the chairmen of the big four banks would all be Old Etonians, while the Home Secretary, the director-general of the BBC, a number of judges and the other two bank chairmen would come from the rival public school, Winchester.
> (adapted from Anthony Sampson, *The Changing Anatomy of Britain*)

Source F

1975 Referendum

To decide whether or not Britain should join the European Economic Community.

Expenditure on campaigning
by those favouring entry   £1,481,583
by those against entry   £133,630

Look at Sources A, B and C (page 284 and 285)

(a)   According to Source A, what *two* features of life in Britain
      suggest that Britain is a Democracy?   (2)

(b)   Examine Source B.
      Roughly what proportion (or percentage) of those who
      voted in the 1987 General Election voted for the
      government which was elected to power?   (2)

(c)   Examine Source C.
      What percentage of the market in daily papers was held
      by those papers supporting the Labour Party?   (2)

(d)   'The report in Source A is biased.' Choose *two* examples
      of apparent bias from the passage and use evidence
      from Sources B and C to support this statement.   (8)

(e)   Is Source C more reliable than Source A? Ensure that
      you indicate clearly what is fact and what is opinion in
      Source C.   (8)

Look at Sources D and E (page 286)

(f)   The evidence in Sources D and E suggests that class
      is still an important factor in determining who
      occupies important positions in British Society. Show
      how the evidence presented could be used to support
      this view.   (6)

(g)   Is the evidence given in Sources D and E enough to reach
      a conclusion that British Society is unequal? Pay
      particular attention to possible deficiencies in the
      evidence presented.   (8)

Sources A to F (pages 284–6)

(h)   Is there any evidence to support the view that 'you
      cannot buy votes in Britain'? Explain your answer.   (4)

(i)   To what extent is Britain a Democracy?
      Use the evidence in Sources A to F to answer this question. (10)

GCSE question from Welsh Board 1988

(a)   Explain what is meant by
    (i)   *equal educational opportunity*, and   (4)
    (ii) *under-achievement*.   (4)
(b)   Identify two groups which under-achieve at school.   (2)
(c)   Discuss the reasons for the under-achievement of the groups
    named in (b).   (10)

GCSE question from Midland Examining Group 1988

Education

Read the following passage carefully and then answer the questions printed after it.

What goes on in classrooms varies widely between schools and within schools. At best teachers and pupils share a sense of purpose and cooperate. Pupils take some responsibility for their own learning and pupils of all abilities achieve at their best levels. Written work is usually well presented and marked helpfully by teachers. Many HMI* reports, however, say that the learning styles in schools are poor. They say that teachers tell pupils what to do too much and give them little choice. There is not enough involvement of pupils in their own learning. There is also not enough oral work – discussion, listening and talking.

*HMI – Her Majesty's Inspectors of Schools.

(Source: adapted from *Education Observed*, published by the Department of Education and Science, 1984)

(a)   According to the above passage, what are *two* of the ways
    in which teaching styles are poor in schools?   (2)
(b)   What does this passage tell you about the position of
    teachers compared to pupils in schools? Give reasons for
    your answer.   (4)
(c)   Give *two* measures of educational achievement used by
    sociologists.   (2)
(d)   Explain the difference between the *curriculum* and the
    hidden curriculum of schools. Give examples of both.   (4)
(e)   In what ways does education influence a person's life
    chances in society?   (8)

GCSE question from Southern Examining Group 1988

The Sociology of the Family

Item A

There is evidence that an increasing number of fathers are taking an active share in the rearing of their children and enjoying it. This is very different from the role of the Victorian father who was in most cases a distant figure to his children and whose attitude was much more formal ... This may be part of the changes in Western society, where differences in role between male and female generally are declining. No longer is the male the provider and the female the home-maker and child-rearer. Inside and outside the home, work is being shared and performed by both.

Item B

Families with Dependent Children 1971–1984 (Great Britain)

Family type	1971–1973 (%)	1982–1984 (%)
Married couple	92	87
Lone mother	7	12
Lone father	1	1
All Lone parents	8	13

(Source: *OPCS Monitor GHS 85/1*, July 1985, Office of Population Censuses & Surveys)

(a) In **Item B** which family type has increased the most? (1)

(b) In **Item B** which family type has decreased? (1)

(c) Look at the extract given as **Item A** and state *two* changes in the role of father which are referred to. (2)

(d) **Item B** draws our attention to a variety of family types. Identify and describe *two* types of families which sociologists have observed. (4)

(e) Identify and explain *two* aspects of family life which have changed since the onset of the Industrial Revolution. (4)

(f) Briefly explain *two* reasons for the popularity of **remarriage** given that divorce is now quite common. (4)

(g) Give *two* reasons why the family may be undergoing change at the present time. (4)

GCSE question from Southern Examining Group 1988

Social Differentiation

Item A

In a perfectly open society everyone has the chance to find his or her own position, restricted only by personal preference and suitability. Individuals, then, find their position by the use of their own talents. Social mobility, in this sense, has increased this century for a variety of reasons, such as personal striving.

(Source: adapted from *Social Stratification*, M. Tumin, Prentice-Hall)

Item B

United Kingdom Distribution of Wealth

Percentage of wealth owned by:	1971	1976	1978	1979	1980	1981	1982
Most wealthy 1% of population	21	14	13	13	12	12	11
Most wealthy 2% of population	27	18	17	17	16	16	16
Most wealthy 5% of population	37	27	25	25	24	24	24
Most wealthy 10% of population	49	37	36	35	33	33	34
Most wealthy 25% of population	71	60	59	58	57	57	57
Most wealthy 50% of population	87	83	81	81	80	80	80

(Source: Adapted from *Business Organisations and Environment, Volume 1*, Glew, Watts and Wells, Heinemann Educational Books Ltd)

(a) Look at **Item A** and state one factor responsible for a person's social mobility. (1)

(b) According to **Item B** what percentage of wealth did the top 5% of the population possess in 1980? (1)

(c) In **Item B** what changes took place in the percentage of wealth ownership held by:
   (i) the most wealthy 1% of the population between 1971 and 1982? (1)
   (ii) the most wealthy 25% of the population between 1971 and 1979? (1)

(d) Identify and explain *two* differences between a caste and a class system of stratification. (4)

(e) Identify and explain *two* changes in society which have affected the class structure in Britain since 1945. (4)

(f) Identify and explain *two* reasons for the increased opportunities for upward mobility for working class children during the 1960s. (4)

(g) A person's social class position is usually based upon his or her occupation. Identify and explain *two* problems of classifying people in this way. (4)

GCSE question from Midland Examining Group 1988

Deviance

Study the information given below and then answer the questions printed after it.

Every eight seconds, there is another innocent victim

CRIME FILE

LAWLESS BRITAIN!

The criminals have never had it so good

RAPE	UP 24%
ROBBERY	UP 9%
BURGLARY	UP 7%
THEFT	UP 6%
VIOLENCE	UP 3%
VANDALISM	UP 8%

The shocking truth about lawless Britain was exposed by official Government figures yesterday.

They show that the country is in the grip of its worst-ever crime wave. There was a 7 per cent overall increase in crime in England and Wales last year.

Crimes of violence, including rape, are soaring. Robberies, burglaries and theft are all up.

What lies behind the tide of lawlessness sweeping Britain and the rest of Europe?

The police say it's being fuelled by the consumer boom, television, drug-taking and unemployment.

TABLE OF SHAME

REGION by region these were last year's biggest crime increases:
1. City of London–up 16%; 2. Avon and Somerset–15%; 3. Cleveland–14%; 4. South Wales–12%; 5. Bedfordshire, Greater Manchester, Suffolk–11%; 6. Cumbria, Essex, Humberside, West Midlands, ten per cent; 7. Lancashire, Surrey, Thames Valley–nine per cent; 8. Merseyside, South Yorkshire, Staffordshire–eight per cent.

Three police forces reported a fall; Gwent –down five per cent; Derbyshire–three per cent; Cambridgeshire–one per cent.

MIRROR COMMENT

A Double disgrace

Two issues cry out for sympathetic and urgent action in today's Budget.

They are the record rise in crime–and the continuing brutality of unemployment, which is the root of much of that crime.

(Source: Quotations from the *Daily Mirror*)

(a) (i) Which area shown in the Table had the greatest fall in the crime rate in 1986? (1)

  (ii) What was the overall percentage increase in crime in England and Wales in 1986? (1)

(b) Why is some deviant behaviour seen as criminal? (2)

(c) Why may statistics for crime be unreliable? (4)

(d) To what extent do you agree with the statement in the information above that unemployment is the main cause of the increase in crime? (6)

(e) Men are six times more likely than women to be convicted of a criminal offence. Explain why this is so. (6)

Author index

The following list of studies indicates the chapter, and section of each chapter, where each study is referred to (for example 14/2 means that the book is referred to in Section 2 of Chapter 14).

14/2 ALDERNAN, G. (1984) *Pressure Groups and Government in Great Britain*, Longman.

5/5 ANWAR, M, (1979) *The Myth of Return: Pakistanis in Britain*, Heinemann.

10/5, 16/3 BALL, S. J. (1981) *Beachside Comprehensive: A Case-study of Secondary Schooling*, Cambridge University Press.

5/5 BALLARD, R. (1982) 'South Asian Families', *Families in Britain* (ed. RAPOPORT, R. N. et al) Routledge & Kegan Paul.

8/2 BELL, D. (1987) 'Acts of Union: youth subculture and ethnic identity amongst Protestants in Northern Ireland', *The British Journal of Sociology*, Volume 38.

13/5 BELSON, W. (1978) *Television Violence and the Adolescent Boy*, Saxon House.

4/3 BETTELHEIM, B. (1969) *The Children of the Dream*, Thames & Hudson

5/5, 7/3 and 4 BROWN, C. (1984) *Black and White Britain: The Third PSI Survey*, Heinemann.

16/3 CAMPBELL, B. (1984) *Wigan Pier Revisited*, Virago Press.

3/5 COHEN, S. (1980) *Folk Devils and Moral Panics the creation of the Mods and Rockers*, Martin Robertson.

14/4 CREWE, I. (1984) *How to Win a Landslide with out Really Trying: Why the Conservatives won in 1983, Papers in Politics and Government*, the University of Essex, Department of Government.

16/5 DANIEL, W. W. (1987) *Workplace Industrial Relations and Technical Change*, Policy Studies Institute.

2/3 DURKIN, K. (1985) *Television, Sex Roles and Children*, Open University Press.

16/4 FAGIN, L. and LITTLE, M. (1984) *The Forsaken Families*, Penguin.

5/5 FARLEY, R. (1984) *Blacks and Whites: Narrowing the Gap?*, Harvard University Press.

16/4 FINNEMAN, S. (1983) *White Collar Unemployment*, John Wiley & Sons Ltd.

3/5 FRITH, S. (1984) *The Sociology of Youth*, Causeway Press.

13/4 GLASGOW UNIVERSITY MEDIA GROUP (1976) *Bad News*, Routledge and Kegan Paul.

13/4 GLASGOW UNIVERSITY MEDIA GROUP (1985) *War and Peace News*, Open University Press.

11/3 GLOCK, C. Y. and STARK, R. (1969) 'Dimensions of Religious Commitment', *Sociology of Religion* (ed. ROBERTSON, R.), Penguin.

15/4 GOLDING, P. and MIDDLETON, S. (1983) *Images of Welfare: Press and Public Attitudes to Poverty*, Martin Robinson, Oxford.

13/4 HALL, S., CRYTCHER, C., JEFFERSON, T., CLARKE, J. and ROBERTS, B. (1978) *Policing the Crisis*, Macmillan.

16/1 HANDY, C. (1984) *The Future of Work*, Basil Blackwell.

10/2 HARGREAVES, D. (1978) 'Power and the Paracurriculum', *Power and the Curriculum: Issues in Curriculum Studies* (ed. RICHARDS, C.), Nafferto Books.

10/4 HARRISON, P. (1985) *Inside the Inner City: Life Under the Cutting Edge*, Penguin

14/4 HEATH, A., JOWELL, R. and CURTICE, J. (1985) *How Britain Votes*, Pergamon Press.

13/3 HETHERINGTON, A. (1985) *News, Newspapers and Television*, Macmillan.

17/3 HIMMELWEIT, H. T., HUMPHREYS, P. and JAEGER, M. (1985) *How Voters Decide*, Open University Press.

8/4 HOYLES, M. (ed.) (1979) *Changing Childhood*, Writers and Readers Publishing Cooperative.

2/2 JOWELL, R. and WITHERSPOON, S. (1985) *British Social Attitudes, The 1985 Report*, Gower.

14/4 JOWELL, R., WITHERSPOON, S. and BROOK, L. (1988) *British Social Attitudes: the 5th Report*, Gower.

13/4 KARPF, A. (1988) *Doctoring the Media*, Routledge and Kegan Paul.

4/2 KENYATTA, J. (1938) *Facing Mount Kenya: the Tribal Life of the Gikuyu*, Secker & Warburg.

2/5 KNIGHT, S. (1983) *The Brotherhood*, Granada Publishing.

12/4 LEA, J. and YOUNG, J. (1984) *What is to be Done About Law and Order?*, Penguin.

2/1 LEES, S. (1986) *Losing Out: Sexuality and Adolescent Girls*, Hutchinson.

2/5 LEONARD, D. and SPEAKMAN, M. A. (1986) 'Women in the Family: Companions or Caretakers' in *Women in Britain Today* (eds BEECHEY, V. and WHITELEGG, E.) Open University Press.

15/2 MACK, J. and LANSLEY, E. (1985) *Poor Britain*, Allen & Unwin.

13/4 MCQUAIL, D. (1987) *Mass Communication Theory*, Sage.

17/2 MARSH, P. (1978) *Aggro: the Illusion of Violence*, Dent.

13/5 MESSENGER DAVIES, M. (1989) *Television is Good for Your Kids*, Hilary Shipman.

13/1 MORLEY, D. (1986) *Family Television: Cultural Power and Domestic Leisure*, Comedia.

13/5 MURDOCK, G. (1978) 'Political deviance: the press presentation of a militant mass demonstration', *The Manufacture of News: Social Problems, Deviance and the Mass Media* (eds. COHEN, S. and YOUNG, J.), Constable.

8/2 NAIDOO, B. (1985) *Journey to Jo'burg: a South African Story*, Longman.

2/2 NEWSON, J. and NEWSON, E. (1978) *Seven Years Old in the Home Environment*, Penguin.

15/3 O'DONNELL, M. (1985) *Age and Generation*, Tavistock.

17/3 OAKLEY, A. (1981) *From Here to Maternity: Becoming a Mother*, Penguin.

8/1 OMOND, R. (1986) *The Apartheid Handbook*, Penguin.

11/5 OWEN, R. J. (1982) *The Moonies: A critical look at a controversial group*, Ward Lock Educational.

16/1 PAGNAMENTA, P. and OVERY, R. (1984) *All Our Working Lives*, BBC.

3/4 PEARSON, G. (1983) *Hooligan: A History of Respectable Fears*, The Macmillan Press Ltd.

7/1 PINKNEY, A. (1984) *Myth of Black Progress*, Cambridge University Press.

14/4 ROSE, R. and MCALLISTER, I. (1986) *Voters Begin to Choose: From Closed-Class to Open Elections in Britain*, Sage Publications.

2/5 ROWBOTHAM, S. (1973) *Hidden from History*, Pluto Press.

10/5 RUTTER, M., MAUGHAN, B., MORTIMORE, P. and OUSTON, J. (1979) *Fifteen Thousand Hours: Secondary Schools and their effects on children*, Open Books Publishing Ltd.

2/1 SHARPE, S. (1976) *'Just Like a Girl': How Girls Learn to be Women*, Penguin

5/2 SHARPE, S. (1984) *Double Identity: The Lives of Working Mothers*, Penguin.

2/5 SPENDER, D. (1982) *Invisible Women: The Schooling Scandal*, Writers and Readers Publishing Cooperative

17/1 TAYLOR, L. (1984) *In the Underworld*, Basil Blackwell.

7/5 TOMPSON, K. (1988) *Under Seige: Racism and Violence in Britain Today*, Penguin.

16/1 TERKEL, S. (1985) *Working*, Penguin.

9/4 TOWNSEND, P. and DAVIDSON, N. (eds) (1982) *Inequalities in Health: the Black Report*, Penguin.

10/5 TURNER, G. (1983) *The Social World of the Comprehensive School*, Croom Helm.

3/1 VAN DER POST, L. and TAYLOR, J. (1984) *Testament to the Bushmen*, Viking Penguin.

14/3 WALKER, J. (1986) *The Queen Has Been Pleased: The British Honours System at Work*, Secker & Warburg.

10/3 WEDGE, P. and ESSEN, J. (1982) *Children in Adversity*, Pan.

16/1 WERNEKE, D. (1983) *Microelectronics and Office Jobs*, International Labor Organisation, Geneva.

17/4 WILLIAMS, J., DUNNING, E., and MURPHY, P. (1984) *Hooligans Abroad*, Routledge & Kegan Paul.

13/4 YOUNG, J. (1971) *The drugtakers*, Paladin.

4/5 YOUNG, M. and WILLMOTT, P. (1973) *The Symmetrical Family*, Penguin.

Index